PRINK

Workers Power

PALESTINE: A MARXIST ANALYSIS

PRINKIPO

First published as: *Against the Racist Endeavour*
Red Flag Publications
© Red Flag 2018

This edition published by Prinkipo Press 2024
© Prinkipo Press 2024
All rights reserved
1 3 5 7 9 10 8 6 4 2

Prinkipo Press
BCM 7750 WC1N 3XX – London – United Kingdom
shop@prinkipo.net
www.prinkipo.net

ISBN-13: 978-1-7395059-1-2

Typeset in Le Monde Livre Std by Prinkipo Press
Printed and bound by ImprintDigital, Exeter, EX5 5HY

Publisher's note:
This volume consists of a reprint of the first section of *Against the Racist Endeavour*, with the correction of typographical errors. The appendices to the first edition have been omitted and replaced with two documents, detailed in the preface. The index, notes and preface are the work of the publisher.

Contents

vii *Preface*

- 11 The Birth of Zionism
- 31 Colony and Settlement
- 49 From the Arab Revolt to the Nakba
- 67 The Apartheid State
- 85 The Arab National Movement
- 99 The PLO and the Armed Struggle
- 109 The First Intifada and the Rise of Hamas
- 121 A Crisis of Leadership
- 133 Peace and Ethnic Cleansing
- 147 Antisemitism, anti-Zionism, and anti-Imperialism
- 167 Towards a Programme
- 187 *Appendix* – Theses on Zionism, Israel, Palestine and Arab Nationalism
- 255 *Appendix* – The Fourth International and Palestine

277 *Index of names*

Preface

The foundation of the state of Israel in 1948 was a key moment in the construction of a new world order after the Second World War. It expressed the decline of the former dominant imperialism, Great Britain, which had arrogantly presumed to 'grant' Palestinian territory to the new state, and the rise of the USA, whose former isolationism had been definitively rejected by intervention, and then victory, in that war.

The form of US global power was to differ from that of the 'old' European imperialists in that it rejected direct control via colonies in favour of an indirect, but certainly no less powerful, dominance via finance and trade, buttressed by strategically placed regional gendarmes. Israel was to become Washington's proxy in the Middle East, playing such a pivotal role that its leaders could depend on effectively unconditional support from Washington.

Today, the war in Gaza signals changes in that world order, changes that threaten to end that unconditional support. With the rise of China, Washington no longer needs Israel as a wedge to keep the region divided but looks to a new alliance that also embraces the oil rich Arab states which have always professed to defend the rights of Palestinians against the rapacious appetite of Israeli expansion. Hamas' attack on October 7, 2023 was designed to scupper US plans for a 'normalisation' of relations between Israel and, in particular, Saudi Arabia.

The war has potentially tumultuous consequences; how long can the Arab regimes suppress the undoubted sympathy for the Palestinians amongst their subjects? Could Israeli provocations encourage retaliation by Iran on such a scale that the USA intervenes directly? If US plans to remove Netanyahu are successful and lead to some new 'peace negotiations', will the fascist wing of the present Israeli government mobilise their armed settler supporters to drive the remaining Palestinians out of the West Bank? If, on the other hand, Netanyahu persists with plans to seize Rafah, will the 'Western' powers finally stop arms deliveries or even withdraw political support?

This book was first published to coincide with the 70th anniversary of the foundation of Israel and the initial expulsion of Palestinians from their lands, al Nakba, the Catastrophe. It does not speculate on those very real possibilities but, rather, investigates the underlying issues and dynamics which first brought Israel into existence and are now putting its future in question. In particular, it deals with the evolution of Zionism from a minority current within the broadly 'assimilationist' Jewish communities in Europe into the driving ideology of the Israeli state. In doing this, it emphasises the mutually reinforcing roles of antisemitism and Zionist nationalism against a background of centuries-old oppression and contemporary imperialist strategy and hypocrisy.

It is not, however, merely a historical accounting. On the contrary, its purpose is to identify the lessons that must be drawn from history if socialists are to elaborate a strategy that can lead to the formation of a revolutionary movement that can challenge and defeat the many competing reactionary forces in the region and beyond. Such a movement needs a leadership that transcends the existing borders, united by a common, internationalist programme that recognises the democratic and national rights of all the populations can only be fulfilled by the overthrow of all the existing regimes and the socialisation of the economies that those regimes currently exploit for their own benefit.

The first section of the book, therefore, concludes with the League for the Fifth International's draft programme for permanent revolution in Palestine. For decades, those who defend the national rights of the Palestinians but certainly do not want to 'drive the Jews into the sea' have concluded that there should be two states between the Jordan and the Mediterranean; Israel and Palestine. The League rejects this as an impossible utopia, the Zionist state will never, can never, cede enough of the land it currently occupies to establish a viable Palestinian state. The League's programme is based on the proposition that only the overthrow of both the Zionist state and the collaborationist Palestinian Authority, by a mobilisation of working class forces inside and outside Israel, can solve the terrible crisis afflicting the country and the region.

It argues that any consistent democratic solution will require workers, both Jewish Israeli and Palestinian, to socialise the economy so that it can be planned in the interests of the entire population. Such a revolution will, like the Arab Spring, spark revolutions in the neighbouring countries, creating the conditions for the foundation of a federation of workers' states of the Middle East.

In a second section, we have included the 1988 'Theses on Israel, Zionism, Palestine and Arab Nationalism', the founding programmatic document of the League for the Fifth International on the Palestinian question. Finally, we include the 'Draft theses on the Jewish Question today', published by the Fourth International in 1947, which show how the then-revolutionary FI attempted to chart a path of permanent revolution, to insist that the project of the Zionist state was a reactionary endeavour, and balance this principled position with an unequivocal opposition to all forms of antisemitism, and especially that of the imperialist states.

We dedicate this book not only to the courageous Palestinian fighters in Gaza and the West Bank and to those Israeli socialists who support them, but also to the anti- and non-Zionist Jews who, despite a torrent of threats and slanders, have campaigned tirelessly to refute the lies, clarify the issues and defend the rights of the Palestinian nation and, in so doing, maintained the best traditions of the Jewish contribution to the internationalist socialist movement.

Peter Main
London, April 2024

The Birth of Zionism

The Palestinian nation was formed out of the struggle of the people of Palestine against the imposition on their lands of the Zionist state of Israel and its subsequent expansion at their expense. It is one of the most tragic of all the ironies of history that Zionism itself emerged as a response to the oppression of Jews in Europe but, while Jews had faced oppression for centuries, this was a new, specifically 20th century response to new forms and causes of oppression as Europe entered the imperialist epoch. This makes it necessary to begin this book about the Palestinian struggle with a brief consideration of the changing circumstances of European Jewry and their consequences.

We do not, however, need to deal with the whole history of the Jewish people, which extends over two and a half millennia. Marxists like Karl Kautsky, Abram Leon, Maxime Rodinson, Enzo Traverso, as well as 'revisionist' Israeli historians, have created a rich literature on this subject. For our purposes, we need only to consider developments since the end of the feudal period, as Europe's scattered Jewish communities emerged into the world of capitalism and the nation state.

The only point about the preceding centuries that has direct relevance to the argument we shall develop is that the states in which the Jews, Sephardic and Ashkenazi, lived, were not nation states. Many had several distinct language communities within them; few had a state language comprehensible to the majority of the population. The concept of national citizenship simply did not yet exist.

Thus, while the Jews were repeatedly persecuted in the Christian states of Europe, it was not because they were members of an alien 'nation' or 'race' but for socio-economic reasons, although expressed in terms of religious bigotry. Persecution certainly included violent repression, confiscation of property and, all too often, bloody massacres, but it also meant denial of rights and exclusion from specific occupations and places. Crucially, ownership of landed property was prohibited but, for religious reasons, Jews were allowed to lend money at interest and to trade. As a result, what wealth Jewish communities or individuals could accumulate could be very easily taxed or, indeed, confiscated. At that time, the only route out of oppression was assimilation into society by conversion to the religion of the rulers, but this was often forced on whole populations.

Emancipation and assimilation

The spread of industrial capitalism in the late 18th and 19th centuries, first in western, then in central, and last of all in eastern, Europe, began the dissolution of the systematic legal and social disabilities afflicting Jewish communities across the continent. In 1782, an enlightened despot, Joseph II of Austria, issued a tolerance decree that removed most disabilities from Jews, although he also tried to force their assimilation by banning the public use of Hebrew or Yiddish.

In Britain, the process began earlier in the 18th century but was carried out in a typically pragmatic and piecemeal way. Jews were not allowed to take degrees at the ancient universities of Oxford and Cambridge until 1870. The more thorough-going bourgeois revolutions, above all that in France, liberated the Jews from their late medieval laws, making them full and equal citizens.

The motivation of those rulers and also prominent Enlightenment thinkers from Locke to Kant, was not so much humane sympathy for a manifestly oppressed people, as a desire to 'make them useful to the state', as Joseph II himself put it. As international, indeed global, mercantile capital began to emerge, first in Holland and Britain, then in other European states, the upper class of the Jewish communities, with their merchant and banking skills and international links, were an asset to those states trying to catch up with the Dutch and the

British.

Beneath them was a substantial stratum within the Jewish communities who had been barred from landownership, excluded from production in hitherto guild-dominated industries and trades and barred from the universities as the route to state employment. They were thus confined to lending to the poor, collecting taxes and small scale trading. The resulting social antagonism (where the peasant or unemployed artisan could not see beyond the Jewish middleman to the gentile landlord or manufacturer) was the basis for the continuation and reproduction of the horrible medieval antisemitic stereotypes of the Jew as usurer and 'blood sucker'.

Parallel to the moves to emancipate Jews from legal discrimination, a rapid process of modernisation and enlightenment developed within the Jewish communities themselves, the Haskallah. It aimed at liberation from the economic conditions of petty trading and loan-mongering but also from the restrictions of Orthodox Judaism. It sought a cultural integration into modern European life. Key figures like the philosopher Moses Mendelssohn (1729–1786) argued for such assimilation but also for the preservation of Judaism as a religion alongside the various forms of Christianity. Haskallah scholars also stimulated the revival of Hebrew for use as a secular language. By contrast, the orthodox Jewish rabbinate were very often opposed to Jewish emancipation. They feared that it would undermine the special social and political role that they possessed within their own communities, in much the same way that capitalist modernity had already eroded the hold of the Catholic priesthood over much of the Christian peasantry and working class.

Once ghetto-like socio-economic conditions began to dissolve, Jewish communities began a rapid social differentiation with a few big bourgeois, a majority of petty bourgeois traders, and, eventually, proletarians. In western and central Europe, this led to the rapid secularisation and assimilation of large numbers of Jews into the various nationalities. Some Jews and gentiles assumed, and even wished, that this would lead to the disappearance of the Jewish religion but in the event it became one religion amongst the others. 'Emancipated' Jews enthusiastically adopted the culture and national identities of the countries where they lived.

Had the development of capitalism proceeded evenly and in the same way across Eastern Europe, a similar process would undoubtedly have taken place there, too. However, although capitalism performed its destructive function, breaking up pre-capitalist relationships and institutions and creating the related impoverishment of peasants and artisans, it did not absorb most of these classes into modern capitalist production.

In Germany and central Europe, the formation of nation states came later and the ideology of nationalism took a different form. Here, the dominant interpretation of nationalism was that the German people (the *Volk*) were a community based on birth and the working of the ancestral land, summed up as 'blood and soil'. This provided the over-arching unity that overcame the myriad divisions caused by feudalism and dynastic wars, presenting the German nation as the reassertion of an original unity of the Germans. This prototype of the nation would be copied wholesale elsewhere in central Europe and the Balkans. There it often acted as a justification for the expulsion or forced assimilation of national or linguistic minorities that often accompanied the consolidation of the new states that emerged from Austrian or Ottoman Turkish rule. In Poland, divided between Russia, Austria-Hungary and Prussia since 1795, it made Polish Jews into conveniently 'alien' scapegoats for the failure to achieve Polish unity and independence, which came about only at the end of the First World War in 1918.

This Romantic method was the very opposite of the French Enlightenment method and created enormous problems for a people who, however long their forbears had lived in the German lands, could hardly claim membership of the ancestral Volk. For German nationalists, the state had legitimacy as the expression of an organic, pre-existing, popular community. They therefore saw the emancipation of the Jews and their entry into prominent positions in German life as a dangerous intrusion. This took on a truly pathological expression when it was combined with pseudo-Darwinian 'racial science' to produce modern antisemitism.

An ominous event bridging medieval and modern antisemitism was the so-called Hep-Hep pogrom in the southern and central states of the German Confederation in 1819, a counter-revolutionary response to the claimed 'insolence of the Jews' as a result of emancipation. Then came the failure of a revolutionary solution to the German Unity problem in 1848–49. The ensuing counterrevolution favoured the flourishing of the anti-Enlightenment Romantic elements within German nationalism which, in the hands of 'culture heroes' like Richard Wagner, became overt antisemitism. Historian and National Liberal member of the Reichstag, Heinrich Treitschke (1834–1896) was the populariser of the slogan, later adopted by the Nazis, 'The Jews are our misfortune!'.

Further East, in the Tsar's Empire, impoverishment also affected the once-prosperous Jewish communities. The Romanovs' absolutist regime, based on a great landowner ruling class and a huge state bureaucracy, resisted the military and economic pressure of western and north European states, maintaining serfdom until 1861, and the nobility's great landed estates until 1917.

The three partitions of the Polish and Lithuanian Commonwealth (1772, 1793, 1795) had resulted in the Tsar occupying territory within which five million Jews lived. The Tsars created a Pale of Settlement that was supposed to limit their eastward migration. Other measures, especially from the 1880s onwards, blocked the absorption of the Jews into Russian economic, social, educational and political life. Thus, whilst the Jews were squeezed out of their old role, they were not allowed to assimilate. They became what various sociologists described as a pariah caste.

Modern antisemitism

It was in the counterrevolutionary era after the failure of the revolutions of 1848 that antisemitism began to develop in France and in Germany. The term was invented by the German gutter journalist Wilhelm Marr in 1879, to express an entirely new idea: that the Jews were not merely the adherents of an alien religion, but a 'Semitic race'.

Racial ideology of course was nothing new. An entirely spurious classification of humanity into 'races' had been necessary to justify the violent European conquests of the Americas and the transatlantic slave trade. But even after the British Empire's formal abolition of slavery in 1807, racial ideology continued to serve a useful purpose in justifying the existence and subsequent massive global expansion of European empires.

Arthur de Gobineau's 1853 work *An Essay on the Inequality of the Human Races*, which featured one of the earliest references to the 'Aryan race', asserted that the aristocratic classes were a superior race whose rule was justified by 'right of conquest', just as that of European colonists in the Americas had been. During the colonial expansion of the late 19th century, this racial ideology was elevated to the 'theory' of Social Darwinism.

Once reimported into Europe, racial ideology encouraged the erosion of the gains made by Jewish people in the countries where they had already been legally emancipated. It also reinforced resistance to any further progress towards Jewish emancipation in those more backward countries where this process was not yet complete, or where it had barely even begun.

This racial form of antisemitism turned the Jews into the ideal imaginary enemies for malicious demagogues: simultaneously invisible, omnipresent and all-powerful. A cottage industry of vile and often absurd conspiracy theories singled out Jewish big capitalists like the Rothschild banking dynasty as somehow being 'more rapacious' and 'more powerful' than their non-Jewish equivalents, as well as being 'unpatriotic' on account of their international ties.

The visible presence of Jewish people in law, banking, medicine and other liberal professions was used to promote the idea that Jews of all classes ruled or aspired to rule over the world. Likewise, the visible presence of Jewish people in the radical, democratic and socialist movements was used to promote the idea that the Jews promoted 'subversion' as part of this grand conspiracy to 'rule the world'.

By redefining the Jews as a 'race', antisemitism made 'assimilation' practically meaningless, by subjecting to scrutiny the however distant Jewish origins of the assimilated. It meant in particular that it was no longer possible to 'stop being Jewish' merely by converting to another religion, or by abandoning religious belief altogether. Antisemites accused the Jews of being responsible for all the social and political conflicts of the 19th century, both for rampant capitalism and for the threat of revolution and communism.

Antisemitism's social roots were in classes declining under capitalism; peasants, artisans ruined by the factories and deprived of their guilds, and small shopkeepers. All these picked on Jewish businesses and professionals as 'unfair' competitors. Such strata did not dare take on the capitalist class as such, gentiles as well as Jews, but the spread of universal suffrage created an opportunity for assembling a reactionary electoral expression of this—so-called Christian Socialism.

The most successful proponent of this was Karl Lueger (1844–1910), founder in 1891 of the Austrian Christian Social Party, who was mayor of Vienna from 1897–1910. He combined anti-Jewish demagogy with carrying out social reforms such as municipal transport and housing. This combination of 'socialism', in the sense of social reforms, with an anticapitalism directed only at Jewish capitalists, particularly 'Jewish financiers', was later taken up by fascism.

It was in Russia that antisemitism became most virulent and gave the world a new term, 'pogrom', a word meaning to beat, to destroy violently. The first anti-Jewish riot to which this term was attached in western reports was in the Black Sea port of Odessa at Easter in 1871. Jewish property was smashed, synagogues burned and Jewish people were beaten and killed. The police and the military authorities did little to stop the pogrom, if they did not actually encourage it.

Following the assassination of Tsar Alexander II by the Narodnik People's Will in 1881, a wave of pogroms spread over the Russian Empire. In 1882–3, these started a process of Jewish emigration towards Germany, France, England and the USA. A tiny group of Jews, Hovevei Zion (Lovers of Zion), emigrated to Palestine where they bought land. In France and England, wealthy and respected leaders of the Jewish community were terrified that mass immigration by 'backward', that is, unassimilated, 'Eastern' Jews would provoke a backlash. They started to fund and encourage colonisation schemes in North Africa and Palestine.

The genesis of Zionism

An early proponent of the idea that Jews could not successfully assimilate but should emigrate to Palestine was Moses Hess, an early colleague of Karl Marx and a member of the Communist League in 1848. He wrote a book, *Rome and Jerusalem* (1862) which set the Jews in the context of the contemporary movements for national unity and independence, in Italy in particular. Zionists later ignored his communist views, which led him to propose that his new Jewish state would be based on communes, and claimed him as an early precursor of their own ideas. Certainly there was a very reactionary side to his argument. In a footnote to *Rome and Jerusalem* he wrote, 'the entire history up to our day has gone through a struggle of races and a struggle of classes. The struggle of races is the primary phenomenon'. But his work did not generate a movement. That had to await the 1880s.

In September 1882, an anonymous pamphlet entitled *Autoemancipation! An Appeal to his People by a Russian Jew*, was published in Berlin. In it, Jews were encouraged to emancipate themselves by rediscovering their national identity instead of making futile attempts to assimilate. The anonymous author was Leon Pinsker (1821–1891), an assimilated Jew from Odessa who had personally witnessed the 1871 pogrom. Responding to even greater atrocities in 1881–2, he concluded that, 'Judeophobia is a psychosis. As a psychosis it is hereditary, and as a disease transmitted for over two thousand years it is incurable'. He went on:

> 'The Jews are not a living nation; they are strangers everywhere and therefore they are despised. Civil and political emancipation of the Jews is not sufficient to raise them in the estimation of the peoples. The correct, the only, solution would be the creation of a Jewish nationality, of a people on their own soil, the auto-emancipation

of the Jews, their equal status as a nation among nations by the acquisition of their own homeland'.

The pamphlet made Pinsker famous and it was one of his supporters, Nathan Birnbaum, who coined the term 'Zionism'. He argued that the attempts at acculturation and assimilation were the real causes of antisemitism. In 1890, the Russian authorities approved the establishment of the Society for the Support of Jewish Farmers and Artisans in Syria and Palestine, and Pinsker became the head of this. Although he died in Odessa in 1891, we can already see in his argument and his practice a pattern that would continue; that virulently antisemitic states would collaborate with Zionist projects to remove their Jewish populations.

Zionism was really founded as an organised international political movement under the inspiration of Theodor Herzl. He was born in Budapest in 1860, into an assimilated bourgeois family. He became a journalist on the famous Viennese liberal paper *Neue Freie Presse*, and was working as a correspondent in Paris at the time of the Dreyfus Affair (1895). The eruption of popular antisemitism in the home of the Enlightenment, of the Revolution of 1789, where there had been the most thoroughgoing emancipation of the Jews, shocked him deeply.

Indeed, the centenary of the Revolution had seen the journalist Édouard Drumont found the Antisemitic League of France with its scurrilous paper *La Libre Parole*. Drumont drew on traditional Catholic antisemitism and the monarchist traditions of hatred of the French Revolution and the Republic and added so-called 'scientific racism' and a pseudo-anticapitalism aimed at international high finance (the Rothschilds etc.)

The frameup, conviction and public degradation of Captain Alfred Dreyfus, an Alsatian Jew, for spying for Germany, with mobs howling 'death to the Jews', was an enormous shock to the liberal, assimilated Herzl. Despite the development of a massive pro-Dreyfusard movement around the novelist Émile Zola, which was supported by the socialist Jean Jaurès and eventually triumphed, Herzl drew the conclusion that assimilation was a failure and that antisemitism was ineradicable.

Worse still, he concluded that in one sense the antisemites were right; the Jews were indeed a 'foreign body' in the national states of Europe, because they had no territorial basis for their national existence. Emancipation and attempted assimilation into a competitive bourgeois society simply made the Jews resented as rivals, by workers, businessmen, bankers, lawyers, journalists. Herzl came to see this hostility as natural, even excusable, with the solution being the exit of Jews to found their own territory and thus become a 'normal' nation.

In June 1895 he wrote in his diary: 'In Paris, as I have said, I achieved a freer attitude toward antisemitism, which I now began to understand historically and to pardon. Above all, I recognized the emptiness and futility of trying to 'combat' antisemitism'.

He became convinced that the threat of a growing antisemitic movement could be a lever to justify the project of creating a Jewish state by emigration and colonisation. He realised, too, that this would have to be done in collaboration with one of the major imperialist powers. These powers, particularly France and Britain, were already taking over former provinces of the Ottoman Empire like Algeria and Egypt. Countries without colonies, like Germany and Italy, had their eyes on other portions.

Herzl's breakthrough came with the publication of his pamphlet *Der Judenstaat* (The State of the Jews) in 1894. It is a powerfully written indictment of the situation facing Jews in mainland Europe in the 1890s:

> 'Attacks in Parliaments, in assemblies, in the press, in the pulpit, in the street, on journeys, for example, their exclusion from certain hotels, even in places of recreation, become daily more numerous. The forms of persecution varying according to the countries and social circles in which they occur. In Russia, imposts are levied on Jewish villages; in Rumania, a few persons are put to death; in Germany, they get a good beating occasionally; in Austria, Antisemites exercise terrorism over all public life; … the position of Jewish lawyers, doctors, technicians, teachers, and employees of all descriptions becomes daily more intolerable.'

Herzl's analysis is that all this is occurring not in spite of emancipation and assimilation but because of it:

> 'In the principal countries where antisemitism prevails, it does so as a result of the emancipation of the Jews. When civilised nations awoke to the inhumanity of discriminatory legislation and enfranchised us, our enfranchisement came too late. It was no longer possible to remove our disabilities in our old homes. For we had, curiously enough, developed while in the Ghetto into a bourgeois people, and we stepped out of it only to enter into fierce competition with the middle classes.'

He believed that the route of assimilation into the professions for educated middle class Jews was blocked by the fierce opposition of their gentile competitors, who responded with the weapon of antisemitism. Because he had a somewhat Nietzschean belief in the positive value of conflict and the triumph of the strong, he did not complain about this. Indeed, in his diaries and letters he had positive things to say about the antisemites. He thought that the Jewish figures in high finance simply aroused the hostility of the masses and even mused as to whether the Christian bourgeoisie might throw them to the socialists. On the other hand, he feared that the rejected Jewish intelligentsia would turn to the revolutionary parties: 'When we sink, we become a revolutionary proletariat, the subordinate officers of all revolutionary parties; and at the same time, when we rise, there rises also our terrible power of the purse.'

The practical proposals for settlement rested on founding a company to accumulate the finances for the settlement project and the plan was that poor Jews would go first to do the hard work of developing the land. Later would come the middle classes. As to where the 'homeland', as he called it at the first Zionist Congress, would be located, he was not dogmatic. Obviously, Palestine was a major option but in *Der Judenstaat* he also considered Argentina. Later, in response to British overtures, he suggested Uganda, which caused a near split at the 1903 Zionist Congress.

Herzl's second major work took the form of a utopian

novel, *Altneuland* (Old-Newland) published in 1902. In it, he dealt with the problems of creating an entirely new society. The problem he outlined was that the immigrants would have to transcend their social demographic as small traders and intellectuals and become workers and farmers.

He realised that the spontaneous working of the market economy would never allow for this so he turned to the ideas of the 19th century utopians such as Robert Owen, Charles Fourier, Étienne Cabet and Pierre-Joseph Proudhon. Indeed, he described the principle by which this society would be run as 'mutualism', defining it as 'halfway between socialism and capitalism'. The land had to be owned by the new state and producer and consumer cooperatives would dominate economic life, housing would be socially owned and constructed, there would be a seven hour working day and a welfare state, too.

Another aspect of his utopia was his attitude to the existing Arab population who, he thought, would peacefully assimilate into this more advanced 'civilisation' and have equal political rights, as would women. It did not occur to him that the indigenous population would not, and could not be expected to welcome the arrival of hundreds of thousands of European immigrants, buying up the peasants' absentee landlords' estates and expelling them. He did not foresee that this would inevitably produce a national movement in resistance to expropriation and oppression.

Even if it became for a period a utopian vision for the settlers, Zionism was always a reactionary ideology. This was obviously the case for the existing population of Palestine, people who had no responsibility for the antisemitism of Europe, but for which they were expected to pay with their homes, their land and their country. Self-determination for the settlers meant no self-determination for them.

But it was also reactionary for the projected settlers, urging them not to resist antisemitism in Europe and converting them from a genuinely oppressed people into an oppressor nation in the Middle East.

The World Zionist Movement

The First Zionist Congress took place in Basel, Switzerland, in August 1897 and was attended by over 200 delegates from at least 17 countries; about one third of the participants came from eastern Europe. The stated goal of the Basel Programme, which was adopted at this congress, was 'the creation of a public, legally secured home in Palestine' by the 'structuring and consolidation of the entire Jewish community through appropriate local and general events in accordance with the laws of the countries'.

The World Zionist Organisation, WZO, would have annual congresses of delegates from national associations in countries with substantial Jewish communities. Its executive was composed of representatives proportional to their relative size. The congress also introduced a membership contribution, the Shekel.

After the congress, Herzl wrote in his diary, 'At Basel, I founded the Jewish State. If I said this out loud today, I would be answered by universal laughter. If not in 5 years, certainly in 50, everyone will know it.'

Over the next seven years, Herzl engaged in a punishing round of visits to European politicians and monarchs and general diplomatic activity with the object of finding a Jewish homeland and arranging the organised transfer of the Diaspora communities to the new state. He attempted to obtain a charter from the Sultan, Abdul Hamid II, for the establishment of a Jewish settlement in Palestine.

He also turned to the Kaiser, Wilhelm II, an outspoken antisemite, since Germany was seeking to oust Britain as the main financial and military 'doctor' to 'the sick man of Europe'. Herzl, always a self-dramatiser, obviously saw himself as a sort of Moses before Pharaoh: 'I will say to the Kaiser: let our people go. We are strangers here. We are neither permitted, nor are we able, to assimilate with the people. Let us go!'

The Kaiser evinced personal sympathy with the idea of ridding Germany of Jews and using them as colonists in Palestine, but he would do nothing without the Sultan's approval. The Sublime Porte (the Ottoman government) had incurred huge debts to British and French financiers in an attempt to modernise its state and army so Herzl dangled the bait of consolidating the entire state debt of the Empire, on more favourable terms, but the wisely sceptical Sultan did not bite. In any case, the Ottomans, having lost control of North Africa and Egypt to the French and British, were not inclined to hand over Palestine to a Jewish-German protectorate.

Herzl's last diplomatic adventure was even more discrediting. On 19 April 1903, a horrendous pogrom broke out in Kishinev, capital of the Russian province of Bessarabia. *The New York Times* reported it thus:

> 'The mob was led by priests, and the general cry, 'Kill the Jews,' was taken-up all over the city. The Jews were taken wholly unaware and were slaughtered like sheep. The dead number 120 and the injured about 500. The scenes of horror attending this massacre are beyond description. Babes were literally torn to pieces by the frenzied and bloodthirsty mob. The local police made no attempt to check the reign of terror. At sunset the streets were piled with corpses and wounded.'

Herzl visited Russia in July 1903, not to protest at the slaughter, which had been facilitated by the Okhrana, the Tsar's secret police, but to persuade the notoriously antisemitic Minister of the Interior, Vyacheslav von Plehve, whose police forged the infamous *Protocols of the Learned Elders of Zion,* to help the Zionists transfer Jews from Russia to Palestine. Von Plehve hesitated because he thought most of Russia's Jews were closer to being narodnik or social democratic revolutionaries than Zionists. Here he was right. Nonetheless, the virulent pogroms, the Okhrana and the Tsar's encouragement did indeed provoke a considerable exodus, mainly to America but this time to Palestine, too. Herzl's visit, however, provoked protests from Russian Zionists.

Herzl received a warmer reaction the same year from Britain's Prime Minister, the Conservative Arthur Balfour, and Colonial Secretary, Joseph Chamberlain. They had little interest in Palestine but were looking for settlers for their African colonies. Chamberlain offered Herzl an area in the highlands in British East Africa, today's Kenya and Uganda, suitable for a 'white' population and from which the native tribes could be driven out. Herzl suggested Cyprus and the Sinai, former Ottoman territories that, together with Egypt, had become de facto British colonies, thanks to the Ottoman debt. However, he was overturned on these by the increasingly influential eastern European Jews, who maintained the focus of the Zionist movement on Palestine, and the following year he died.

The WZO now pursued a strategy of building a homeland through persistent small-scale immigration and the founding of such bodies as the Jewish National Fund, a charity that bought land for Jewish settlement, and the Anglo-Palestine Bank, which provided loans for Jewish businesses and farmers.

The Second Aliyah and the rise of Socialist Zionism

A fresh wave of antisemitic pogroms in Russia, which followed Kishinev, led to another wave of immigration with more going to Palestine than in 1882–3. This became known as the Second Aliyah (going up to Zion).

The early 1890s had seen a rise in the revolutionary movement in the Tsarist Empire in which Jewish workers played a pioneering role in western Russia, specifically around the Lithuanian capital, Vilnius. Out of this was founded, in 1897, the General Jewish Labour Federation, more generally known as the Bund, which was the most sizeable and impressive social democratic organisation before the 1905 revolution.

The example of the Bund inspired the development of several socialist groupings within Zionism and amongst those emigrating to Palestine. Many migrants dedicated to socialist ideals arrived in Palestine. What came to be known as Labour Zionism was represented by the non-Marxist Tolstoyan Aaron David Gordon and the Marxist Ber Borochov.

Gordon emigrated to Palestine in 1904, becoming an agricultural labourer but at the same time writing copiously on the theory of a labour-based Zionism. Like other Zionists he considered the life of Jews in the Diaspora to be 'abnormal' and 'unnatural'. Inspired by 19th century romanticism, he called for a Jewish return to the soil and virtually made a religion of work:

> 'The Jewish people has been completely cut off from nature and imprisoned within city walls for two thousand years. We have been accustomed to every form of life, except a life of labour—of labour done at our behalf and for its own sake. It will require the greatest effort of will for such a people to become normal again. We lack the principal ingredient for national life. We lack the habit of labour ... for it is labour which binds a people to its soil and to its national culture, which in its turn is an outgrowth of the people's toil and the people's labour.'

Gordon founded Hapoel Hatzair, (The Young Worker) and inspired the creation of agricultural collective farms (kibbutzim), the first of which was Degania in Galilee, where he worked.

Ber Borochov started his political career as a convinced Zionist although, for a few months in 1900–1, he was a member of the Russian Social Democratic Labour Party, RSDLP, which, at that time, included the Bund. He helped found a local group under the name Poale Zion (Workers of Zion). The 1905–7 revolution had a powerful impact on him and he became organiser and coordinator of the local groups and helped centralise them into a party, founded in February 1906 under the name Jewish Social Democratic Labour Party (Poale Zion).

It demanded 'personal autonomy' and a Jewish parliament as steps towards territorial independence within Russia and it participated actively in the 1905 Revolution against Tsarism. On tactical questions in this period, it stood closer to Bolshevism than Menshevism.

Borochov developed the theory that life in the Diaspora concentrated Jews in economically backward, small scale workshops and rendered them politically helpless. The normal organisation of capitalist society, he said, was a pyramid, with a large body of workers and peasants at its base, the smaller groups of intelligentsia above that, and a pinnacle of landowners and capitalists. The Jewish Diaspora had created an 'inverted pyramid' with no significant Jewish peasant or worker class. In Palestine, he believed, this could be solved by settling in communities engaged in productive agricultural and industrial labour. Thereby, the over-large bourgeoisie and petit bourgeoisie would disappear and a 'normal' labour movement would move on to socialism. For all Borochov's 'Marxism', this was clearly nearer to the utopianism which we have seen in Herzl's novel.

It was this utopian communal settler ethos that triumphed as Labour Zionism. During the 1920s, Poale Zion developed branches in America, in Western Europe and in Palestine. In Russia, however, Poale Zion took a principled anti-war stand in 1914 and rallied to the defence of the USSR after 1917, organising Jewish brigades in the Red Army.

The new immigrants to Palestine had the ideals of socialist Zionism but no training in agriculture and were ill suited to compete with Palestinian workers. In addition, the latter were able and willing to work for lower wages because their families made a large part of their income from sharecropping. The socialist Zionist movements initially tried to force plantation owners to pay higher wages, but soon turned to trying to force them to hire only Jewish workers. This aspect of the 'conquest of labour' was controversial within the socialist-Zionist movements. Some Labour Zionists resisted the conflict with Palestinian labour and tried to build a united labour movement. Many of these later became communists, but the contradiction already showed the utopian and reactionary character of the 'socialist' settler project.

Perfidious Albion

The foundations of mass Zionist settlement in Palestine were actually laid in Britain in the years immediately before and during the First World War by a new figure who was to prove himself a worthy, and more successful, successor to Herzl, Chaim Weizmann. He was Russian born and brought up in a traditional Jewish home and schools where he learned Hebrew from an early age. He was introduced to Zionism by a Hovevei Zion group. He then emigrated to Germany to study chemistry in Berlin, became active in the Zionist movement and attended the Second Zionist Congress in Basel. He also became a lecturer in organic chemistry, first in Geneva and then, in 1904, in Britain, at the University of Manchester. He became a British citizen in 1910.

Weizmann cultivated friendships with Conservatives like the former Prime Minister, Arthur Balfour and Liberals like David Lloyd George, Herbert Samuel and Winston Churchill, who all proved sympathetic to Zionist ideas. As the inventor of the process of producing Acetone, used in the manufacture of explosive propellants, which were important to the Allied war effort, Weizmann was appointed Director of the British Admiralty's laboratories during the First World War. In a conversation with David Lloyd George, he suggested the strategy of a British Palestine campaign against the Ottoman Empire and how a colony there could support the Empire's post war geostrategic interests. The British, having just before the war started the conversion of their fleet from coal to oil were already aware of the oilfields the region could contain.

Many of the leading members of Britain's Jewish community regarded Weizmann's ideas with open hostility and a major debate took place in cabinet. The former Viceroy of India, Lord Curzon, and Edwin Montague, Secretary of State for India, strongly opposed the whole plan because it would alienate both Arab and Indian Muslim opinion. Montague, the only Jew in the cabinet, also thought it would undermine the assimilated Jewish bourgeoisie in Britain and actually called it antisemitic.

Weizmann, now president of the British Zionist Federation, nevertheless worked with Arthur Balfour to win the cabinet over. Almost immediately, Balfour sent his November 2, 1917, letter, known to history as the Balfour Declaration, to Baron Rothschild, a prominent leader of Britain's Jewish community and Zionist movement who, in fact, helped with its wording. The Declaration famously stated that:

> 'His Majesty's government view with favour the establishment in Palestine of a national home for the Jewish people, and will use

their best endeavours to facilitate the achievement of this object, it being clearly understood that nothing shall be done which may prejudice the civil and religious rights of existing non-Jewish communities in Palestine, or the rights and political status enjoyed by Jews in any other country'.

This deceitful and totally ambiguous document became the charter of the Zionist colonisation project. Its terms were quoted explicitly in the British Mandate granted by the League of Nations in 1922. To the Arabs, the British insisted that 'a national home' did not mean a Jewish state in Palestine. To the Zionists, they privately indicated quite the opposite.

In fact 'the existing non-Jewish communities', that is, the near 90 per cent Palestinian majority, were denied their right to self-determination and the 10 per cent Jewish minority were offered a 'national home' without the majority's consent or even consultation. At the same time, by allowing continuous immigration by Zionist settlers, this started the process that led to the Nakba of 1948; the ethnic cleansing of Palestine.

The Balfour Declaration, alongside the broken promises of sovereignty and independence made to the leaders of the 'Arab Revolt', is probably the most infamous example of the actions that earned Britain the title 'perfidious Albion'. No wonder Theresa May celebrated its centenary in the presence of Benjamin Netanyahu in 2017 and claimed not only that she was proud of 'our pioneering role in the creation of the state of Israel' but, even more astoundingly, 'proud of Balfour's vision of a peaceful coexistence'.

Colony and Settlement

Prior to the First World War, 'Palestine' consisted of three sub-provinces within the Ottoman Empire: El Kuds (Jerusalem), Nablus and Akka (Acre). The population was 84 per cent Muslim, 10 per cent Christian, 5 per cent Jewish and 1 per cent Druze. With the defeat of the Ottomans by the combined forces of France and Great Britain in 1918, it became one part of a larger territory, including the East Bank of the Jordan, under the control of the British. Military control was replaced by a civilian administration in 1920 and in 1922 the League of Nations 'legitimised' British control by granting a Mandate to administer the whole territory 'until such time as (it is) able to stand alone'. This was given a formal status by the League as the British Mandate for Palestine, in 1923.

Even before that, however, British policy had set in motion the conflicting forces that were to dominate the development of the whole region right down to the present day. In July 1915, Britain's High Commissioner in Egypt, Henry McMahon, had promised British support for an independent Arab state to Arab nationalists and to the Hashemite Sharif of Mecca, Hussein bin Ali, in return for their support for the British-sponsored 'Arab Revolt' against Ottoman Turkey during the war.

Less than a year later, in May 1916, British diplomat Mark Sykes agreed with his French counterpart, François Georges-Picot, that Britain and France would divide the whole region between them. Britain would receive today's Israel-Palestine, Jordan and most of today's Iraq. France was promised today's Syria and Lebanon, most of northern Iraq including Mosul and, indeed, much of today's Turkey.

Several British politicians within the Liberal Party were already sympathetic to the Zionist project. David Lloyd George had acted as legal advisor to Theodor Herzl when he was pursuing the Uganda Scheme in 1903. Winston Churchill, as a Manchester MP, had befriended Herzl's successor Chaim Weizmann. In the war cabinet, too, was Herbert Samuel, who, as early as March 1915, had been the author of the memorandum, *The Future of Palestine*, which first suggested a British occupation and the settlement of Jews there.

The year 1917 was a critical one in Britain's war effort. The Russian Revolution of February overthrew its ally, Tsar Nicholas II, and weakened the war effort. The October Revolution saw the Bolsheviks leave the war altogether. Britain desperately needed to raise new loans in New York. Both Churchill and Lloyd George, and the Tory leader Arthur Balfour had bought the antisemitic trope that wealthy Jews constituted a powerful force world wide and in the USA in particular. They believed access to major funding would be made easier by supporting the Zionist settlement project.

As we have seen, it was also in November 1917 that Britain's Foreign Secretary, Arthur Balfour, promised Walter Rothschild that Britain would support 'the establishment in Palestine of a national home for the Jewish people'. This promise, by a government of a foreign country to one of its own citizens about the fate of another country altogether, was hedged only with the proviso that 'nothing shall be done which may prejudice the civil and religious rights of existing non-Jewish communities in Palestine, or the rights and political status enjoyed by Jews in any other country'.

True to past form in Ireland, India, Cyprus and elsewhere, Britain would spend much of the Mandate period playing Jews and Arabs off against each other, the better to justify her own continued presence there as a 'peacemaker' between them. Needless to say, these conflicts repeatedly went beyond what the British administrators had bargained for but then they cheerfully blamed the barbarism of the 'natives'.

The Arabs' principal complaint was not a difficult one to

understand. As early as the late 19th century, the nascent Arab nationalist movement in Beirut, Damascus and Baghdad was outraged by the suggestion from the European Zionist movement that a significant part of the Arab-majority territory of the decaying Ottoman Empire might be given over, not to the self-rule of its inhabitants, but to primarily European Jewish colonists who did not yet even live there.

This, however, was now not only the official policy of a ruling European colonial power but also part of the overall re-ordering of the former Ottoman lands in which the more economically and culturally developed Arab-majority regions were placed under British and French rule (in Syria, Lebanon and Iraq), with the pretence that a period of benign foreign tutelage was necessary to prepare them for 'independence'.

To add insult to injury, the first Arab states to be granted formal independence and international recognition following the end of the First World War did not include any of these countries. Nor did they include Egypt, Algeria or Tunisia, which had come under British or French rule or domination over the course of the previous century. Rather, it was the economically backward kingdoms of Saudi Arabia and Yemen that became 'independent', both of them effectively remaining British satellites long afterwards.

After the British took over, the Muslim-Christian Associations in Palestine summoned the first of a series of Palestine Arab Congresses which met from 27 January to 10 February 1919, with 27 delegates. Most delegates were from the landed and merchant propertied class, some were pro-British and others supported pan-Arab or Greater Syrian nationalist factions. The conference sent a memorandum to the Versailles Peace Conference, calling for renunciation of the Balfour Declaration and the inclusion of Palestine as 'an integral part of … the independent Arab Government of Syria within an Arab Union, free of any foreign influence or protection.' It was fiercely opposed to a French takeover of Syria but hoped to maintain friendly relations with Britain.

How mistaken they were was revealed when the Allied authorities blocked their sending a delegation to the Peace

Congress in Paris and refused to discuss the memorandum. Instead, the Balfour Declaration, at British insistence, was included in the Mandate for Palestine as drafted by the San Remo Conference. The second congress was held in secret on 31 May 1920, because British military authorities had banned all Arab political gatherings.

Zionism under the British Mandate

In 1918, the population within the larger Mandate territory was approximately 85 per cent Arab and 15 per cent Jewish. The 'Arab' population included sizeable minorities of Christian Arabs, Armenians, Druze and Circassians (originally Muslim refugees from the north Caucasus). There were even small communities of 'Templars', a German Protestant sect who had arrived some four or five decades earlier, hoping thereby to hasten Christ's Second Coming.

The Jewish minority included a large number of Arabic-speaking Sephardi Jews, whose forebears had fled the expulsion of Jews from Spain and Portugal by the Inquisition in 1492. It also included some Arabic-speaking Mizrahi Jews who had been there since the defeat of the Crusaders by the Muslim ruler Saladin in the twelfth century.

Much larger Sephardi and Mizrahi Jewish communities also existed in Beirut, Damascus, Aleppo and Baghdad (in today's Lebanon, Syria and Iraq). These were often bound to their Palestinian counterparts by familial ties and by trade relations. However, contrary to Zionism's rewriting of Jewish history, according to which the Jewish people had spent almost two thousand years waiting to 'return home', these Jewish communities had remained in place for centuries under Ottoman Turkish rule, despite the absence of any legal impediment to their moving to Palestine at all.

Jerusalem had a fairly large Jewish minority, possibly even a narrow majority, in 1918. However, most were not Zionists but religious Orthodox Jews from Tsarist Russia and central Europe. Their forebears had trickled slowly into Palestine over the course of the previous century or more, long before the modern Zionist movement even existed.

These Orthodox Jews and others had long coexisted with the indigenous Arab population, in a way that their Zionist counterparts elsewhere rarely would. The newer Zionist settlers generally preferred to live apart from the Arabs; for example in Tel Aviv, founded under Ottoman rule in 1909 as an explicitly 'Jewish only' city, and as an economic rival to its Arab-majority neighbour, the port city of Jaffa.

Many of Jerusalem's Orthodox Jewish residents had come there in old age, although enough had brought their families that their descendants maintained a community there. They came to Palestine not to live, but to die within the confines of, or at least close to, Jerusalem's Old City, a belief in whose holy status they shared with Arab Muslims and Arab Christians alike.

Their deep religious belief, their aversion to capitalist modernity and their lack of interest in the building of a 'Jewish State', alongside their poverty, their dependence on the charity of Jewish communities abroad and their relatively friendly relations with the Arabs, all stood in stark contrast to the thrusting, pioneering and 'enterprising' spirit of the Zionist colonists. They frequently regarded Orthodox Jews with some hostility and derision, seeing in them a prime example of the 'old Jew' that Zionist ideology had set itself the goal of relegating to the dustbin of history.

The Zionists' language in describing these 'old Jews' borrowed more than a little from the stock of hostile Jewish stereotypes promoted by antisemitic racists in Europe. The Zionist colonists similarly saw themselves as archetypes of the 'new Jew' that Zionism advocated in their place: carrying a rifle in one hand and a spade in the other, speaking Hebrew, 'redeeming the land' and 'negating the diaspora'.

A 'Jewish State' however, required a Jewish majority, and the objective of building up and securing a Jewish majority in Palestine would shape the struggle that took place there over the next three decades. This struggle involved not only the Zionists and Palestine's Arab majority, but also the British authorities, the neighbouring Arab regimes and British imperialism's French, Italian, German and US imperialist rivals.

Revisionist and Labor Zionists

Although the British had broken their promise to the Arab nationalists by accepting Jewish claims to a 'homeland', they also did two things that angered Zionist Jewish opinion. The first was that they hived off the whole of their Palestine Mandate east of the River Jordan to form the Emirate of Transjordan in September 1922, under the rule of Hussein bin Ali's son Abdullah. This entirely artificial entity, today's Jordan, was to be a 'buffer state' in the classical sense of the term. Its creation set an eastern limit on Zionist aspirations for Jewish settlement, as well as a southern limit on French territorial ambitions.

The other British action that angered the Zionist movement was to place annual quotas on Jewish immigration into Palestine, as a cynically motivated sop to Arab opinion. These two actions combined caused an ultranationalist minority, the 'Revisionist Zionists', to split both from the mainstream Zionist movement led by Chaim Weizmann and also from the dominant 'Labor Zionist' trend in Palestine, led by David Ben-Gurion.

The Revisionists, so called because they demanded the revision of the British Mandate, possibly through its transfer to the control of Benito Mussolini's Fascist Italy, were the precursors of today's Likud party, and wanted an 'Eretz Yisrael' (Land of Israel) on both sides of the Jordan. Their leading figure, Ze'ev Jabotinsky, developed cordial relations with Mussolini's regime, which provided refuge and material support. Indeed, it even allowed the Revisionists' youth organisation, Betar, to establish a naval academy at Civitavecchia, whose graduates produced numerous future commanders of the Israeli Navy. An openly fascist wing of Ze'ev Jabotinsky's Revisionist movement developed around the journalist Abba Ahimeir, and waged a sporadic, low-level, street-based 'civil war' against their 'leftist' counterparts within the Zionist settler community.

Both Labor Zionists and Revisionists formed various illegal or semi-legal armed militias, albeit primarily for use against the Arabs rather than against the British. Of the two, it was the Revisionists who were the more notorious for their open militarism. Jabotinsky's seminal 1923 article, "The Iron Wall", set the tone for this. Its central argument was that it would take an 'iron wall' of Jewish military strength to force the Palestinian Arabs to accept both unlimited Jewish immigration and the eventual establishment of a Jewish state.

While the Revisionists concerned themselves with establishing the conditions for the creation of such an 'iron wall', the more mainstream Zionists concentrated on promoting Jewish immigration and on building up quasi-state institutions, in collaboration with the British authorities. In this, their behaviour closely resembled that of the Israeli-collaborationist Fatah leadership of today's Palestinian Authority under Mahmoud Abbas, who presumably imagine that they can 'negotiate' their way to a Palestinian state via a similar route.

This, however, is only one part of the story; the Labor Zionists were little better than the Revisionists in their attitude towards the Arabs, and in many ways were actually far worse. Most adherents of Labor Zionism had their political origins in continental European social democracy. Their half-remembered 'Marxism' had taught them that, in any class society, the majority of the population would consist quite naturally of the principal class of direct producers, be it farmers, agricultural labourers or industrial and service workers.

This meant that the Labor Zionists were far more concerned than the Revisionists with ensuring that Jews should form a majority not only of Palestine's population as a whole, but also of each of the principal classes of capitalist society there; workers, peasants, small business owners, professionals, bureaucrats and big capitalists alike.

Israel's national poet Hayim Nahman Bialik once expressed this outlook quite crudely by saying, 'we will be a normal state when we have the first Hebrew prostitute, the first Hebrew thief and the first Hebrew policeman'.

The Labor Zionists, however, translated this outlook into more acceptably 'left-wing' language, with the demagogic claim that they were in favour of a Jewish Palestine for Jewish workers and peasants, and not just for Jewish bosses. They similarly poured scorn on 'selfish' Jewish capitalists who 'exploited'

Arab workers. The practical implication of this was an exclusivist racism to the effect that there could be little or no place for Arab workers or peasants in a future 'Jewish Palestine', at least not in those parts of the economy over which the Zionist movement's adherents had any degree of control.

In particular, this placed Labor Zionists at the forefront of the apartheid-like exclusion of Arab goods and Arab labour from the 'Jewish economy'. The Labor Zionist trade union federation, the Histadrut, sent trade unionists to drive out Arab workers from mixed Arab and Jewish enterprises, and led boycotts of Jewish businesses that hired Arab workers, or that bought or sold Arab goods.

Nor was this project entirely original to Labor Zionism. The Zionist movement's founder, Theodor Herzl himself, had once dreamed of establishing a Jewish majority in Palestine by spiriting 'the penniless population across the border by procuring employment for it in the transit countries, while denying it any employment in our own country'.

Beyond their racist politics, however, there was also a far more practical reason for the Labor Zionists' focus on Arab exclusion. The vast majority of potential Jewish immigrants to Palestine came from countries in central or eastern Europe that had far higher standards of living, even if those same countries were still poor and backward compared to western Europe or north America.

Any politically or ethnically 'neutral' capitalist class in Palestine would therefore quite naturally be inclined towards hiring much cheaper Arab labour. Equally, only a small and ideologically-committed minority of Jewish immigrants would be willing to remain there if they had the option of higher standards of living elsewhere.

The creation of a sizeable Jewish working class in Palestine, under the conditions of British rule and Zionist colonisation, was therefore impossible without assuring it a privileged social and economic position over the native Arabs. While a small urban Arab working class did come into existence, its development was retarded by this early precursor of apartheid, which meant it was concentrated in the British-controlled parts of the economy, like the railways and the oil-refining industry in the port city of Haifa.

By contrast, the Revisionists had no such qualms about being seen to be 'exploiting' the Arabs, and far less immediate interest in driving them out. Jabotinsky's infamous "The Iron Wall" had even emphasised that his attitude towards the Arabs was "the same as it is to all other peoples—'polite indifference', adding that 'the expulsion of the Arabs from Palestine is absolutely impossible in any form' and that 'there will always be two nations in Palestine'.

Rural Revisionist settlers living on moshavim (private farms) therefore often hired Arab workers, and enjoyed formally polite, if exploitative and domineering, relations with their Arab neighbours. On the other hand, rural Labor Zionists generally lived in the much-romanticised 'socialistic' kibbutzim (collective farms), from which practically any Arab presence was excluded altogether.

Even now, this tension, between the priorities of militaristic territorial expansion and the priorities of maintaining an ethnic majority, still shapes Israeli politics. Today's Israeli rightwing 'settler camp' may no longer aspire to ruling over the Jordanian East Bank, but it still wants Israel to settle and annexe as much of the West Bank as it can. For its part, the 'peace camp' continues to fret about the 'demographic threat' posed to Israel by the higher birthrates of the Arab Palestinians, even if it couches its 'solution' to this problem in the form of a Palestinian pseudo-state that would allow Israel to avoid having to grant formal citizenship to the Palestinians under its present rule or domination.

If anything, the tragedy is that the worst elements of both Zionist ideological traditions have become part of a malign consensus across Israel's political spectrum. Militarism, expansionism and exclusivist racism all inform the politics of each of the major Zionist parties, if to varying degrees. Ultimately, they could be reconciled through a colossal act of ethnic cleansing that would make the last century of atrocities in Israel-Palestine pale by comparison.

Jewish immigration, the Arab bourgeosie and the Zionist project

Despite the Zionists' repeated complaints about Britain's duplicity, British policy massively favoured them, at the Arabs' expense. Britain's first Military Governor of Jerusalem in 1918, Ronald Storrs, was quite openly enthusiastic about the Zionist project as was Herbert Samuel, Britain's first High Commissioner for Palestine in 1920. Though a convinced Zionist himself, in a private letter to Lord Curzon, the former Viceroy of India, he wrote:

> 'The decisions accorded neither with the wishes of the inhabitants nor with the unqualified end-of-war undertakings about freedom of choice. They were pieces of unabashed self-interest, suggesting to many onlookers that all talk of liberating small nations from oppression was so much cant'.

While neither Jews nor Arabs had any collective political representation at national level, the Zionists at least enjoyed a functioning quasi-state administration of their own, in the form of the Labor Zionist-dominated Jewish Agency for Palestine. Jewish towns and settlements enjoyed roads, schools, hospitals and even modern facilities like electricity, all paid for by taxes levied on the Jewish settler community as a whole, and by the donations of Zionist organisations in Europe and north America.

The revenue raised from British taxation of Arabs and Jews alike, however, found its way into the small towns and villages in which most Palestinian Arabs lived mainly in the form of police stations and tax collecting offices. Thus, the majority of Palestine's population remained in a state of social and economic backwardness while, all around them, new Jewish settlements sprang up from which they were all but excluded, except very occasionally as a source of cheap labour.

The British awarded no comparable form of limited self-rule to Palestine's Arab majority. They did, however, allow influential families of Arab notables to take up bureaucratic and religious appointments. The two most important of these were the Husseinis and their rivals, the Nashashibi clan. Musa al-Husayni had been the Ottomans' mayor of Jerusalem and the British appointed his relative, Amin al-Husseini, to the newly-created post of Grand Mufti of Jerusalem shortly after their arrival. Raghib al-Nashashibi was subsequently mayor of Jerusalem from 1920 to 1934.

The rivalry between the two families reflected the insular world of urban Palestinian Arab politics, cut off as it was from any mass constituency. Nonetheless, in the main cities, an Arab middle class and big bourgeoisie did emerge. It drew its wealth from its parasitic relationship with the British authorities and from its subordinate role as a partner with Jewish capital, both 'private' and 'collective'. Many of its members came from landowning families, who profited enormously from the inflation of land prices brought about by land purchases conducted by the Jewish National Fund. This body had been founded in 1901 to centralise Jewish land acquisition, and like the Jewish Agency was given formal recognition by the British authorities.

This rising Arab bourgeoisie's members rubbed shoulders with their Jewish counterparts, and often shared with them a British or European-style education and outlook. Their more prominent political figures were often on first-name terms with their British and Zionist equivalents. Although they toyed hypocritically with 'nationalism', primarily as a means of securing rather more bureaucratic appointments and big government contracts, alongside the Zionist leaders and their Jewish immigrant mass base, theirs was a different world from that of the great bulk of Palestinian Arabs.

The Arab peasants found themselves squeezed on one side by Zionist land purchases (which brought about their ejection from lands that they had worked and lived on for generations), and on the other by their near-total exclusion from the developing 'Jewish economy' in the cities.

In their role as 'nationalist leaders', the Arab bourgeoisie also very often found themselves in competition with the rulers of Britain's surrounding Arab client regimes. King Faisal of Iraq in particular had established friendly relations with the Zionist leader Chaim Weizmann as early as 1918. Faisal saw Zionist colonisation both as a source of economic development for a future Arab state, and as a potential ally in European capitals for the advancement of Arab 'political independence'.

Faisal's older brother, Abdullah, similarly saw his own neighbouring Emirate of Transjordan as being the natural ruler of the Palestinian Arabs. Like Faisal, he saw his route towards this objective as coming through behind-the-scenes negotiations with the British and with the Zionists, using his statelet's proximity (and thus his dynasty's political influence over the Palestinians) as a bargaining chip.

This triangular struggle between the British, the Zionists and the Arabs occasionally burst out into open conflict. Riots in Jerusalem in 1920, in Jaffa in 1921 and in Jerusalem and Hebron in 1929, all saw the murder of Jewish residents by Arab mobs. However, most of Hebron's ancient Sephardi Jewish community were protected by their Arab neighbours from a mob of Husseini-led pogromists, who had gathered there intending to travel to Jerusalem to join the riots taking place there.

The British authorities typically responded to disturbances like this with a characteristic cynicism. On the one hand, they placed limits on Jewish immigration. On the other, they tolerated the growth of the Zionist movement's armed militias, and even recruited Jews into the Mandatory administration's own security forces. Together, these would spread a murderous terror amongst Arab peasants in the countryside, much less-publicised by historians than the rarer, if often more spectacular, Arab riots in the cities.

Zionism, Fascism, and Jewish emigration

Although the Zionists bridled at Britain's immigration quotas, they actually struggled to fill them for most of the first decade and a half of the British Mandate. For all Zionism's romanticisation of it as the Jewish people's 'real home', Palestine was not a very attractive place for Jewish immigrants to live during the postwar economic boom of the 1920s. The USA, western Europe, South Africa and Latin America were all far more inviting destinations.

The single largest source of Jewish emigration from Europe before the First World War had been the Tsarist Russian Empire, which included most of today's Poland and Ukraine. However, the Russian Revolution of 1917 very systematically liberated the Jews of the former Russian Empire from their previous position as a hunted pariah caste. Russian, Ukrainian and Polish Jews, among them Leon Trotsky, Grigory Zinoviev and Lev Kamenev formed a visible component of the leadership of Russia's revolutionary movements, in particular the Bolshevik party and its successor, the Communist Party.

Soviet Jews likewise were absorbed into the new Soviet state's planned economy, both as bureaucrats, professionals and administrators and as white-collar and industrial workers. Their dreams of emigration were now largely at an end, at least until the revival of antisemitism by Joseph Stalin's counterrevolution in the 1930s.

This left only interwar Poland (which included much of today's western Ukraine and Belarus) and the sizeable Jewish minorities in Romania, Hungary and elsewhere as serious pools of potential Jewish immigration to Palestine. However, where they could, these prospective Jewish immigrants far preferred to go to Britain, France, Germany or the Americas.

By contrast, Jewish people in economically advanced and industrialised countries like Germany, Austria and the Czech region of Czechoslovakia saw little reason to emigrate anywhere; although Jews from Slovakia often did migrate, either to the Czech lands or to the West. Jewish people in Britain, France and the USA had even less reason to emigrate, least of all to Palestine.

Left to its own devices, therefore, Zionism would probably have left behind little more than the relics of a failed project of colonisation, like Britain's attempt in that same period to populate the Kenyan highlands with white European farmers. Palestine would have been left with a sizeable minority of Jewish former colonists and their descendants, occupying a relatively privileged social position, but living alongside an Arab majority that would sooner or later seek to shake off British rule.

What changed this picture was the rise of Fascism in Europe and, more particularly, Nazism in Germany. Against the background of deepening economic crisis after the Wall Street Crash of 1929, and taking full advantage of the criminal refusal of the leaderships of the two mass working class parties, the Social Democrats and the Communists, to join forces against his storm troopers, Adolf Hitler came to power in 1933. Within a year and a half, the Nazi regime had not only liquidated the working class organisations, parties and unions, but effectively eliminated, or 'coordinated' as they put it, all independent political, cultural and social organisations.

Hitler himself was a pathological antisemite who argued in *Mein Kampf* for the 'extermination' of the Jews as the 'poisoners' of the German people. One of the first actions of the Nazi regime after taking power was a campaign to boycott Jewish businesses and antisemitic propaganda was systematically circulated not only in newspapers and on the radio but in schools and universities. At first sight, therefore, it seems unbelievable not only that the Zionist Federation of Germany, ZVfD, was allowed to maintain a legal existence, but that it built a uniformed, pro-Nazi youth organisation of its own.

There was, however, a logic to this that was accepted, at least temporarily, by Zionist and Nazi alike. Just as Herzl had hoped to negotiate with von Plehve, so some Zionists believed that the Nazi programme to 'rid' Germany of Jews could be channeled into support for emigration to Palestine. While Hitler himself never endorsed the policy—indeed he had opposed the idea of a Jewish state in *Mein Kampf* as 'a central organisation for their international world swindler, endowed with its own sovereign rights and removed from the intervention of other states: a haven for convicted scoundrels and a university for budding crooks'—in the early years of the Nazi regime, actual policy was the product of more pragmatic calculations. This included doing all they could to disrupt any international campaign against the new regime whilst it was still in the process of establishing itself.

German state policy and official propaganda, therefore, affected a hypocritical degree of enthusiasm for this suggested solution to Germany's 'Jewish problem'. As late as September 1935, the preamble to the Nazi regime's Nuremberg Laws made the following argument:

> 'If the Jews had a state of their own in which the bulk of their people were at home, the Jewish question could already be considered solved today, even for the Jews themselves. The ardent Zionists of all people have objected least of all to the basic ideas of the Nuremberg laws, because they know that these laws are the only correct solution for the Jewish people too.'

The turning point in official Nazi policy towards Zionism came in 1936, when a mass revolt of Palestine's Arab majority presented German imperialism with an opportunity to try to weaken its British rival, by switching from an affected 'pro-Zionist' propaganda position to an equally affected 'pro-Arab' one.

The Haavara Agreement and the Anti-Nazi Boycott

The Nazis' apparent indulgence of German Zionism went alongside a similar indulgence towards the Zionist movement's mainstream leadership in Palestine. The ZVfD and the Jewish Agency's leaders between them agreed to strike a deal with the Nazi regime between August and November 1933, the so-called 'Haavara' (Transfer) agreement.

Under the terms of this deal, the Anglo-Palestine Bank agreed to allow German Jewish emigrants to Palestine to use their liquidated assets to buy German-manufactured goods, whose subsequent sale in Palestine would then be used to compensate them for their losses of property in Germany. This turned Palestine into a major export market for German products. It also effectively undermined the boycott of German goods that had been proposed by numerous American-Jewish and other progressive organisations in March 1933.

The German Zionist movement opposed the anti-Nazi boycott quite openly, and found a willing audience amongst their counterparts in Palestine. The Central Association of German Citizens of Jewish Faith, whether through coercion or by faulty political calculation, even denied that 'the responsible government authorities' were aware of the violent attacks on Jewish businesses, arguing that 'we do not believe our German fellow citizens will let themselves be carried away into committing excesses against the Jews'.

The Haavara Agreement was, of course, an extremely unequal deal, at least from the standpoint of most German Jews. It was made at a time when Jewish people in Germany were already being cruelly attacked and discriminated against; and the various parties to this deal would have had very different subjective motives for pursuing it.

For the Zionist movement in Palestine, however, it provided a critical mass of Jewish immigrants who had nowhere else to go; and this gave the Zionist project a demographic viability that it had lacked until then. The agreement also brought to Palestine an influx of investment capital from the better-off section of Germany's Jewish minority who, under its terms, were thus able to emigrate to Palestine with at least some portion of their former property. At a time when most of the rest of the world was still struggling with the aftermath of the Great Depression, British-ruled Palestine enjoyed an investment-led boom.

This in turn helped to make Palestine a more attractive prospect for Jewish emigrants from Poland and elsewhere, a case reinforced by the Western imperialist democracies' response to the growing refugee crisis in Europe. This was to close their own borders to Jewish and other refugees from the wave of fascist and antisemitic reaction that Hitler's regime inspired across continental Europe.

The Zionist movement shared with the British, French and US ruling classes an interest in ensuring that Jewish refugees had nowhere to go but Palestine. In the USA, it was only the Communists and the small Trotskyist movement who demanded the lifting of immigration controls. Both the major Zionist organisations and the longer-established Jewish 'community leaders' largely stood aside, fearing that an influx of Jewish refugees would 'encourage' antisemitism.

In Britain, prominent Zionist leaders opposed similar calls

to 'open the gates' as late as the aftermath of the Nazis' notorious, nationwide Kristallnacht pogrom in November 1938.

This opposition extended even to the Kindertransport programme, in which the British government agreed to allow in some 10,000 Jewish children from Germany, Austria and Czechoslovakia, albeit without their parents.

Of the Kindertransport, David Ben-Gurion said the following:

> 'If I knew that it would be possible to save all the children in Germany by bringing them over to England, and only half of them by transporting them to Eretz Yisrael, then I would opt for the second alternative. For we must weigh not only the life of these children, but also the history of the People of Israel.'

Ben-Gurion's priorities here are quite clear: the building of a Jewish state took precedence over the actual wellbeing of Europe's oppressed Jewish minorities.

The Haavara Agreement should rightly be considered a source of shame and embarrassment for the Zionist movement. However, contrary to former Labour Mayor of London Ken Livingstone's notoriously misjudged comments in April 2016, this is not because this episode proves that Hitler 'was supporting Zionism'. Rather, the crime of this agreement was that it saw the Zionist movement's mainstream leadership act consciously to demobilise Jewish and progressive opinion worldwide from any attempt to undermine the Nazi regime, on the pretext of 'not making things difficult' for Germany's beleaguered Jews (and indeed only those who had sufficient property to take advantage of it).

Worse still, this came at a time when Hitler's regime was still only in the process of consolidating both its domestic power and its international acceptance, and therefore could still have been hurt by any movement of international solidarity. The Haavara Agreement also allowed Nazi Germany to deport a large portion of its Jewish citizens with minimal interference. This situation lasted until the outbreak of the Second World War in September 1939, which disrupted practically all trade and migration.

In the light of recent controversy, it should also be noted that there was opposition to this agreement even within the Zionist movement. With Hitler and Mussolini then at each other's throats over the fate of German-speaking Austria, Jabotinsky's partiality towards Fascist Italy meant that he could be quite vocal in his anti-Hitlerism. Revisionist Zionists thus denounced the Labor Zionists for their 'treason' in breaking the anti-Nazi boycott, and even tried to arrange a boycott campaign of their own.

This controversy provided grist to the mill of the occasionally violent rivalries between Labor and Revisionist Zionism in Palestine. In the course of this rivalry, two followers of Jabotinsky's openly fascist former comrade Abba Ahimeir assassinated the Labor Zionist politician Haim Arlosoroff on a beach in Tel Aviv in June 1933. Arlosoroff had been involved in the negotiations for the Haavara Agreement, and was a reviled hate figure in the Revisionist press.

However, tainted as they were by their association with Mussolini, Revisionist Zionists were neither credible nor especially attractive allies for any Jewish (or indeed non-Jewish) progressives, who might otherwise have continued the anti-Nazi boycott against official Zionist objections. Jabotinsky's proposed boycott therefore proved to be little more than a damp squib.

From the Arab Revolt to the Nakba

Some 150,000 new Jewish immigrants came to Palestine in the two years after Hitler came to power in Germany in 1933. This brought the Jewish population up to 443,000, or 27 per cent. In the previous six years, Jewish immigration had averaged only around 7,200 per year. Palestine might not yet have acquired the Jewish majority that would be necessary for the completion of Zionism's dreams of a 'Jewish state', but its eventual emergence was now no longer unthinkable.

The revival of Zionism's fortunes by the rise of fascism in Europe had an almost immediate effect in Palestine. It greatly exacerbated the conflict over land and alerted the Arab middle class and working class of the towns to the risk that their hopes for national independence following the end of British rule might be thwarted.

Amid booming economic conditions in the country as a whole, the Arab peasants faced increasing landlessness and penury. In the cities to which they migrated in search of casual work, they faced worsening unemployment and underemployment stemming from their racist exclusion from urban economic life. Arab workers became more militant and more organised while the Arab middle class was given a rude awakening about the timid complacency of the bourgeois and landowning leaders of Palestinian Arab nationalism.

Characteristically, it would be events in the Arab world outside of Palestine that provided the inspiration for revolt. In neighbouring Syria, the French authorities arrested the poet Fakhri al-Barudi and the politician Sayf al-Din al-Mamun following a memorial service for the recently deceased nationalist leader Ibrahim Hananu. Both had been prominent leaders of the National Bloc, whose offices were closed at the same time as their arrest.

What followed was a 50-day general strike, in the course of which the French arrested some 3,000 people and shot hundreds of demonstrators. It came to an end on 2 March 1936, when nationalist leaders agreed to accept negotiations. These led, six months later, to a Franco-Syrian treaty that formally recognised Syria's independence, albeit ceding the province of Alexandretta (today's Iskenderun and Antakya) to Turkey. Although the treaty granted it a continued role in Syria for the next 25 years, France failed to ratify it, fearing German influence in an independent Syria.

All the same, this was a first sign of rising unrest in the European imperialist powers' Arab colonies. Another was a wave of riots across Egypt in October 1935 when Britain attempted to renegotiate its 1922 unilateral declaration of Egypt's independence following Mussolini's invasion of Ethiopia. However, these failed to prevent the subsequent Anglo-Egyptian treaty in August 1936, which more or less preserved the status quo of Britain's military and political role there.

In November 1935, Palestine's British colonial police killed the itinerant Syrian Muslim preacher Izz ad-Din al-Qassam in a shootout in the village of Nazlet Zeid in today's West Bank, following the death of a Jewish policeman. Unaware of Qassam's identity, the British authorities were shocked when some 3,000 mourners attended his funeral. Famous across the Arab world for having fought the Italians in Libya in 1912 and the French in Syria in 1919, Qassam's death drew eulogies in the Egyptian press. He had spent the previous decade mainly in the Palestinian port city of Haifa, preaching to the new class of dispossessed peasants streaming in from the countryside, whose armed resistance to rural Zionist settlers and the British he then helped to lead.

The Arab Revolt of 1936

Amid rising urban unrest and the emergence of rural guerrilla war in Galilee and the West Bank, the Arab capitalists and landowners stepped in to 'lead' the Arab national movement in Palestine, before it got out of hand.

Amin al-Husseini called an all-Palestine 'Arab general strike' on 19 April 1936. He formed the Arab Higher Committee, AHC, the following week, stuffing it with representatives both of his own clan and of his Nashashibi rivals, who later withdrew from it. Across the country, Arab 'National Committees' were formed at local level, less clearly under the AHC's control but broadly professing allegiance to it.

The British responded by demolishing hundreds of houses in Arab-majority Jaffa, and authorising Jewish-majority Tel Aviv to build its own seaport to reduce Jaffa's importance. In the countryside, the British carried out thousands of house demolitions and imposed fines as collective punishments on resistant villages, in an eerie preconfiguration of Israel's later tactics during the Palestinian uprisings of 1988–91 and 2000–5.

Eventually, Arab dock workers in the port of Haifa went on strike in October 1936. This was a strategically vital location for British imperialism, given the nearby oil refineries which processed oil from Britain's Iraqi client state. The Histadrut then stepped in and showed the true class character of its Labor Zionism by replacing the striking Arabs with Jewish scabs, thus allowing Britain to maintain its control of this strategic resource.

This display of Arab working class militancy, albeit one cruelly undermined by Zionist racism, alongside the uncontrollable social anger of the Arab peasants, was enough to panic the AHC into calling an end to the general strike the following month.

The AHC leaders were given vital cover for this treachery by Abdullah, the Emir of Transjordan, by his nephew, King Ghazi of Iraq, and by the Saudi monarch, Abdulaziz ibn Al Saud. In an open letter published in the Palestinian Arab press, they urged the Palestinian Arabs to accept negotiations, adding that: 'We rely on the good intentions of our friend Great Britain, who has declared that she will do justice'.

Husseini, having been amongst the most pro-British of Palestine's Arab leaders, was now a marked man. He fled to the sanctuary of the Al Aqsa Compound in Jerusalem in July 1937 following tip-offs about his impending arrest, and then fled to French-ruled Lebanon three months later. During the Second World War, he would become an ally of Nazi Germany, and was a leading figure in promoting anti-British unrest in Egypt and Iraq both before and after this.

The AHC and the local National Committees were forcibly dissolved by the British, with many of their leaders deported to the Seychelles and elsewhere across the British Empire. By Britain's own estimates, around 1,000 Arabs were killed during the general strike. Britain also sealed Palestine's borders and established an internment camp for Arab prisoners near Acre, while building fortified police and army stations across the countryside, modelled on their equivalents in British-ruled India and Ireland.

None of this, however, was enough to put an end to the war in the countryside. In fact, this escalated, as the illegal Revisionist Zionist militia, Irgun, began a campaign of indiscriminate attacks on Arab civilians, fearing that the British authorities' repression would not be enough to put an end to the Arab uprising. The Irgun conducted a massacre of Arab bus passengers in Jaffa and Jerusalem on 'Black Sunday' on 14 November 1937. Not to be outdone, Ben-Gurion allowed the Haganah's special operations squads, the Peulot Meyuhadot, to conduct similar actions from early 1939 onwards. Even so, Arab rebels were able to storm into Jerusalem's Old City in October 1938, before being driven out by three British army regiments.

The British also stepped up the recruitment of Jews into their security forces, establishing the Jewish Settlement Police in the countryside and the Jewish Supernumerary Police in the cities. These were recruited primarily from the Labor Zionists' semi-legal Haganah militia, as also were the Special Night Squads, led by the British army officer, Orde Wingate.

Coming from a deeply religious family of Plymouth Brethren, this convinced Christian Zionist developed a reputation both for sadism in his dealings with Arab civilians, and for a degree of daring and initiative in thwarting Arab guerrilla attacks on the now-defunct Mosul to Haifa pipeline, which brought oil from Iraq to the Mediterranean through Transjordan and Palestine.

The British also established the 'peace bands', unofficial Arab militias led by local landlords and by the Nashashibis' National Defence Party, who conducted repression on the Arab majority from within. These, however, were later disarmed, their veterans regarded as outcasts by their own communities.

At the height of Britain's repression of the Revolt, there were up to 50,000 British and Australian soldiers in Palestine, almost three times as many as in India. This went alongside some 20,000 Jewish policemen, 3,000 British policemen, 15,000 Haganah militia fighters and around 2,000 from the Irgun. For such a small country, Palestine stretched the resources of the world's then most powerful empire to keep it under control. Even with the uprising facing certain defeat by early 1939, it was clear that Britain would have to make concessions.

The Peel Plan and the White Paper

Britain's initial political response to the Arab Revolt was to toy with the idea of dividing Palestine into an Arab state and a Jewish state, as per the Peel Commission's proposals in July 1937. The Jewish state would have contained most of Palestine's coastline, stretching from halfway between Jaffa and Ashkelon (then known by its Arabic name al-Majdal Asqalan) up to the Lebanese border, and would have contained the whole of Galilee in today's northern Israel. Gaza, the West Bank and the Negev desert would all have been part of the proposed Arab state, apart from a British-controlled corridor from Jaffa to Jerusalem, which would have remained under a permanent British mandate.

Needless to say, this proposal outraged the Arabs and failed to satisfy the Zionists. Nonetheless, Weizmann and Ben-Gurion convinced the World Zionist Congress in August 1937 to accept the Peel plan as a basis for future negotiations, not feeling especially bound by its proposed borders. The plan at least had the merit from their standpoint of accepting that there would be a 'Jewish state' in Palestine after all, if not yet in all of it.

A pan-Arab summit called by the exiled AHC in Bloudan in Syria's Damascus suburbs the following month, however, overwhelmingly rejected the Peel plan. Three months later, in December, the British Cabinet voted secretly to abandon the Peel plan. The British Woodhead Commission later backtracked both from the Peel plan and from two proposed alternatives in November 1938, on the basis that any viable partition of the country would require large scale forced movements of populations. The Peel plan itself had advocated the forced transfer of some 225,000 Arabs.

With the threat of war in Europe looming, Britain went through the motions of consulting Arab and Jewish political delegations separately at a conference in London's St James's Palace in February and March 1939. This predictably failed to establish any consensus between the parties; on the continuation of the Mandate; on continued Jewish immigration; on the commitment to a 'Jewish national home'; or on full independence for an undivided Palestine.

Hitler's invasion and occupation of Czechoslovakia took place during the last two days of this conference. With this in mind, Britain's Colonial Secretary, Malcolm MacDonald, hastily announced a shift in British policy. Britain was now committed to a ten-year transition period towards Palestinian independence, during which Jews and Arabs would both be recruited gradually into the senior ranks of Palestine's British colonial civil service. The British promised to maintain the existing quotas on Jewish immigration by agreement with recognised Palestinian Arab leaders, and promised to restrict further land purchases in some parts of the country.

This was then formalised in an official White Paper on 23 May 1939. The bloody defeat of the Arab Revolt was thus followed by an entirely illusory political victory for it. Britain, that 'Perfidious Albion' rarely known for keeping its promises, now promised to give the Palestinian Arabs almost all of what they wanted, having spent the previous three years killing 5,000 of them, wounding 15,000 and imprisoning 13,000 to prevent them from getting it.

Meanwhile, it was still the British who controlled and ruled the country, although with the Zionist movement's armed militias playing a much-increased direct and indirect role in assisting them. Britain could only have kept its promises to the Arabs by disarming or by making war on its Zionist allies, something that it showed no obvious inclination towards doing.

Alongside the events of 1947–49 and of June 1967, the Arab revolt of 1936–39 was one of the three defining tragedies of modern Palestinian history. The next came less than a decade later. In between, the European Jews suffered what was to become their own defining tragedy of the same century, namely, Nazi Germany's meticulously planned attempt to exterminate the whole Jewish population of Europe, which claimed some six million Jewish lives.

The World War and the Holocaust

Needless to say, Britain's sudden switch of policy caused much more than just annoyance to the Jewish colonists who had supported British colonial rule against the rebellious Arabs. The outbreak of war in Europe in September 1939, however, forced most Zionists in Palestine to bide their time, despite the inclination of a minority towards immediate confrontation with Britain.

Many Jewish colonists were recruited into the British war effort in Lebanon and Syria, through the British-sponsored Zionist paramilitary organisation, Palmach. This became the main legal cover for the Haganah until the British stopped funding it in 1942. Alongside the previous recruitment into Palestine's British colonial security forces during the Revolt, this helped to turn the Haganah into a disciplined and professional fighting force.

However, a small minority within the Revisionist Zionist movement conducted a terrorist campaign against both British and Arab targets in protest at the White Paper, even during the Second World War. Represented by Lehi's leader, Avraham Stern, this extremist minority succeeded in assassinating Britain's Minister Resident in the Middle East, Lord

Moyne, in Cairo, in November 1944.

They had previously approached German officials in Lebanon and Turkey with an offer to join the war on Germany's side in late 1940 and early 1941. In return, they requested German support for the creation of a pro-German fascist state in Palestine under their leadership, to which Hitler would then be able to deport German-occupied Europe's Jewish populations en masse.

The Nazis, however, never even deigned to respond to this proposal, which they evidently did not take at all seriously. Less than a year later, it would have been seen as little more than a minor distraction from the genocidal 'Final Solution to the Jewish Question' that Nazi Germany was already undertaking in Europe. Stern himself was captured and killed in a shootout with British police in February 1942, only a month after the Wannsee Conference in Berlin at which the Nazi regime set about planning its genocide of the European Jews.

After the end of the Second World War in Europe, however, Lehi were joined in their armed campaign to coerce Britain into accepting a Jewish state in the whole of Palestine by the more 'mainstream' right-wing Irgun, from which Lehi had originally split in August 1940. By far the most famous of the attacks conducted by these two groups was the King David Hotel bombing in Jerusalem in July 1946, which killed 91 people including 41 Arabs, 28 British government employees and 17 Jews.

The aftermath of the Second World War and the Nazi Holocaust produced a refugee crisis in Europe on an even larger scale than its prewar equivalent. The Western imperialist democracies, predictably, reprised their former heartless role by doing as little as possible to relieve this crisis. There were up to 11 million people in camps for displaced persons in Italy, Germany and Austria alone, but only 60,000 were registered as Jewish refugees by the Western allies. However this figure later more than doubled, as Polish Jewish refugees in Poland fled to the West, especially after the murder of 42 Jews in a pogrom in Kielce in July 1946.

Just two months later there were only some 12,000 Jews left

in Poland, despite the previous agreement to return to Poland 200,000 displaced Polish Jews in the USSR, who had survived the war by fleeing to Soviet-held territory.

The Jewish refugee crisis in Europe, large as it was, could have been resolved easily if the victorious Western Allies had agreed to take in and rehabilitate Jewish refugees themselves. Britain took in up to 120,000 Polish citizens in the aftermath of the war. These were mainly exiled supporters of the former Polish government-in-exile, who chose not to return to the new 'Communist' Poland that had been established by the Soviet occupation that followed Germany's defeat. Britain also took in around 12,000 Ukrainian former prisoners of war, who had fought alongside the Nazis during the German occupation of Ukraine. Canada, too, took in comparable numbers of Ukrainians, including hundreds who would subsequently be accused, or suspected, of having committed war crimes.

As was the case before the war, the Zionist movement in Palestine had every interest in ensuring that these refugees had nowhere to go but Palestine. Alongside the resumption of an armed campaign against British rule and Arab independence, the Revisionist Zionists, and later also the Haganah, began a campaign of illegal Jewish immigration to Palestine, hoping to shame the British into dropping the immigration quotas imposed under the White Paper.

It is of course neither condemnable nor difficult to understand that many traumatised and desperate European Jews heeded Zionism's siren calls to Palestine in this period, given the indifference to their plight of the Western powers and of Joseph Stalin's USSR alike. Equally, however, from the Palestinian Arabs' standpoint, it was very clearly an injustice that they should be called upon to abandon their aspirations for national independence in their own country, in order to shoulder a burden that much larger and much wealthier states would not.

The Revisionist Zionists' armed campaign against the British also enjoyed the occasional, if indirect, support of the official Labor Zionist leadership around Ben-Gurion. The combination of the armed campaign and illegal immigration threw

British policy into crisis. Unwilling to be seen to 'take sides' between Jews and Arabs, and in order not to disturb its relations both with the Zionist movement in Palestine and with its own client Arab regimes, British imperialism cynically handed over the 'Palestine problem' to the newly-formed United Nations, then still dominated by European powers with large colonial empires of their own.

What followed was a war, celebrated today by Israelis as a 'War of Independence', and commemorated by Palestinians as the 'Nakba' (Catastrophe). In the course of it, between 750,000 and 900,000 Palestinians were driven from their ancestral lands, villages and cities to create a state in which relatively recent Jewish settlers would be a majority. Before these events, Arabs still formed two thirds of Palestine's population, and still owned 90 per cent of its land.

The Partition of Palestine

Israel's official story of how and why this happened is that the surrounding Arab states broadcast radio messages urging the Palestinian Arabs to flee. This, supposedly, was to allow the armies of four Arab states to invade Palestine and 'drive the Jews into the sea'. David Ben-Gurion, the 'founding father' of the Israeli state, in effect claimed that the Palestinian Arabs fled so that the Arab armies could carry out a second Holocaust.

Over decades, however, not only Palestinian historians but even a handful of courageous Israeli historians have exposed this account as a pack of lies. Zionist paramilitary forces, many armed and trained by the British in the 1930s and 1940s, were by far the strongest of all of the armies on the ground. By early 1948, the mainstream Labor Zionist movement's militia, the Haganah, stood at around 50,000 rising by the summer to 80,000. It included a small air force, a navy and units of tanks, armoured cars and heavy artillery.

Against this, the Palestinians had only 7,000 poorly equipped irregulars, most of them locals, alongside some volunteers recruited from Syria and Iraq. The Haganah could also rely on the support of the more right-wing Zionist militias, like the Italian fascist-inspired Irgun and Lehi.

The surrounding Arab states; Transjordan, Iraq, Syria, Lebanon and Egypt, had all only just emerged from British or French colonial rule or domination and their governments were still dominated by British and French interests. Their armies, good for little more than palace coups and for shooting strikers and demonstrators, had been created for the purpose of internal repression, rather than for serious wars with other states.

Of these five countries, Lebanon's main role in the 1947–49 war in Palestine was to round up and disarm Palestinian refugees and fighters on its territory, rather than to assist them. Only Transjordan had a well-trained professional army, the Arab Legion, and it was still commanded by a British general, Sir John Bagot Glubb ('Glubb Pasha'). At the time, however, Transjordan's Abdullah was secretly negotiating with Ben-Gurion for a Jordanian occupation of the West Bank, and for its annexation to his resource-poor statelet. Both sides wanted to prevent the emergence of a separate state for the Palestinian Arabs under Amin al-Husseini's leadership or, even worse from their standpoints, under the leadership of the Palestinian guerrilla leaders who had fought the British and the Zionists during the Arab Revolt.

Adhering closely to the 'red lines' of Abdullah's understanding with Ben-Gurion, which the British clearly had prior knowledge of, Glubb saw to it that the Arab Legion never at any point in the war occupied any of the territory that had been set aside for a 'Jewish state' by the United Nations. The Arab Legion even allowed Tiberias and Safed in the north of the country to fall to the Haganah in April and May 1948, to prevent Husseini establishing a provisional Palestinian government there. As a result, most of the fighting between the Haganah and the Arab Legion took place because the Zionists tried to occupy areas well beyond this pre-agreed division of the spoils.

The Nakba, or Catastrophe

The United Nations had arrived at a detailed plan for the partition of Palestine into Arab and Jewish states in November

1947, although it stipulated only voluntary 'transfers' and 'exchanges' of populations were to take place. Arab governments and Palestinian Arab leaders overwhelmingly rejected the plan, awarding as it did roughly half of Palestine to the Jewish one-third of its population, for a proposed 'Jewish state' in which Arabs, even then, would still form a slim majority. Assuming, of course, that they remained there.

As with the Peel plan in 1937, Ben-Gurion and the mainstream Labor Zionist movement accepted the United Nations Partition Plan, seeing it as a springboard for future Zionist aspirations in Palestine as a whole, while the Revisionist Zionist Irgun and Lehi both rejected it. For the right-wing Revisionists, this plan fell far short of their original demands in 1922 for a Jewish state on both sides of the River Jordan.

Both wings of the Zionist movement, however, had the full intention of turning Jews into an overwhelming majority of the population there by 'redeeming' the land from its indigenous Arab population, that is, by expelling Arabs and importing Jewish immigrants and refugees from Europe, the Arab world and elsewhere.

In fact, the Partition Plan gave the Zionist movement far more land than was then owned or controlled by Palestine's Jewish settler minority. To achieve the Jewish majority that would give a Jewish state in Palestine any political or demographic viability, it was necessary to put into operation a number of plans that had been drawn up years, or decades, beforehand, to drive out the Arabs.

The most comprehensive of these was known as Plan Dalet (or 'Plan D'), which informed most of the Haganah's military actions in 1947–49. This envisaged the forced transfer from their lands of hundreds of thousands of Palestinian Arabs in the Arab-majority rural Galilee region and in the Negev desert as well as the ethnic cleansing of Palestine's major towns and cities, especially the ports like Haifa, Jaffa and Acre.

Britain's immediate response to the Partition Plan was to 'wash its hands' like the Biblical Roman governor of Palestine, Pontius Pilate, announcing unilaterally and in advance that Britain would terminate its former League of Nations Mandate over Palestine less than six months later on 14 May 1948. The Jewish Agency, then led by Ben-Gurion himself, then unilaterally declared the independence of the new State of Israel from the same day as Britain's formal withdrawal.

In the intervening six months, however, Britain was still officially responsible for maintaining 'law and order' in Palestine. But British forces had in effect withdrawn to their camps, and British-officered police stations did absolutely nothing to protect civilians (overwhelmingly Arabs, but also some Jews) from being massacred or displaced.

Britain also dismantled its colonial administration in Palestine right down to the last paperclip, taking Palestine's land records with it, which remain in British possession to this day. This did not harm the Zionists at all, because they had an effective state bureaucracy-in-waiting in the form of the Jewish Agency and their armed militias were more than capable of preserving 'law and order' in the areas that fell under their control during Britain's staged and ponderous withdrawal of its forces. It did, however, create a sudden power vacuum for the Arabs. They were left leaderless as the Arab upper classes fled to the neighbouring Arab states, leaving Arab workers and peasants behind to face attack almost undefended.

This perfidy was entirely of a piece with Britain's actions during the Partition of India only a few months before, when Britain stood aside and did nothing to prevent the terrible communalist slaughter and expulsions of millions, having previously spent decades setting Hindus, Muslims and Sikhs against each other. Both exits from Empire remain terrible stains on the record of Clement Attlee's much-lionised Labour government of 1945–51.

In the actual event, the new Israeli state's well-armed and trained militias seized 78 per cent of the former British Mandate territory, far beyond the 56 per cent awarded to them by the Partition Plan. In the process, some 530 Arab villages were destroyed or emptied of their Arab residents, as well as the Arab quarters of all the major urban areas, even including the western parts of Jerusalem. Jaffa was attacked on 25 April 1948 by the 'official' Haganah, acting alongside the even more murderous Irgun. Its Arab population of 100,000 was reduced to 5,000 in the space of a few days.

These atrocities were not simply carried out in the hot blood of combat, but were designed coldly and deliberately to spread panic, and thus to induce the indigenous Arab population to flee. According to the Israeli military historian Arieh Itzchaki, there were ten major massacres and about 100 smaller massacres perpetrated by various Zionist militias during the Partition.

Caesarea ('Qesarya' in Arabic) was the first village to be expelled in its entirety, on 15 February 1948. Another four villages were 'cleansed' on the same day, all recorded by watching British troops stationed in nearby police stations. Another village attacked that same night was Sa'sa' near the Lebanese border, where the officer in charge, Moshe Kelman, later recalled: 'We left behind 35 demolished houses (a third of the village) and 60–80 dead bodies (quite a few of them were children)'.

The most infamous Zionist massacre of all, however, took place at the village of Deir Yassin near Jerusalem on 9 April 1948. It was carried out by the Irgun and Lehi militias, whose national commanders respectively were Menachem Begin and Yitzhak Shamir. Both later became politicians for the Benjamin Netanyahu's right-wing Likud party, serving as prime ministers in 1977–83 and in 1986–92, respectively.

The responsibility for this massacre has generally been placed solely on these two militias alone. In part, this is because Ben-Gurion admitted to, and 'apologised' for, the massacre at the time, in a bid to shift international blame onto his right-wing rivals. But Israeli 'New Historians', like Ilan Pappé, have shown that Haganah commanders approved of their plans, and even sent the Palmach to Deir Yassin to help them finish it off.

This massacre however had an immediate effect on Arab civilian morale. Its scale (exaggerated from the actual figure of 107 to some 254) was used to terrify other villages and city districts. Trucks carrying loudspeakers broadcast the news and urged Arabs elsewhere to flee to escape a similar fate. This village of only 600 people lay just a few miles to the west of

Jerusalem. Its inhabitants had signed a non-aggression pact with neighbouring Jewish settlements and even with Lehi commanders. It had at most around 30-odd armed villagers for its defence.

Some 132 Irgun and 60 Lehi commandos stormed into it as dawn was breaking. Ilan Pappe's 2006 book *The Ethnic Cleansing of Palestine* sums up what happened:

> 'As they burst into the village, the Jewish soldiers sprayed the houses with machine-gun fire, killing many of the inhabitants. The remaining villagers were then gathered in one place and murdered in cold blood, their bodies abused while a number of the women were raped and then killed'.

Born in Deir Yassin, a 2017 documentary film by the Israeli director Neta Shoshani, collected a series of eyewitness accounts, including from some Israelis involved in the events. One was Yehoshua Zettler, the Jerusalem commander of Lehi. In a candid but unapologetic interview, he described the way in which Deir Yassin's inhabitants were killed:

> 'I won't tell you that we were there with kid gloves on. House after house … we're putting in explosives and they are running away. An explosion and move on, an explosion and move on and within a few hours, half the village isn't there any more.'

Another witness was Professor Mordechai Gichon, who was a Haganah intelligence officer sent to Deir Yassin after the massacre ended:

> 'To me it looked a bit like a pogrom. If you're occupying an army position—it's not a pogrom, even if a hundred people are killed. But if you are coming into a civilian locale and dead people are scattered around in it—then it looks like a pogrom. When the Cossacks burst into Jewish neighbourhoods, then that should have looked something like this.'

Despite Ben-Gurion's and the Labor Zionists' attempts to

present this and other massacres as the exceptional results of the actions of a few extremists, these 'extremists' were not punished in any way. Indeed, they eventually succeeded the Labor Zionists in power in Israel in the 1970s, and continued the same murderous methods in southern Lebanon in the 1980s. These very 'respectable' extremists never apologised once for their actions in 1948. Quite the opposite.

Menachem Begin, who was later awarded the Nobel Peace Prize in 1978, wrote in in his memoir *The Revolt: Inside Story of the Irgun*, in 1951, as follows: 'the massacre was not only justified but there would not have been a state of Israel without the victory at Deir Yassin.'

He went on:

> 'The legend of Deir Yassin helped us in particular in the saving of Tiberias and the conquest of Haifa. ... All the Jewish forces proceeded to advance through Haifa like a knife through butter. The Arabs began fleeing in panic, shouting "Deir Yassin!"'

The Result of the 'War of Independence'

The state of Israel was consolidated during a year of war, both against the resistance of the Palestinian Arabs and against the interventions of the surrounding Arab states. The defeat of these states was sealed in July 1949 by a series of ceasefires and armistices. It resulted in the mass expulsion of the most of the indigenous population.

Only some 160,000 Arabs remained inside the borders of the new state in 1949, about a third of them internal refugees. By then there were nearly 800,000 Palestinian refugees in camps in the neighbouring Arab states, many of them close to Israel's new borders. Despite United Nations resolutions and US President Harry Truman's wishes, the new state refused point blank to consider the return of these refugees.

And whatever they said in public, many of Israel's top leaders privately recognised that their state had been established by expelling the Palestinian population, just as they had planned. Nahum Goldmann, chair of the World Jewish Congress, recounted in his memoirs in 1978 that Ben-Gurion had once admitted as much to him in the following terms:

> 'If I were an Arab leader, I would never sign an agreement with Israel. It is normal; we have taken their country. It is true God promised it to us, but how could that interest them? Our God is not theirs. There has been Anti-Semitism, the Nazis, Hitler, Auschwitz, but was that their fault? They see but one thing: we have come and we have stolen their country. Why would they accept that?'

Moshe Dayan, a commander in the 1947–49 war who later served as Chief of Staff and as minister of defence, once summed up this unapologetic settler mentality during a funeral oration for an Israeli farmer killed near the Egyptian border in April 1956:

> 'Let us not today fling accusations at the murderers. Who are we that we should argue against their hatred? For eight years now, they sit in their refugee camps in Gaza and, before their very eyes we turn into our homestead the land and the villages in which they and their forefathers have lived. We are a generation of settlers, and without the steel helmet and the cannon we cannot plant a tree and build a home. Let us not shrink back when we see the hatred fermenting and filling the lives of hundreds of thousands of Arabs, who sit all around us. Let us not avert our gaze, so that our hand shall not slip. This is the fate of our generation, the choice of our life—to be prepared and armed, strong and tough—or otherwise, the sword will slip from our fist, and our life will be snuffed out.'

In the very week of the 70th anniversary of the partition of Palestine on 15 May 2018, Israel Defence Forces snipers once again were killing dozens of unarmed Palestinian demonstrators and wounding hundreds more on the border with the Gaza Strip. These demonstrators were trying to use their commemorations of the anniversary of the Nakba to break through the Israeli and Western media's blackout of their desperate situation.

Only the day before, the appallingly racist and pro-Israel US President Donald Trump sent his daughter Ivanka and his son-in-law Jared Kushner to open the new US embassy in Jerusalem, in defiance of an international consensus against recognising Israel's illegal annexation of Arab East Jerusalem following Israel's occupation of it in June 1967.

It therefore continues to be vital that the global movement of solidarity with Palestine makes clear that a state born out the expropriation of an entire people, a racist state created on the basis of a hundred Deir Yassins, has no right to continue to exist on this basis.

The Apartheid State

Ever since its establishment by war in 1948, the Zionist state has faced a fundamental dilemma. On the one hand, as a self-described 'Jewish and democratic state', Israel cannot be stable or complete as long as the people that it displaced and continues to oppress are still present in significant numbers within the territory under its control.

On the other hand, Israel has not yet been able to complete the obliteration or, to use the correct term, the genocide, of the Palestinians as a distinct people, despite seven decades of trying, four major wars with its neighbours and the generous investment and military aid it receives from the so-called Western democracies.

Like Australia or the USA before it, Israel could only manage the demands of its dispossessed and disenfranchised indigenous population, perhaps even effect some future 'reconciliation' with them, if its colonist-descended population possessed an unassailable ethnic majority. Until that is achieved, the national aspirations and the historic memory of the Arab Palestinians, both those under occupation and Israel's own minority Arab citizens, pose an existential threat. Ultimately, this dilemma will bring about the downfall of the Zionist state.

Israel faces three fundamental options. A decisive choice between them has merely been disguised and delayed by the pretence of a 'peace process' towards a 'two-state solution' that no Israeli government yet has ever agreed to, and probably never will. This choice has been complicated further by the conquests that Israel undertook in 1967.

Israel's fundamental choices

The 'maximum programme' of Zionism requires a state with a sizeable Jewish majority in a defensible territory large enough to satisfy the social and material aspirations both of its current Jewish citizens and of future Jewish immigrants who are essential to Israel's continued development.

The expulsion of much of the existing population in the war that accompanied Partition in 1947–49 provided Israel with this large Jewish majority within the borders that it acquired at that time. This territory, however, did not fit the bill as far as the need for new Jewish immigration was concerned.

The conquest of Gaza, East Jerusalem and the West Bank in June 1967 'solved' this second problem by providing Israel with new resources and new land for Jewish settlement. This time, however, the bulk of the existing population of these territories did not flee, leaving an expanded Israel with a new 'Palestinian problem'.

Thus, although that war gave Israel control of all of Britain's former Mandate of Palestine, plus the Syrian Golan Heights, occupied in 1967 and annexed unilaterally in 1981, it also placed under Israel's rule Arab and Jewish populations of roughly equal size, the former with a higher birthrate than most of the latter. This meant that Israel could not, and still cannot, simply 'annexe' Gaza or the West Bank in the way that it subsequently annexed East Jerusalem and the Golan Heights.

The resulting anomaly, of occupied Palestinians possessing neither formal citizenship nor a separate state of their own, was justified as merely being a temporary 'security measure', pending a comprehensive peace settlement. In the meantime, the illegal Jewish settlement of the 1967 territories has allowed Israel to break up the physical continuity of the West Bank's areas of Palestinian habitation, thereby creating a de facto piecemeal assimilation of the occupied territories into Israel, without any formal annexation.

In practice, the 'Area A' parts of the territories that were handed over to the Palestinian Authority under the Oslo Accords after 1993, have played much the same role as Apartheid South Africa's 'Bantustans', keeping the occupied

Palestinians under control in the ever-shrinking portion of their lands into which they have been herded.

This tension, between the imperatives of expansion and the imperatives of a Jewish ethnic majority, is what lies at the heart of the biggest controversies in Jewish Israeli electoral politics, including the often arcane controversies over 'who is a Jew' for the purpose of Israeli citizenship.

The most obvious route to the completion of the 'Zionist dream' would be for Israel to 'finish the job' that it began in 1948 by expelling the majority of Palestinians from the West Bank and the Gaza Strip. But this would require much more than just a 1948-style war, and remains unlikely, if not impossible, except under the conditions of a generalised regional war across the Middle East.

Of course, such a war is not entirely beyond imagination, but, if it were to come to pass, in its aftermath there would be little to attract new Jewish immigrants from around the world. Opinion polls, in the USA in particular, already show a sharp decline in the Jewish diaspora's support for aggressive Israeli policies.

Short of such a war, Israel's second-best option is to continue its current programme of settlement expansion, with an intensified 'separation' of Jewish Israeli and Arab Palestinian populations, while putting off indefinitely any negotiated 'final agreement' with the Palestinians. This has been the effective programme of all three of Israel's prime ministers since 2001; Ariel Sharon, Ehud Olmert and Benjamin Netanyahu.

This course, however, reveals increasingly clearly the character of Israel as an Apartheid state. Already, the total number of Arab Palestinians in historic Palestine very slightly exceeds the total number of Jewish Israelis, if one includes Israel's 1.7 million Arab citizens alongside the 4.8 million Palestinians in the 1967 occupied territories. Given relative birth rates, the passage of time will fatally undermine Israel's claim to be the only democracy in the Middle East and, as a result, much of its popular support in the West.

Israel's third option, of course, would be to accept completely equal citizenship for Jews and Arabs in a democratic and fully secular bi-national state. This, however, would mean the end of Zionism's reactionary utopia of an ethnically exclusive state for the world's Jews in Palestine. It would mean the 'normalisation' of a state created by colonisation on the basis of abandoning its colonising project, instead of on the basis of completing it.

The Arabs in Israel

For Israel's apologists in the West, however, any reference to Israel as a 'colonial-settler state' is automatically offensive. This might seem curious, given the early Zionist movement's open identification with the projects of European colonisation and the frequent references to colonial themes made by many Israeli politicians today, at least when addressing an Israeli audience. What this reflects is a recognition that 'colonialism' and 'colonisation' no longer possess the respectable status they had before 1945. As a result, Israel has to justify its existence in today's world by claiming an entirely unique status, as a 'national homeland' for the Jews, supposedly 'recovered' after its loss some 2,000 years ago, underpinned by the exceptional character of the Nazi Holocaust, the latter having become a key component of this ideological self-justification.

Similarly, the near-universal condemnation of South African apartheid makes Israel's advocates hypersensitive to any comparison with that regime, as witnessed in the synthetic furore stirred up around the IHRA definition of antisemitism. Such distancing from South Africa is all the more ironic, given that Israel was quite possibly apartheid South Africa's closest and friendliest ally. Israel partnered white South Africa in their joint pursuit of nuclear weapons, and provided the material support for the apartheid regime's repression of its black majority that the Western imperialist democracies could not provide openly.

For Israel's apologists, the basis for their 'defence' against accusations of 'colonialism' and 'apartheid' is the existence in Israel of a sizeable Arab minority. They argue that, unlike South Africa, where whites were only about a tenth of the population, Israel has a Jewish majority, at least within its 1967 borders. They also point out that (again, unlike South Africa's black majority) Israel's Arab inhabitants are voting citizens of the same state.

An examination of the place of Arabs, and Jews, within Israeli society, however, readily makes clear Israel's continuing 'colonial' character. The position of Israel's Arab minority reflects the fact that, within the Green Line, Israel's project of colonisation is far more advanced than in the West Bank. Their second-class status, and their enforced separation from their expelled kith and kin elsewhere, demonstrate what Israel would impose on Palestinians in the West Bank as well, if only it could get away with it.

Equally, although the conditions of Israel's Arab citizens are quite visibly 'less harsh' than those of Palestinians in the 1967 territories, it should not be forgotten that, of the roughly 950,000 who lived on the territory that is now Israel before Partition, only some 160,000 were still there after it. Israel was then able, magnanimously, to 'allow' this fraction of the original population to become Israeli citizens or, from their standpoint, to impose Israeli citizenship on them.

Israel's Arab citizens in effect enjoy only individual civil rights, while only Jewish citizens enjoy collective national rights from the standpoint of a state that defines itself as belonging to the Jewish people worldwide, rather than to its actual citizens. This already makes their citizenship unequal in its nature. To add insult to injury, even Arab citizens' individual rights are not on a par with the individual rights of Israel's Jewish citizens, especially in the sphere of property rights and the inheritance of citizenship.

The Legal Centre for Arab Minority Rights in Israel (Adalah) has identified 55 laws that discriminate explicitly against Arab citizens. In particular, the same laws that stripped Palestinian refugees of their citizenship and property after 1948 also created the bizarrely Kafka-esque legal category of 'present absentees', to which just under a third of Israel's Arab citizens were relegated. Like the refugees themselves, these 'absentees' also had their property seized by the state, on the pretext of their having been 'absent' from their homes at some point or another during the war.

Other laws placed expropriated Arab land under the control of the Israel Land Authority, whose covenants with the (non-state) Jewish National Fund require it to lease state-controlled land only to Jews. This means that up to 93 per cent of Israel's land is off-limits for use by Israel's Arab citizens, to whom much of it once belonged.

This all helped the Israeli state in its early years to enforce a physical segregation between Arab and Jewish citizens that more or less continues today. For example, just under half of Israel's Arab citizens today live in villages and small towns in the Galilee, a region in which Arabs constitute just over half of the population overall. They often enough live in predominantly Arab localities usually only a short distance from their expropriated former lands, on which almost exclusively Jewish towns and settlements have since been built.

About a fifth of Israel's Arabs live in the Jerusalem area, where some considerable proportion of the residents of occupied and annexed Arab East Jerusalem have opted to apply for Israeli citizenship rather than risk losing the precarious status of 'legal residents' that was imposed on them after 1967. About one-seventh live in the 'Little Triangle' region near Haifa, and constitute about 10 per cent of Haifa's urban population (and about 70 per cent of the population of its city centre). Almost all of the 54,000 residents of Umm al-Fahm in the 'Little Triangle' are Arabs, as also are almost all of the the 76,000 residents of Nazareth in the Galilee.

An amendment to Israel's Basic Law allows the state to prohibit parties from standing in elections if they engage in 'a denial of the existence of the State of Israel as the state of the Jewish people, a denial of the democratic nature of the state, or incitement to racism'. This has periodically been used to threaten bans on Israel's four Arab political parties, namely the National Democratic Assembly (Balad), the United Arab List, the Islamic Movement in Israel and the Arab Movement for Renewal (Ta'al).

Until the emergence of these parties from the 1960s onwards, Arab electoral politics in Israel was dominated by the

Israeli Communist Party (which acted almost as a surrogate party for Israel's Arab minority) and by the Arab satellite parties of Israel's ruling Labor Party. The latter were formed so that Labor could use the Arab minority as voting fodder, while excluding Arabs from the party's own formal membership. The Zionist Histadrut trade union federation similarly excluded Arabs from membership until 1959, and is still regarded as a bastion of Israel's more privileged European-origin Ashkenazi Jews.

Arab citizens of Israel are exempt from the military service that is compulsory for Jewish citizens, although many Druze and Bedouins volunteer for military service in pursuit of livelihoods that would not be available to them otherwise.

This 'exemption' of Arab citizens is hardly surprising given that the Israeli state in its own eyes does not even 'belong' to them to begin with. Anyone taken in by the common suggestion that this too demonstrates Israel's 'magnanimity' should bear in mind that access to social security benefits, to skilled jobs and even to public housing in Israel often depends on having done military service. This 'exemption' therefore provides the state (and non-state bodies) with a disguised means of conducting an entirely legal racial discrimination, justified obliquely by reference to the evident 'disloyalty' of its Arab 'fifth column'.

By contrast, ultra-orthodox Jews who refuse military service on religious grounds are allowed in its place to attend religious schools, 'yeshivot', and are treated as if they had performed military service for the same purpose of access to jobs, benefits, housing and so forth. This underlines the racial basis of this 'exemption', and also indicates the bravery of the tiny but vocal number of Jewish Israelis who refuse military service in the occupied territories, not on 'religious' grounds but on the basis of political principle.

Finally, the Citizenship and Entry into Israel Law prevents Arab citizens of Israel from passing on citizenship or residence rights to spouses from the 1967 territories. Originally passed in 2003 as a supposedly 'temporary' and 'defensive' measure during the Second Intifada, this law in fact underlines the entirely unequal and racist basis on which Israeli citizenship is held or acquired.

The aftermath of partition

This state of affairs has not emerged out of thin air but has a history. Israel's Arab minority were subjected to a military administration from the armistice of 1949 right up until 1966, despite nominally being citizens of the new state. This regime of martial law restricted their movements between localities in much the same way that the occupation restricts freedom of movement within the West Bank today, while imposing internment without trial, curfews and the expulsion of 'infiltrators' on a regular basis.

The near-totalitarian surveillance that was imposed on Israel's Arab citizens by its Shin Bet security service after 1949 was aimed at their intimidation and demoralisation. Odeh Bisharat, an Arab former leader of the Israeli Communist Party, graphically described the spying and the provocations that he experienced in his youth during those years in an interview in June 2013, saying it was as if 'the military administration settled in our homes, nestled between the sheets of our beds, between father and son, man and wife, until everything seemed suspect'.

Commenting on the Arab citizens killed during the Land Day protests in March 1976, and at the beginning of the Second Intifada in October 2000, Bisharat added that 'the military administration may have come to an end, but its spirit still hovers above us'.

But he also pointed out that the Arabs were not simply passive and atomised victims:

> 'The other side of the coin is the staying power of those that remained. The key word was 'sumud', steadfastness, and it was expressed in the building of homes, most of them without permits. The entire village would join in the construction work. It was also expressed in the exhausting daily struggle to obtain an exit permit to work in Jewish cities, the struggle to pave a road, to connect a village to the water and electricity grids and to build a school.'

Nor can the repression of Israel's Arab minority be seen in isolation from Israel's ongoing conflict with the Palestinians and with the Arab states in general. Between 1949 and 1956, a series of incidents occurred as Israeli security forces shot at Arab 'infiltrators' who tried to cross the Green Line, often to harvest crops or to join their families on the other side. On the very first day of Israel's 1956 war with Egypt over the Suez Canal, the Israel Border Police shot dead 48 Arab citizens in the border town of Kafr Qasim. Regarded as a 'hostile population' in times of war, they had been subjected to a curfew that most of them knew nothing about until they were killed for violating it.

Israeli special forces carried out numerous 'punitive raids' in Egyptian-occupied Gaza and the Jordanian-occupied West Bank during this same period, usually on the pretext of deterring or responding to raids conducted by Palestinian guerrillas. The most notorious such 'reprisal' took place in October 1953 in the village of Qibya in the West Bank, barely 20 kilometres from Kafr Qasim and, like it, on the 1949 armistice line with Jordan. At least 69 Palestinians were killed and 45 houses blown up, as well as the village's school and mosque. Two thirds of the victims were women and children.

Commanding the special forces Unit 101 that perpetrated this massacre was none other than Israel's future prime minister, Ariel Sharon. Dubbed the 'Butcher of Beirut' for his role as defence minister at the time of the September 1982 Sabra and Shatila massacres in Lebanon, Sharon was also responsible for the Temple Mount provocation in September 2000 that triggered the Second Intifada. As prime minster between 2001 and 2006, he began the construction of the notorious 'separation barrier' in the West Bank, and was responsible for the killing of 497 Palestinians in the various massacres across the West Bank that were part of 'Operation Defensive Shield' in the spring of 2002.

Israeli citizenship but Jewish nationality

Even the plethora of terms used to describe the Arabs in Israel is itself an indication of their anomalous status, as the descendants of those Palestinians that Israel had not yet expelled by the time its 'War of Independence' came to an end. In Western media, the most commonly used term to describe them is that they are 'Israeli Arabs' or 'Arab Israelis'. This term is rejected by most 'Israeli Arabs' themselves, who in general regard it as pejorative. Nor is it used much by Jewish Israelis. For them, it carries the suggestion that it is possible to be 'an Israeli' without being Jewish, and also that there is an Israeli nation that is distinct from 'the Jewish people' at large. Both of these things stand in direct contradiction to the claims of Zionist ideology.

A more commonly used euphemism in Israeli media is of 'the Arab sector', as opposed to the majority 'Jewish sector'. A more neutral term, used by Arabs in Israel as well, is of 'Arab citizens', here meaning 'Arab citizens of Israel' rather than citizens of some unnamed Arab state.

More nationalistic Arabs in Israel may use the term 'Palestinian citizens' to emphasise that they are not merely nondescript Arabs who happen to live in Israel, but part of the Palestinian people. Others still use the term '1948 Arabs' or '1948 Palestinians', to distinguish themselves from the '1967 Arabs' or '1967 Palestinians' across the Green Line.

By contrast, the intentionally provocative term 'Palestinian-Israeli' is used only by a small left-wing minority to emphasise their support either for a future bi-national state, or for their own complete absorption and normalisation as a recognised national minority in some future post-Zionist Israeli state.

It is easy enough from a distance to assume that this maze of terminology reflects an entirely natural identity crisis on the part of Israel's Arab minority but any such identity crisis is not at all theirs. On the contrary, it is the byproduct of an identity crisis of Israel's majority Jewish citizens, who have not yet squared their current material reality as a new nation of colonists with their own state's dominant national ideology.

As bizarre as this might sound to activists in the West, used to receiving lectures about 'Israel's right to exist', neither Zionist ideology, nor even Israel's own legal system, recognise the existence of an 'Israeli nation'. Israel, after all, is the state of the Jews, not the state of the Israelis.

This finds its most absurdly logical conclusion in Israel's citizenship and nationality laws. The identity cards that all Israeli citizens are obliged to hold all listed 'citizenship' and 'nationality' as distinct categories, at least until the introduction of biometric identity cards in 2005. Israel's internal population registry continues to record 'citizenship', 'nationality' and 'religion' separately.

All, by definition, have 'Israeli citizenship', but, in the category 'nationality', Israeli citizens can be Jewish, Arab, Druze, Circassian or one of roughly 130 other recognised 'nationalities', not all of them coterminous with origin in an existing nation-state. Citizens with 'Arab' nationality can be registered as being 'Muslim' or 'Christian' by religion; but citizens with 'Jewish' nationality can only ever be 'Jewish' by religion and vice versa.

Numerous court cases have been brought over the years by secular and irreligious Jewish Israelis who object to having any reference to religion in their official documents, as well as by non-Zionist Jewish Israelis who insist that they be allowed to list their nationality as being 'Israeli' rather than 'Jewish'. All such cases have come up against the objection that 'there is no Israeli nationality'.

In one such case in October 2013, Supreme Court judge Hanan Melcer argued that the creation of an inclusive Israeli nationality 'was against both the Jewish nature and the democratic nature of the State'. His colleague Asher Grunis added that 'the existence of an Israeli ethnic nationality has not been proven'.

More tellingly, in the earliest of these cases in 1971, Supreme Court judge Shimon Agranat argued that it was not legitimate 'just 23 years after the establishment of the state' for people to 'ask to separate themselves from the Jewish people and to achieve for themselves the status of a distinct Israeli nation', comparing the advocates of an inclusive Israeli nationality with the Southern Confederate separatists during the US Civil War.

The Israeli linguist Uzzi Ornan, who brought many of these court cases, has noted that these rulings allow Israel 'to continue being a very peculiar country indeed, one that refuses to recognise the nationality of its own people'. He added that they also tell Israel's Arab citizens 'that they have no real recognition in their own country, that they will always be treated as foreigners and they will always face discrimination'.

However, seen in the context of Netanyahu's repeated demands that Palestinian leader Mahmoud Abbas recognise Israel 'as a Jewish state', it should be clear that this message is entirely intentional.

Israel's Jewish citizens are Israeli citizens by right, while its Arab citizens are Israeli citizens only by sufferance, under permanent suspicion of disloyalty. Jewish Israelis enjoy citizenship by dint of being Jewish, while Jews outside of Israel are future such citizens by right, again by dint of being Jewish and nothing more.

That Jews outside of Israel are not yet Israeli citizens is solely a result of the unhappy accident that they have not yet 'returned home', something that Israel's ruling class hope one day in the future to rectify. By contrast, Israel's Arab citizens are citizens solely by virtue of the equally unhappy accident that they and their offspring have not yet left the country, something else that many in Israel's ruling class hope one day in the future to rectify.

Last, but not least, Zionism's identification of Jewishness with the Israeli state involved a massive assault on the culture and traditions of Jewish communities worldwide, religious and secular, liberal and socialist. It meant the rejection of their previous languages, in particular Yiddish, which many Zionists associated with a Jewish working class movement in Europe towards which they were quite instinctively hostile, and with the culture and ideological outlook of the much-derided 'old Jew' in Europe that Zionism hoped to replace with a modern, militaristic and Hebrew-speaking 'new Jew' in Palestine.

Many of the founding figures of Zionism expressed hostility to what they referred to as 'the Diaspora mentality' in terms that echoed the racism of the antisemites. By contrast, anti-Zionists, both Jewish and non-Jewish, far from being hostile to Jewish people, defend their best historic traditions, and in particular their contributions to the elements of a universal human culture, as well as to the culture of the various countries within which they lived.

Marxists likewise not only fought antisemitism but also recognised the progressive features of international Jewish culture. As the Russian revolutionary, Vladimir Ilyich Lenin, put it in 1913, referring to the Jewish minorities in western Europe and north America:

> 'There the great and universally progressive features of Jewish culture have made themselves clearly felt; its internationalism, its responsiveness to the advanced movements of our times (the percentage of Jews in democratic and proletarian movements is everywhere higher than the percentage of Jews in the general population).'

This has been seen throughout the twentieth century, not least in the role played by many young American Jews in the struggle for black civil rights against Jim Crow, the apartheid-like segregation of the US South. It is also witnessed today in the increasing number of Jewish people supporting the Palestinian struggle.

The Apartheid question

Does this mean then that Israel is 'an apartheid state'? The appeal of this designation to the many activists who make use of it is obvious, given the emotive character of this label. Like any analogy, the comparison of Israel to apartheid South Africa should not be taken to imply complete duplication; as well as many obvious points of similarity between the two, there are significant differences.

The most obvious of these is that Israel does not fundamentally depend on exploiting cheap Palestinian labour, as South Africa exploited the black population of its townships. This is something that has obvious consequences for any strategy for combating and overthrowing the Zionist state. In particular, it means that the Palestinians cannot throw the system into crisis solely by withdrawing their labour, as South Africa's black trade unions did in the late 1980s with their mass stay-aways. It does not, however, mean that Israel's forms of apartheid and colonisation are any less reactionary or morally condemnable than South Africa's.

The Israeli state's own official language frequently leads it into trouble on this score. 'Apartheid' in Afrikaans literally just meant 'separateness' or 'separate development'. State-sponsored segregation during the Jim Crow era in the US Deep South similarly relied for its justification on the claim that the segregationist states afforded 'separate but equal' protection to black and white citizens alike.

The Israeli government's own official description of its current policy towards the Palestinian population of the 1967 territories is referred to as 'hafrada', which means... separation. This policy's most notorious and concrete expression lies in Sharon's 'separation barrier', now widely and justly called the 'Apartheid Wall'. This word and the reality that it describes have quite rightly been compared to South African apartheid, including by the United Nations Special Rapporteur Richard A. Falk in his August 2010 report, which was met by great outrage from the 'friends of Israel'.

Nor is this the first time that representatives of the 'international community' have made this comparison. The United Nations General Assembly adopted an International Convention on the Suppression and Punishment of the Crime of Apartheid in November 1973. It defined apartheid as 'inhumane acts committed for the purpose of establishing and maintaining domination by one racial group of persons over any other racial group of persons and systematically oppressing them'.

The July 2002 Rome Statute of the International Criminal Court further defined 'inhumane acts' for this purpose as including 'torture, murder, forcible transfer, imprisonment, or persecution of an identifiable group on political, racial, national, ethnic, cultural, religious, or other grounds'.

The supporters of this charge point to the following features: the forcible transfer of Palestinians to make way for illegal Israeli settlements; preventing expelled Palestinians from returning to their homes and lands; systematic and severe deprivation of fundamental human rights of Palestinians based on their non-Jewish identity; denying Palestinians their right to freedom of movement and residence; murder, torture, unlawful imprisonment and other severe deprivations of physical liberty, especially of Palestinians living in Gaza.

The alarm of Israel's friends and allies

While the world has become accustomed to Israel rejecting almost everything that the United Nations and other international bodies have to say about its policy, many of its own friends abroad are starting to say much the same thing. In April, 2014, US Secretary of State John Kerry said in a private meeting with top Israeli officials that:

> 'A two-state solution will be clearly underscored as the only real alternative. Because a unitary state winds up either being an apartheid state with second-class citizens, or it ends up being a state that destroys the capacity of Israel to be a Jewish state.'

Like former US President Jimmy Carter before him, however, Kerry was soon forced to apologise profusely for using this analogy. It has not only been foreign politicians who have made this warning, however. The former Israeli prime minister, Ehud Barak, argued in February, 2010, during his tenure as Netanyahu's defence minister, that 'if this bloc of millions of Palestinians [in the 1967 territories] cannot vote, that will be an apartheid state'.

Going even further, Michael Ben Yair, Israel's Attorney General between 1993 and 1996, argued as follows in March 2002:

> 'We enthusiastically chose to become a colonial society, ignoring international treaties, expropriating lands, transferring settlers from Israel to the occupied territories, engaging in theft and finding justification for all these activities. Passionately desiring to keep the occupied territories, we developed two judicial systems: one, progressive, liberal, in Israel; and the other cruel, injurious, in the

occupied territories. In effect, we established an apartheid regime in the occupied territories immediately following their capture. That oppressive regime exists to this day.'

One way in which Israel differs significantly from South Africa under Apartheid is that it is far less capable of self-sustaining itself. Israel received about $125 billion in US financial assistance between 1949 and 2016, making it the single biggest recipient of US aid since the Second World War. This is even set to rise to $170 billion by the end of the most recent package of military aid agreed for 2019 to 2028. Israel depends on US aid for a fifth of its total defence budget, and for almost all of its weapons procurement.

With this observation, Israel's former deputy national security advisor Chuck Freilich argued in July 2017 that:

'No other permanent member of the Security Council would repeatedly use its veto, as the United States has done, to shield Israel from such resolutions, including possible sanctions, even over policies with which it has sometimes disagreed. Between 1954 and 2011, the US vetoed a total of some 40 one-sided or clearly anti-Israeli resolutions. Nothing better demonstrates Israel's dependence on the US in international forums, where America is often nearly its sole supporter, than the angst and distress it experienced when the US merely abstained, for the first time, from a Security Council resolution condemning the settlements in December 2016. As Israel's international isolation has grown, its dependence on US diplomatic cover has become almost complete.'

In February 2017, Freilich had previously warned the Netanyahu government against ignoring the importance of continuing US support in the following terms:

'There is simply no alternative to American weapons, and our dependence on the United States is almost complete; the bitter truth is that without the United States, the IDF would be an empty shell. [...] No other power so consistently defends Israel in almost every international organization and leads the battle against its delegitimization and diplomatic isolation.'

Pointing to the risk that US support for Israel might be undermined by changes in public opinion in the West, he continued:

> 'So maybe Israel can survive without the United States, significantly reduce its standard of living, withdraw into itself. Maybe. What is abundantly clear is that it would be a far less secure and far poorer existence, with severe isolation and a lifestyle fundamentally different from that which most Israelis have become accustomed to. Significant changes are underway in American society that do not bode well for the future of the bilateral relationship, inter alia, the rise of population groups that are less identified with Israel (Hispanics, those with no religious identification, the young) and the dwindling numbers of the secular Jewish population, Israel's traditional base of support.'

Indeed, a poll conducted by Pew Research in 2013 found that only 38 per cent of American Jews agreed that the Israeli government 'was making a sincere effort to establish peace with the Palestinians'. Numerous US Jewish organisations have emerged in recent years to show solidarity with the Palestinians or, at least, to protest against Israeli state violence; amongst them IfNotNow, Jewish Voice for Peace, J Street and Jews for Racial and Economic Justice.

This is why the global movement for Boycott, Divestment and Sanctions (BDS) has provoked such a vitriolic response, both from the Israeli state and from Israel's apologists in the USA and Europe. It is why the election of Jeremy Corbyn as leader of the Labour party and, therefore, his emergence as a potential future British prime minister, threw the 'Israel lobby' into such a frenzy of activity to discredit a veteran defender of the rights of the Palestinians. It is also why accusations of 'antisemitism' were thrown around with such abandon against Corbyn's supporters in the Labour party, including against an increasingly vocal number of Jewish pro-Palestine activists.

What this demonstrates is not the unassailable strength of

the Zionist state and its imperialist backers, but their own increasing awareness of Israel's vulnerability. For all of their own myths on this score, they are now seen to be the Goliaths, and the young Palestinians on the Gaza border the Davids.

While it will take far more than stones and slingshots to bring down the monstrous force of Israel's military, its asymmetrical power will not last forever. Above all, this power relies on the continued support of Israel's Western allies who, in turn, have to keep their populations behind them. Israel's undeniable brutality and remorseless expansionism is undermining this support.

That is why the BDS movement and the broader Palestine solidarity movement within the Western imperialist countries have such a tremendous role to play in aiding the struggles of the dispossessed Palestinian people. In the following chapters, however, we will examine the struggles of Palestinians themselves over the last seventy years.

The Arab National Movement

At the beginning of 2017, the two rival Palestinian leaderships announced their intention to form a united Palestinian Authority administration for the first time since 2007. By that time, Hamas had been in control of Gaza for almost ten years, while Fatah had been in at least nominal control of the West Bank since 1994.

Throughout the year, Israel continued to expand its illegal settlements, making ever more obvious that it would never allow a separate Palestinian state. And to cap it all, US President Donald Trump then announced that the US embassy was to be moved to Jerusalem, in defiance of an international consensus against recognising Jerusalem as Israel's 'capital'. Thus the year demonstrated that the two rival leaderships were no more able to advance the Palestinian cause in concert than they had been able to individually.

This is not solely a failure of the current leaderships, but the outcome of 70 years of struggle that have thrown up a series of political leaders and organisations. These have fought, often heroically but ultimately without success, against the imposition of Israel's colonial settler state on the Palestinian people's erstwhile homeland. Each wave of struggle has taken up and developed the ideas, slogans, organisations, strategies and tactics that had already been developed in earlier struggles, modifying them either in the light of experience or of the influences of other struggles of the oppressed.

As Karl Marx once observed in the aftermath of the defeat of the revolutions of 1848:

'Men make their own history, but they do not make it as they please; they do not make it under circumstances of their own choosing, but under circumstances existing already, given and transmitted from the past. The tradition of all dead generations weighs like a nightmare on the brains of the living.'

The experience of the Palestinians has certainly been a recurrent nightmare. Strategic failures and defeats have consequences, most important amongst them being Israel's continued expansion, to the point where it is even conceivable that the remaining Palestinian population of the West Bank could be forced out altogether. Yet, the existing Palestinian leaderships remain tied to political programmes that have proved worse than useless, each in their own different ways hugely dysfunctional to the gigantic tasks that they face.

This is not a new phenomenon, and neither is it unique to Palestine. Rather, it is an expression within the Palestinian struggle of an almost universal phenomenon that the Russian-Jewish revolutionary Leon Trotsky once described as 'the crisis of leadership'.

That is to say that, while the struggles of the oppressed and the exploited erupt and re-erupt spontaneously out of the material conditions of their oppression and exploitation, time and again they are also thwarted by the very same organisations that lead them. They run repeatedly into the obstacles thrown up by the failures and sometimes even by the outright betrayals of the institutions and the individual leaders that they have inherited from history.

The casual observer, struck by the supine character of today's Palestinian Authority, of its dominant faction Fatah and of its leader Mahmoud Abbas, may even wonder how these leaders ever had any popularity at all, and how they still maintain a base of support today. The Western media, which rests content with labelling Palestinian movements and leaders as 'moderates' or 'extremists' does not provide any useful guide.

It may therefore surprise some readers to learn that Mahmoud Abbas is the inheritor of a movement that was once regarded as a model for national liberation movements worldwide. It may similarly surprise them that Hamas (or rather, its predecessors) have not always represented the principle of 'resistance' in Palestinian politics, but were once regarded as harmless and apolitical 'moderates', including by the Israeli occupation's own security forces.

The building of a new Palestinian leadership will depend on a struggle for a new political programme within a movement that is still being led by its current leaders. The first requirement in this struggle to create a new leadership, therefore, is an understanding and a critique of the political strategies of the different factions that have led the Palestinian struggle in the past.

George Habash, Nasserism, and Pan-Arabism

Even before the Partition of Palestine and the foundation of Israel in 1948, there was already a history of Palestinian struggle against both British rule and Zionist colonisation, within which many of the seeds of today's organisations first took root. At that time, however, this was one part of a wider struggle against the domination of the whole region by French and British imperialism.

A specifically Palestinian national struggle could be dated to Palestine's Arab Revolt of 1936–39, or at the latest to the outbreak of the civil war in Palestine in November 1947, after the United Nations voted in support of Partition. However, its character as part of a wider Arab struggle was evidenced by the Arab-Israeli war of 1948–49, which began after the formal end of the British Mandate and the declaration of the State of Israel.

Almost all of the 'independent' Arab states that existed at that time were relatively recent creations, whose durability and legitimacy were open to question. Almost all of them saw major (and often violent) changes of regime in the decades after Israel's creation: Egypt in 1952, Iraq and Lebanon in 1958, Iraq again in 1963 and 1968, and Syria once almost every two or three years between 1949 and 1970.

Syria's first such coup itself took place in the closing stages of the war with Israel, and was followed by a bloody counter-coup barely a few months later. Many of today's Arab states had not yet become formally independent, while others were ruled by families that acted as barely-disguised satraps for the Western powers that had placed them in power. Some of these survive today, in Jordan, Kuwait, Bahrain, Qatar, Oman and the United Arab Emirates.

British and French imperialism had carved up the region between them in the aftermath of the First World War, creating today's Syria, Lebanon, Jordan, Iraq and Saudi Arabia as well as, of course, Britain's Mandate of Palestine. These new states had boundaries that had no logic from the standpoint of their own populations.

Arab nationalism, with its programme of uniting these regions into a single state or, in its more ambitious Baathist variant, of uniting the entire Arabic-speaking world, was a popular movement across the region. It threatened almost all of the Arab regimes, some of whom began to adopt its themes and its rhetoric as a means of legitimising their own rule.

This is the Arab world into which between 750,000 and 900,000 Palestinian refugees found themselves expelled, literally and politically homeless, in the aftermath of 1948. It was an Arab world of weak, quarrelling, repressive, unstable and unpopular regimes that had just suffered a massive defeat in war barely after coming into existence themselves.

In Syria, Lebanon, Iraq and Egypt, there were sizeable working class movements led by large or at least significant Communist Parties that competed with Arab nationalists for popular support. However, the fortunes of Arab Communism were damaged significantly by the support given to Israel by the USSR's dictator Joseph Stalin in 1948. Many of the emerging Arab nationalist parties would begin to take on a 'socialist' colouration to compete with the Communist left.

In Syria and Iraq, the most prominent of these would come to be the Arab Baath Socialist Party founded by the Christian Syrian schoolteacher (and former Communist) Michel Aflaq. Its quarrelling successors would later become the ruling parties in Iraq under Saddam Hussein and in Syria under Hafez al-Assad and his son, Bashar al-Assad.

Amongst the Palestinians, however, the biggest of these movements was the Arab Nationalist Movement, ANM, led by the charismatic Christian Palestinian children's doctor George Habash (1926–2008). Habash had studied medicine in Lebanon, where his organisation was founded, and later practised in the Palestinian refugee camps in Jordan and the West Bank, where the ANM acquired a mass following.

The ANM's basic thesis was that the Palestinians had been the principal victims of the disunity of the 'Arab nation'. Their liberation would therefore require a series of revolutions in the Arab world to bring to power regimes committed to 'Arab unity', who would then wage a revolutionary 'people's war' against Israel for the liberation of Palestine. To this end, the ANM's cadres engaged in numerous coup plots and intrigues, in particular in Jordan (whose ruling dynasty was regarded by many Arab nationalists and by most Palestinians as a national enemy) and in Syria, Habash's frequent refuge from the vicissitudes of Jordanian politics.

Like Habash himself, many of the ANM's leading lights were drawn from the educated secular middle classes and had a Western, or at least a Western-style, education. They were secularists, modernists, democrats (of a sort) and radicals with regard to the established Arab order, with all of its semi-feudal backwardness. They were not, at this stage, self-identified 'socialists' of any description; although this would change under the impact of events elsewhere.

In 1952, in Egypt, a military coup conducted by the nationalist Free Officers' Movement brought to power Gamal Abdel Nasser (1918–70). His regime overthrew the pro-British monarchy, nationalised a large part of Egypt's industry and redistributed much of the country's agricultural land to the peasantry. This peasantry's struggles against their parasitic absentee landlords had been a problem for British imperialism, and for Egypt's wealthy ruling class, for almost a century.

Nasser's status as a pan-Arab hero was further enhanced by his nationalisation of the Suez canal in 1956. This resulted in a joint invasion of Egypt by Britain, France and Israel, who were then forced to withdraw by the intervention of US President

Dwight Eisenhower. This gave Nasser the mantle of being the only Arab leader to have successfully 'confronted Israel'. In his competition for influence in the Arab world with Saudi Arabia's ruling dynasty, Nasser capitalised on this image by posing as an Arab Napoleon Bonaparte or Simon Bolivar, a progressive and modern-minded strongman who would 'unite' the Arab world against Israel and the Western powers.

As part of this, Nasser began to sponsor friendly movements like the ANM that could provide him with a popular base to lean on in his dealings with hostile Arab regimes. The ANM in turn became Nasser's almost-uncritical cheerleaders in the Arab world, helping to provide him with the sort of popularity paralleled in recent times only by Venezuela's Hugo Chávez in Latin America. Under Nasser's influence, Habash and the ANM moved left with the Egyptian regime's own 'socialist' rhetoric and its popular social measures. The ANM's Egyptian branch dissolved itself without trace into Nasser's ruling Arab Socialist Union, ASU.

The limits of Nasserism

Under Nasser's leadership, Egypt moved towards the Soviet-led bloc in the Cold War, with a military programme involving the supply of Soviet weapons and advisers. Containing and defeating Nasser's Egypt therefore became a key priority both for US imperialism and for its British and French rivals and junior partners, with Israel a key component of this alliance. British and Israeli propaganda in particular depicted Nasser as a sort of Hitler on the River Nile.

In fact, Nasser was far less concerned with 'pan-Arab' considerations than is depicted in the popular image of him promoted by his cheerleaders. He accepted an 'Arab union' with an unstable Syria in 1958 only reluctantly and with many reservations. Syria's oligarchic capitalist and landowning elites practically handed Nasser power in a bid to forestall the rise of the Baath and of the Syrian Communist Party. This 'United Arab Republic', however, lasted barely three years, after Nasserist rule in Syria moved first right and then left in a way that satisfied precisely no one.

In 1961, Nasser's rule in Syria was overthrown by the same elites that had begged him to save them from communism in 1958. It had by then already fallen foul of the resentment of Syria's state bureaucracy and officer caste at being dominated by their counterparts in Cairo. Nasser's repression of the Syrian Communist Party, and his forced dissolution of the Baath into Syria's own ASU-style 'National Union', also left him without any allies to his left who could have supported him.

In 1963, another coup overthrew Syria's restored and landlord-dominated parliamentary regime and brought to power the 'left wing' of a now reconstituted Baath Party. This regime then set about competing with Nasser for the leadership of Arab nationalism. A central element of this challenge was its sponsorship of Palestinian guerrilla organisations; one of which, Fatah, went on to play a central role in the Palestinian national struggle.

Two other developments also served to tarnish Nasser's credentials. The intrigues of homegrown Nasserist republican officers against Yemen's pro-British monarchy embroiled Egypt in a costly war in Yemen from 1962 to 1970. This war sapped Egypt's political energies and military resources in a way that left it ill-prepared for Israel's provocations and blitzkrieg in 1967.

Most importantly of all, Egyptian rule of the Palestinian Gaza Strip under Nasser differed very little from its counterpart under the Egyptian monarchy between 1948 and 1952. Like the regime that preceded it, Nasser's regime would alternate between repressing and encouraging the Palestinian fedayeen (guerrillas) that tried to defend Gaza from Israel's frequent aggressions, according to the changing priorities of state, as opposed to the needs of the Palestinian movement.

Nasser shared in the discrediting of all of the Arab regimes by the 1967 defeat. He 'resigned' as Egypt's President in the days immediately after it, and then resumed his position shortly thereafter, following (partly genuine and probably partly staged) mass demonstrations demanding his return. He would die a broken man only three years later, at the height of the 'Black September' crisis in Jordan. While he retained his status as a symbol of radical Arab nationalism, Nasser had by then already lost his influence on the Palestinian movement, which shifted to a more radical and militant perspective in the aftermath of that war.

For the ANM, rapidly losing support to Fatah and other Palestinian guerrilla organisations, this meant reorganising itself and orienting towards armed struggle. In 1968, the ANM's Palestinian cadres, together with a number of smaller groups, formed the Popular Front for the Liberation of Palestine, PFLP. This then evolved towards a heavily Stalinist-influenced 'Marxism', albeit one that owed far more to Che Guevara, Amilcar Cabral and Régis Debray than to Leonid Brezhnev's USSR.

Habash himself, together with the PFLP's public spokesperson Ghassan Kanafani (1936–72), a talented and prolific journalist, novelist and poet, and its female guerrilla fighter and airplane hijacker Leila Khaled, became icons of the Palestinian struggle for many on the global left, in a way that Fatah's Yasser Arafat also did for those less ideologically-inclined.

However, the stage for Palestinian disaffection with Nasserism had already been set in the course of the previous fifteen years and a new Palestinian movement would come to embody its politics.

Fatah and the armed struggle

This new movement's founder and leader, Yasser Arafat (1929–2004) was a civil engineer from a minor branch of a wealthy Muslim Palestinian family originating in Jerusalem, who had spent most of his formative years in Gaza and in Cairo. He had been a leading figure in the Palestinian student movement in exile, leading the General Union of Palestinian Students for four years and representing it at a conference in Prague in 1956. He was, by some accounts, briefly sympathetic to Egypt's conservative Islamist Muslim Brotherhood and by all accounts was not remotely a 'social radical' of any description.

Neither Nasser's 'socialistic' pretensions nor his rhetorical 'pan-Arab' ambitions held any special appeal for Arafat or for the social class that he hailed from, many of whom lost property and businesses as a result of Nasser's nationalisation programmes. This was especially the case when set against Nasser's actual record regarding Palestinian liberation. Arafat himself was one of the Palestinian fedayeen that Nasser forced to withdraw from Gaza in the aftermath of the 1956 Suez crisis, when a United Nations Emergency Force was placed in Gaza to preserve continued quiet with Israel.

Like many Palestinians in that period, Arafat emigrated to the booming oil-rich Arab Gulf countries, in his case to a Kuwait that was then still a British protectorate in 1957. He reportedly made a millionaire's fortune in construction and civil engineering contracts but lived a fairly modest lifestyle, at least by the standards of the rising Gulf and Arab expatriate bourgeoisies. He preferred to sink his newly acquired wealth into financing the Palestinian National Liberation Movement, better known by its reversed Arabic initials as Fatah.

Arafat founded this political grouping in 1959 alongside other expatriate Palestinians from Egypt, in particular Salah Khalaf (1933–91), known as Abu Iyad and Khalil al-Wazir (1935–88), known as Abu Jihad. Its principal message was that the Palestinians could only be liberated by their own actions, and not by any reliance on any distant future 'Arab revolution'.

In a testament to the power of the written word to assist the birth of new political movements, this grouping's first serious activity was to produce a regular journal, *Filastinuna, Nida' al-Hayat* ('Our Palestine, the Call to Life'), produced mainly by Abu Jihad. Editions of this journal were exported (or smuggled) from Kuwait to every Arab country with a Palestinian presence. It would be followed by numerous other cultural and political magazines, books and pamphlets pushing the same basic message.

Both Nasser and the conservative Arab regimes were alarmed by the growing popularity of this and similar radical currents within the Palestinian diaspora, which were seen as potentially destabilising. In response, the Arab League's first summit meeting in Cairo in January 1964 proposed the foundation of a Palestinian National Council, PNC. This then met in Jerusalem in May 1964 and founded the Palestine Liberation

Organisation, PLO.

Contrary to the PLO's later reputation as a 'resistance movement', it was originally created to play a role for the Arab regimes comparable to the role that the Palestinian Authority plays for Israel today. Their intention was that the PLO would contain Palestinian national aspirations by giving them some form of political 'representation', and thus would channel those aspirations harmlessly away from any practical struggle towards their achievement.

Fatah's armed wing officially began its 'armed struggle' with Israel from the Jordanian-ruled West Bank on New Year's Eve in 1964, meeting both with armed Israeli reprisals and the Jordanian Hashemite monarchy's own state repression. It was then only the latest of many small and ineffectual Palestinian fedayeen groupings engaged in similar activity.

However, Fatah would acquire a most unlikely pair of state sponsors. One was the Syrian Baathist regime of Amin al-Hafiz after 1963 (and his more left-wing Baathist successor Salah Jadid after 1966). The other was the ruling dynasty of Saudi Arabia. Each of these had their own reasons for wanting to outflank and embarrass Nasser on the Palestinian issue.

Syrian-trained and Syrian-hosted Fatah fighters conducted frequent armed raids into Israel from Jordan and from Lebanon, using arms and materiel acquired with oil dollars from Saudi Arabia and Kuwait. In later years, many Palestinians would complain of the PLO's corruption and of the malign influence of the Arab regimes and their 'support' on the Palestinian cause; but this problem was already present in embryo at this early stage.

However, it was after the Six Day War in June 1967, and in particular after the Battle of Karameh in 1968, that Fatah established itself as the leading force both in the Palestinian struggle and in the PLO, which it had joined in 1967. Both Fatah and the PFLP acquired a mass following, especially in Jordan with its majority Palestinian population. Between them, they came respectively to represent the PLO's 'moderate' and 'rejectionist' wings.

There were, however, numerous other Palestinian resistance factions both inside and outside of the PLO. Almost every Arab regime sponsored one or more them, in order to buy nationalist or Islamic credentials in regional politics, and to influence the Palestinian movement itself. This would reproduce within the movement the same divisions that existed between the Arab regimes. It would also give those regimes a means of settling bloody scores with each other, far away from their own territories.

Today's PLO and the Palestinian Authority

The PLO is now almost forgotten in day to day news coverage of the Israeli-Palestinian conflict. It has long been eclipsed in that sphere by its own creation, the Palestinian Authority. Since the 1993 Oslo Accords, this Authority has had the unedifying role of 'ruling' over those Palestinians who still live in the territories occupied by Israel in 1967, and of taking part in endlessly stalled 'peace negotiations' with Israel for the end of that occupation.

The PLO's first leader, Ahmad Shukeiri, was a Palestinian lawyer and diplomat-for-hire who at various times had represented Syria, Saudi Arabia and the Arab League at the United Nations and elsewhere. He was known for giving noisy speeches about the impending 'liberation of Palestine', and for very little else.

However, the Arab regimes that sponsored the creation of the PLO suffered an irreparable blow to their prestige in the June 1967 'Six-Day War', in which Israel occupied all of the remaining territory of the former British Mandate of Palestine, plus the Syrian Golan Heights and the Egyptian Sinai peninsula. This affected not only the conservative Arab regimes in Jordan and Saudi Arabia, but also the more radical nationalist regimes in Egypt, Syria, Iraq and Algeria.

Originally established to forestall the rise of the Palestinian guerrilla movements, the PLO now fell under their leadership, and that of Arafat's Fatah movement in particular. Arafat himself became the PLO's third Chairman in February 1969, and remained in that position until his death. Henceforth, the PLO's history would be inseparable from Arafat's own political career and from the politics of the movement that he founded.

Arafat and Fatah, however, did not represent the first port of call for Palestinian national liberation in the aftermath of the 1948 Nakba, but came to prominence only after the first wave of post-1948 Palestinian radicalism had already been seen to have reached the limits of its potential.

For much of the three decades before Oslo, the PLO was the central political institution of the Palestinian struggle, one that posed as a sort of 'state-in-exile' for the Palestinian people as a whole. Yasser Arafat, with his sunglasses, his designer stubble beard, his olive-green uniforms and his keffiyeh headscarf twisted carefully into the shape of a map of pre-1948 Palestine, was for many people across the world the personification of Palestinian nationalism, right up to the time of his death in November 2004. Indeed he was still harried by the Israel Defence Forces until his last days in his West Bank compound, and may even have been murdered by Israeli agents.

In theory at least, the PLO represents the whole Palestinian people, including the refugees and other emigrants outside of Palestine; while the Palestinian Authority represents only the Palestinians in the 1967 occupied territories. The PLO therefore still plays a role in conferring a form of 'legitimacy' on the Palestinian Authority's own leadership.

While the latter are, at least in theory, subject to regular elections in the territory under the Palestinian Authority's shared 'control' with Israel, the PLO's leadership, again, at least in theory, consists of representatives of the Palestinian resistance factions affiliated to it, of the PLO's own various mass institutions and of the Palestinian Authority's parliament.

Moreover, the PLO's bureaucracy and leadership are closely intertwined with the Palestinian Authority's. Like his mentor Arafat before him, Mahmoud Abbas is both President of the Palestinian Authority and Chairman of the PLO's Executive Committee. The core of the Palestinian Authority's security forces on its creation was initially composed of Arafat's personal bodyguard and special commando operations unit, then called 'Force 17'.

Today's PLO appears to have reverted to the role that the

Arab regimes originally intended for it in 1964. It harmlessly 'represents' the Palestinians at the United Nations and in the Arab League, dispenses various services to the Palestinian refugee camps and to Palestinian expatriate communities, helps certain Arab regimes to control the Palestinians under their own rule, and provides a source of sinecures for office-seekers. However, the role, the lingering popularity and the politics of Fatah and of other Palestinian factions today cannot be understood without an understanding of their role in the PLO's history.

The PLO and the Armed Struggle

Fatah's programme was eventually replicated in the programme of the PLO after 1969. George Habash and the ANM had advocated a regional 'Arab revolution' as a necessary precondition for the liberation of Palestine, and intervened in the politics of other Arab countries. Arafat and Abu Jihad, however, insisted on Palestinian liberation first, and 'Arab unity' only afterwards.

Fatah also declared that it was interested only in a 'Palestinian revolution', and that it would work with any Arab regime that wanted to support the Palestinian cause. Where the ANM and later the PFLP had promoted 'pan-Arab' illusions in nationalist regimes like Nasser's, Fatah claimed to represent Palestinian independence from all of the Arab regimes, while adding that the regimes nevertheless had an 'Arab duty' to provide the Palestinians with material support.

In practice, this meant that Habash's strategic dependence, first on Egypt and then on Syria, was replaced in Fatah's schema with a strategic dependence on a consortium of the Arab regimes as a whole. In particular, Fatah became dependent on the richest and most pro-Western Arab regime of all, the backward but oil-rich Saudi kingdom. Saudi Arabia even imposed a 'liberation tax' on expatriate Palestinians to finance Fatah and the PLO's growing bureaucracy, in return for Arafat's good behaviour with regard to Saudi interests in the region.

While the PFLP sided with the Soviet-led bloc in the Cold War, and with the radical nationalist regimes in regional Arab politics, Fatah declared its official 'neutrality', while leaning in practice towards the more pro-Western conservative Arab states. Arafat sought out audiences with the 'respectable' leaders of major Third World and 'non-aligned' countries like India, Pakistan, Indonesia and Malaysia. Habash by contrast sought alliances with other radical left-wing national liberation movements in the Third World, in Latin America in particular. Similarly, while the Fatah-led PLO's orientation in the West was towards finding interlocutors in respectable mainstream political parties, the PFLP's sights were focused firmly on the radical left. In particular, the PFLP found itself drawn towards groups that shared its own vision of elitist 'armed struggle' in place of the class struggle (a vision ultimately borrowed from Fatah), like Germany's Baader-Meinhof grouping, the 'Red Army Faction'.

By contrast, Fatah's profoundly un-ideological character allowed it to pose as a broad movement of all Palestinians committed to national liberation. Devout Muslims, social conservatives, pro-Western liberals, disillusioned Baathists and Nasserists and self-identified Marxists could all be part of Fatah. All that was required of them was that they accepted its 'armed struggle' strategy and its minimalist political programme: a 'democratic secular state' in Palestine for Muslims, Christians and Jews.

Defects of the PLO strategy

That this programme of a 'democratic secular state' would have been an advance from Zionism's ethnically exclusive 'Jewish state' should be obvious. It nevertheless suffered from a number of fatal defects.

One was that the PLO and Fatah in effect imagined that Jewish Israelis could be absorbed into a post-Zionist Palestine as members of a confessional minority, like Christians, Sunni Muslims, Druze and Shiites in Lebanon. Any recognition that Zionism had created a new, Hebrew-speaking Israeli nation in Palestine, albeit a nation of colonists, was studiously avoided.

Another defect was that the PLO's programme said nothing about the nature of the economy and of property rights in a future 'democratic Palestine'. Would it be capitalist or socialist?

This left the programme's advocates with little beyond good

intentions and the promise of fair and equal treatment to offer to the less privileged layers of Jewish Israeli society. This in turn deprived the Palestinian movement of the ability to exploit Zionism's internal class contradictions and thus to win over a part of Israel's Jewish-majority working class, in particular the recent immigrants from the Arab countries.

Many of these immigrants had been subject to racist discrimination by the established European-origin Jews in Israel that they eventually came to outnumber. This made their social and ethnic discontent a genuine threat to Israel's ruling class if related to correctly. Equally, however, many of them had been subjected to similarly vile treatment (or worse) by the same Arab regimes to which the PLO appealed for support. This helped to reinforce the national and communal nature of the conflict, to the advantage of the Zionist state.

Finally, this programme had no strategy for tying the Palestinian struggle to the badly-needed democratic and social transformation of all of the countries of the region. Indeed, it was predicated quite explicitly on a rejection of Palestinian involvement in the 'internal affairs' of the Arab regimes.

The PFLP's effective programme differed from this only in that it still maintained the ANM's previous 'pan-Arab' perspective, and on this basis looked forward to 'national-democratic' revolutions in Jordan and Lebanon in particular. The PFLP's popular slogan therefore had it that 'The road to Jerusalem goes through Amman, Damascus and Cairo'. However, Nasser's Egypt and Baathist Syria for this purpose were assumed already to be in the throes of an (uncompleted) 'national-democratic' revolution themselves.

One Maoist-inspired PFLP offshoot, the Democratic Front for the Liberation of Palestine (DFLP) began to develop a 'two state' programme in the early 1970s, advocating a struggle for an independent Palestinian state in the 1967 territories as an interim step towards the liberation of Palestine as a whole. While the DFLP itself was small, its turn on this question gave Arafat and Fatah enough political cover to move slowly, cautiously and pragmatically towards a coded acceptance of the 'two-state solution' that has since become part of the hypocritical repertoire of the diplomacy of almost every Western government.

Fatah, the PFLP, and the various other PLO-aligned factions therefore had many differences: on one state versus two; on their attitude towards the Arab regimes and the Cold War; on their interest, or lack of it, in diplomatic negotiations; and on their competing visions of what a post-Zionist Palestine would look like.

However, they also had much in common, including the lack of any serious strategy beyond the 'armed struggle' for the overthrow of the Zionist state. To varying degrees, they all neglected the building of a mass popular movement against the 1967 occupation in the occupied territories themselves. Instead, they prioritised the creation of an armed guerrilla movement in the refugee camps outside of Palestine, and an armed underground resistance movement in the occupied territories.

Very few took any interest in exploiting Israel's own class and ethnic contradictions, with Arafat and Fatah in later years preferring instead to relate to the precursors of Israel's Zionist 'peace camp'. Almost none of them paid any attention to the politics of Israel's own Arab Palestinian minority, which was by then undergoing a political reawakening. And, beyond the level of rhetoric, none of them had any revolutionary strategy for the Arab countries from which they had to conduct their 'armed struggle'. It would not take long for this movement to suffer its first major defeats, although its effective liquidation took almost 25 years. The first defeats, however, were inflicted on it not by Israel but by the Arab regimes.

Black September and the 1973 War

Jordan's British-educated King Hussein had been forced to tolerate the Palestinian guerrilla movement in Jordan after the 1967 war, hypocritically declaring that 'we are all fedayeen now'. But this standoff with an armed threat to his own state's authority could not possibly last.

The very fact of tens of thousands of society's most exploited and downtrodden people taking up arms in a struggle to overthrow the oppressive rule of a neighbouring state was a direct threat to Jordan's minority ruling class, and indirectly to the ruling classes of all of the Arab states. This remained the case however much Arafat insisted that his was a purely Palestinian revolution, and that Palestine and not Jordan was the homeland of the Palestinians. Hussein merely bided his time before striking at the Palestinian fedayeen.

The pretext for a crackdown came in September 1970, when the PFLP hijacked three Western airliners and blew them up, minus passengers, in front of the world's television cameras in a former British airbase near Zarqa, an event that was the 9/11 of its day. Graffiti scrawled by the hijackers contained slogans against 'Zionism, imperialism and Arab reaction', emphasising their understanding of the Palestinian people's common enemies.

The next few weeks would see the Jordanian army try to drive out or disarm almost all of Jordan's 40,000 or so Palestinian fedayeen. Iraq's new Baathist regime declined to get involved on the Palestinian side, despite having around 17,000 troops in Jordan that had been there since 1967. Syria's airforce minister Hafez al-Assad also refused to provide air cover to Salah Jadid's planned military intervention in Jordan, depriving the Palestinians of support at a critical moment.

Nasser's attempt to mediate between Arafat and Hussein produced a brief ceasefire, although Nasser himself died of a massive heart attack only the day after. This ceasefire, however, did not result in an end to what was now a war to expel the PLO from Jordan altogether. Fighting continued under martial law conditions until July 1971.

Assad used his unpunished act of mutiny against Jadid to stage a right-wing coup against him in November 1970, bringing to power a dynastic regime whose bloody rule in Syria continues to this day. And Syria under the Assads would clash repeatedly with the PLO. Assad wanted a Palestinian national movement in his own image and under Syria's domination; and Arafat, for all his many other faults, was too popular and too independent a leader for this role.

Palestinian fedayeen displaced from Jordan flooded into

Lebanon, which became the new front line in the 'armed struggle'. In the meantime, Assad's Syria and Egypt under Nasser's successor Anwar Sadat conducted a surprise attack on Israel in October 1973.

Known in Israel as the Yom Kippur War, these two Arab regimes failed in the course of it to achieve their stated objectives, of recovering the Syrian Golan Heights and the Egyptian Sinai Peninsula from Israeli occupation. However, the fact that they had caught Israel off-guard, and had managed to continue fighting for almost three weeks, allowed them to recover enough of their lost prestige that both regimes were now able to pursue intrigues and negotiations with Israel without being too vulnerable to Palestinian criticism.

The same war saw both superpowers, the USA under Richard Nixon and the USSR under Leonid Brezhnev, re-supply their Israeli and Arab allies respectively, emphasising Israel's character as a frontline state in the Cold War. It also saw a Saudi-led Arab oil embargo of Israel's Western allies, provoking a global rise in oil prices that produced a shock to oil-dependent Western economies.

In Egypt's case, the political consequences of the October War allowed it to leave its Syrian and Palestinian allies in the lurch. Sadat signed the Camp David Accords with Israel's prime minister Menachem Begin and US President Jimmy Carter in September 1978. Henceforth, Egypt would become part of the Western camp in the Cold War, albeit at the cost of its temporary isolation in regional Arab politics.

This in turn produced a regional power vacuum that would come to be filled by Iraq's rising Baathist dictator Saddam Hussein. Saddam would become an ally of US imperialism, the USSR and the conservative Gulf Arab monarchies against Iran, following the 1979 'Islamic Revolution' against Iran's pro-US Shah.

Egypt's military would be funded to the tune of billions of dollars a year by the USA, making it one of the world's biggest recipients of US military aid, alongside Israel and Saudi Arabia. But this largesse was not to ensure Egypt's 'defence' against an Israel with which it was now officially at peace, but to hold down and repress its own people. With the PLO's 'armed struggle' now restricted to Lebanon, the Palestinians now faced a new 'Black September' on far less favourable terrain.

Black June and the invasion of Lebanon

The sectarian leaders of Lebanon's privileged Christian Maronite minority saw the mainly Muslim Palestinians as a threat to the domination that they had enjoyed over the state ever since France artificially separated Lebanon from Syria in the 1930s. Palestinians in Lebanon were thus the most badly mistreated of all of the Palestinian refugee communities. They were legally excluded from all except the most menial jobs and possessed no secure rights of residence, and only second-class property rights.

Many of the right-wing Christian parties had long possessed armed militias of their own, most notoriously the fascist-inspired Phalangist movement of former Olympic athlete Pierre Gemayel. These militias began to receive arms and training from Israel, in pursuit of a quasi-genocidal programme of reasserting 'Lebanese sovereignty' by putting an end to the Palestinian presence in Lebanon altogether.

On the other hand, most Muslim Lebanese, and leftists and Arab nationalists in Lebanon of all religious affiliations, supported and identified with the Palestinian struggle. Many joined the Palestinian guerrillas themselves, or formed leftist, Muslim or secular nationalist militias of their own.

Lebanon finally exploded into civil war in April 1975. The Lebanese National Movement, a pro-Palestinian coalition of leftist, Muslim and Druze parties and militias, quickly found itself in control of almost all of the south of the country and of the mainly Muslim Western half of Beirut. There was the serious prospect of a revolution that would bring to an end Lebanon's undemocratic sectarian power-sharing system, perhaps accompanied by a secessionist right-wing pro-Israeli Christian state in the north.

Syria's Assad, however, decided to forestall this by invading Lebanon in support of its right-wing Christian President Suleiman Frangieh in June 1976, turning on Syria's historic

Palestinian and Lebanese leftist allies in the process. Two months later, Assad allowed his new Phalangist allies to conduct a massacre of some 2,000 Palestinians at Tel al-Zaatar refugee camp in Christian-controlled East Beirut.

Israel's prime minister Yitzhak Rabin noted with approval that Syria had killed more fedayeen in Lebanon in the course of a few months than Israel had managed in the course of the previous decade. Lebanon's civil war however would last for another fifteen years, and degenerated into a bloody spectacle of communal massacres and counter-massacres between Christians, Muslims and Druze.

Six years later, Israel under Menachem Begin invaded Lebanon up to and including West Beirut. This forced the PLO to accept the evacuation of its fighters and its bureaucracy, under international supervision, to distant Tunis. This left the unarmed Palestinian refugees who remained behind at the mercy of Israel and its allies.

Israel then acted to install a new Lebanese President, Pierre Gemayel's bloodthirsty warlord son Bachir Gemayel, in September 1982. He, however, was assassinated only a few days later. Israel's then defence minister, Ariel Sharon, took revenge by allowing the Phalangists to repeat their 1976 performance at Tel al-Zaatar in the Sabra and Shatila refugee camps in Israeli-occupied West Beirut, killing up to 3,500 unarmed men, women and children.

The PLO's armed struggle was effectively at an end, although Israel failed to bring about a stable Lebanese regime that was capable of signing any credible peace treaty. A new armed struggle began against Israel's occupation of the south of the country. It was led at first by the Lebanese Communist Party, although this in turn was soon surpassed by the rise of the new Iranian-sponsored Lebanese Shiite Islamist movement, Hezbollah.

Assad returned to the job of finishing off what remained of the Palestinian resistance in Lebanon in the 'War of the Camps' in 1985–88. He hoped thereby to prove to the West and to the conservative Arab states that a re-stabilised Lebanon under Syrian domination would not be a threat to their interests. By then, however, the West and the Arab regimes were far less concerned with the Palestinians than with containing the ambitions of Iraq's Saddam Hussein, who was then in the process of defeating Iran in a destructive eight-year war that he had conducted with their encouragement and support.

By this point, the failures and inadequacies of all the different factions and would-be leaderships of the Palestinian struggle had brought the movement to its lowest ebb. And so things might have remained, had the Palestinian people themselves not intervened.

The First Intifada and the Rise of Hamas

The word *Intifada* is now internationally recognised as a synonym for unarmed popular mass uprisings. In Arabic, appropriately enough, it literally means a 'tremor' or a 'shaking off'; and the first Palestinian Intifada of 1987–91 was indeed something like an earthquake in the region.

In place of the image of the Palestinian guerrilla with his keffiyeh and his semi-automatic rifle, the new popular symbol of Palestinian resistance came to be that of a Palestinian child or teenager pelting stones at Israeli soldiers and tanks. A popular slogan in the Arab world, replicated in numerous pieces of art and on innumerable items of clothing, had it that 'the future belongs to the children of the stones'.

The Intifada began as a riot in Jabalia refugee camp in the Gaza Strip in December 1987, after Israeli forces killed four Palestinians in what appeared to be a traffic accident. Such incidents had been common in the occupied territories for twenty years. Spontaneous protests then spread quickly across the 1967 territories, and mushroomed into a mass movement of civil disobedience.

Its methods included general strikes by the hundreds of thousands of Palestinian workers then employed in the Israeli economy, boycotts of Israeli goods and of work on the illegal Jewish settlements, a boycott of the Israeli occupation's labyrinthine civil bureaucracy, tax strikes, the throwing up of barricades to impede the day-to-day operation of the occupation's armed forces, and even a boycott of cars with Israeli licence plates.

The routine brutality of Israel's military occupation, obscured from Western view by tendentious rhetoric about 'terrorism' and the morality of armed struggle, suddenly became regular television viewing in the Western countries that enabled Israel's state violence. Defence minister Yitzhak Rabin's infamous call for a policy of 'force, might and beatings', and for 'breaking the bones' of civilian protesters, exposed the imbalance of power between the parties to many who previously had been oblivious to it.

Around 1,900 Palestinians and 300 Israelis were killed between the beginning of the uprising and the Oslo Accords in September 1993, about 300 of those Palestinians in the first year of the Intifada. Between 24,000 and 30,000 Palestinians were wounded in the same period, while almost every Palestinian family had members in Israeli prisons at some point during the uprising.

The defence and sustenance of the uprising required, and quickly produced, a mass network of locally-based self-help organisations. These dealt with the wounded, with the maintenance of strikers and their families, with legal assistance, food, education and other necessities. A new generation of mostly younger activists emerged from obscurity to provide leadership to this movement.

As much as the 'armed struggle' had possessed a mass base in its heyday, this movement sank far deeper roots into the ordinary people. It was precisely this, and not the Intifada's much-romanticised 'nonviolent resistance', that led it to achieve political results where the 'armed struggle' had achieved only lofty diplomatic resolutions. Like any popular rising, however, the Intifada did need some form of armed self-defence and its absence allowed Israel gradually to wear down the uprising, through acts of collective punishment that targeted the population as a whole.

Many or most of the new activists were not necessarily formal members of any political faction. However, in their overwhelming majority they still expressed their allegiance to the exiled PLO leadership as their ultimate political representatives. At a national level, Fatah, the PFLP, the DFLP and the Palestine Communist Party all jointly played a role in coordinating mass protests and other actions, forming the Unified National Leadership of the Uprising, UNLU, in January 1988. This leadership issued regular communiques to the population at large, providing instructions, advice and political direction.

The recognisable public faces of the uprising came to be the Christian Palestinian academic Hanan Ashrawi, the Jerusalem-based publicist and researcher Faisal Husseini and the Gaza-based clinician Haidar Abdel-Shafi, the last of these previously associated with the PFLP. The central political demand of the movement was one that was easily understood by all: the immediate and unconditional end of the 1967 occupation.

With Israel facing growing international criticism and a loss of resolve by conscript soldiers unprepared for dealing with sustained and unarmed mass protests, the Intifada forced open a debate in Israeli society about the occupation. A small but politically significant movement emerged of Israeli youths who refused military service in the 1967 territories, some of whom were imprisoned for this.

Betrayal at Oslo

The PLO leadership in Tunis, however, saw the Intifada both as an opportunity and as a threat. Arafat had successfully convinced a November 1988 meeting of the PLO's National Council in Algiers to adopt a 'declaration of independence'. This proclaimed a Palestinian state in the 1967 territories with East Jerusalem as its capital, and was drafted by the iconic Palestinian national poet Mahmoud Darwish.

The Western diplomatic consensus around a 'two-state solution' thus became official PLO policy for the first time. The remaining obstacles to its acceptance by the major Arab regimes had already disappeared four months earlier, when King Hussein finally relinquished Jordan's territorial claims to the West Bank. This deprived Israel of the long-pursued and always illusory 'Jordanian option' as a means of getting around the PLO.

Arafat hoped by this declaration to use the uprising as leverage to pursue a diplomatic path towards a Palestinian state, through negotiations with Israel and with its US and other

Western allies. At the same time, the West Bank-based leadership around Ashrawi and Husseini had much more detailed knowledge of local conditions, and a much closer organic relationship with the mass base of the uprising than the PLO's distant bureaucracy. This made them into a threat to Arafat's authority, despite their support for, and association with, his Fatah faction in the PLO.

This projected 'diplomatic path' eventually took shape in the form of the US-sponsored Madrid conference in November 1991, albeit not without unprecedented pressure on Israel from the USA. US President George HW Bush's Secretary of State, James Baker, had to threaten to withhold $11 billion in loan guarantees to force Israel's prime minister Yitzhak Shamir to attend. However, the USA also made repeated humiliating demands that Arafat and the Palestinians officially 'renounce terrorism'.

In the meantime, world events were conspiring to weaken and isolate the PLO. Arafat had supported Saddam's Iraq following its August 1990 invasion of Kuwait and the US-led 'Operation Desert Storm' that followed it, in which Bashar al-Assad's Syria joined the US-led coalition against Iraq in return for a free hand in Lebanon. This was followed by the expulsion of 400,000 Palestinians from Kuwait after the restoration of its ruling dynasty in March 1991.

Saudi Arabia and Kuwait both cut off funds to the PLO in revenge, placing pressure on its now cash-strapped bureaucracy. Then the failed August 1991 coup attempt against the Soviet leader Mikhail Gorbachev set in motion a chain of events that led to the collapse and disintegration of the USSR four months later. This deprived the Palestinians of the potential support of a global superpower.

In the occupied territories, Israel escalated its repression as the Intifada appeared to be losing momentum. The exiled PLO leadership found itself increasingly desperate to maintain its relevance, and to preserve its hold over its own people. It began secret negotiations with Israel behind the backs of the official Palestinian delegation after Shamir was replaced by Labor's Yitzhak Rabin in July 1992. These secret negotiations led eventually to the September 1993 Oslo Accords.

It is worth emphasising here that Arafat's biggest betrayal at Oslo was not that he accepted the reduced ambition of 'two states'. Rather, Arafat's crime was that the PLO leadership made such unprincipled and wide-ranging concessions that they left the future of the 1967 territories at the mercy of Israel's internal politics, in a way that would seal off the possibility even of 'two states' in the future. It took another another seven years, however, and a new Palestinian uprising, to make the nature of this betrayal abundantly clear.

Hamas and the Muslim Brotherhood

The origins of Hamas lie in the Palestinian adherents of Egypt's Muslim Brotherhood, in Gaza in particular. Founded in Egypt in 1928 by the schoolteacher and cleric Hassan al-Banna (1906–49), the Muslim Brotherhood established branches in many other Arab countries. Its Palestinian supporters under the British Mandate played a role in the formation of the Young Men's Muslim Association, one of whose leaders was the itinerant Syrian preacher Izz ad-Din al-Qassam (1882–1935), after whom Hamas's armed wing is named.

Qassam became a leading figure in the armed struggle against both the British and the Zionist settlers in the early 1930s, and was killed in an ambush by British forces at the end of 1935. He thus became an iconic figure for the 1936–39 Arab Revolt in Palestine against British rule and Zionist colonisation. However, his Association was less subordinate to the Brotherhood than it was to the British-appointed Grand Mufti of Jerusalem Amin al-Husseini (1895–1974), who became the leading Arab enemy of the British in Palestine following the Revolt.

Husseini notoriously visited Adolf Hitler in 1941, offering to unleash an Arab revolt against their common enemies: 'the British, the Jews and the Communists'. He did not, however, give Hitler the idea for the Holocaust, as Israeli prime minister Benjamin Netanyahu claimed in a speech to the 37th Zionist Congress in October 2015. The Nazi leader had already begun his genocide of the European Jews more or less simultaneously with Germany's invasion of the USSR in June 1941, five months before the Mufti's visit. Hitler, as a racist and an imperialist himself, politely rejected Husseini's idea of a pan-Arab uprising against British imperialism.

Husseini, however, did maintain good relations with the Muslim Brotherhood, which helped to recruit Egyptian volunteers to his irregular 'Army of the Holy War' during the 1947-49 Partition. The Brotherhood's mainstream variant of Islamism, therefore, already had a presence in Palestine long before the Partition. However, Egypt's occupation of the Gaza Strip between 1948 and 1967 ensured that Palestinian Islamism would be far more closely tied to political developments in Egypt than its counterparts elsewhere.

This continued to be the case even after 1967. For example, an offshoot of the Egyptian Brotherhood called Islamic Jihad, which assassinated Egypt's President Anwar Sadat in October 1981, spawned an armed, Gaza-based Palestinian movement of the same name, whose leaders were disillusioned former members of the Brotherhood themselves.

Less a political party than a social and religious movement, the Brotherhood's practice has alternated between two poles. One involved practical engagement in politics, for example, through support for the Arab Revolt and involvement in Egypt's independence movement. Where Muslim Brothers became involved in politics with its official backing, the Brotherhood often established special organisations for that purpose, like Hamas in Palestine, former Egyptian President Mohamed Morsi's Freedom and Justice Party, and the Islamic Action Front in Jordan.

The other pole of the Brotherhood's practice involved promoting the 'Islamisation of society' through its network of mosques, charities, schools, hospitals, and other institutions. These dispensed services to a poverty-stricken mass base often neglected by state-funded equivalents. In this latter role, the Brotherhood has often been tolerated by Arab governments as a useful safety valve for social discontent, and as a means of cushioning the social impact of their own policies on the poor.

In its former role, however, the Brotherhood has often been

quite severely repressed, in Egypt and Syria in particular. This dynamic has frequently produced dissidents from within the Brotherhood's own ranks who, in effect, have declared war on their governments of the day, and violent offshoots that have engaged in armed campaigns against those governments.

For example, Sayyid Qutb (1906–66), a leading figure in the Egyptian Brotherhood, was hanged for his role in an alleged plot to assassinate Nasser. He would become the most well-known exponent of the outlook of this 'Qutbist' trend within Brotherhood-derived Islamism. His 1964 book *Milestones* has become the acknowledged inspiration for many of the Brotherhood's more extreme and more explicitly political competitors since.

The Muslim Brotherhood has members and adherents from all classes of society. However, its main organised base and its leading cadres are most frequently conservative Muslim university students and university-educated professionals. Conversely, its mass base, especially in Egypt, is very often amongst the urban poor. The Brotherhood seeks to unite and to reconcile rich and poor through charity and through the promotion of a common adherence by both to 'Islamic values'. It has therefore often been quite violently hostile to the organised left, to secular nationalists and to any notion of class struggle.

Palestinian Islamism has followed the same pattern as the Muslim Brotherhood's history in Egypt but with one major difference. Shorn by the Israel occupation after 1967 of any possibility of exercising any influence over the state, the Palestinian Brothers were able for much longer than elsewhere to maintain a detachment from profane politics, and to stick to a policy of 'Islamising society' by disseminating their social and cultural values through their network of institutions.

For that same reason, they were tolerated by the Israeli occupation forces for a much longer and more continuous period than they were in any Arab country at the same time. The number of mosques in Gaza tripled in the twenty years under Israeli occupation before the First Intifada, while Hamas's founding spiritual leader Sheikh Ahmed Yassin (1937–2004) established a charity in 1973, Mujama al-Islamiya, that Israel allowed to operate across the Gaza Strip.

For context, one should understand that, in the same period, Gaza was a stronghold of Fatah's 'armed struggle' and then, as now, was the site of some of Israel's bloodiest reprisals against both armed and unarmed resistance. The Arab states similarly regarded PLO-aligned Palestinian emigrants on their territory as potential troublemakers, and kept them under surveillance. By contrast, Palestinian Islamists like the former Hamas leader, Khaled Mashal, who studied and worked in Kuwait for twenty-odd years until the 1991 Gulf War, were treated almost as harmless and apolitical moderates.

The Palestinian Brothers were thus able to grow in influence and to expand their institutions. But they were very much out of tune with the mood of most politically active and politically conscious Palestinians for almost two decades.

From Muslim Brothers to Islamic resistance

That changed with the First Intifada in 1987. This mobilised far too deep and far too broad a cross-section of Palestinian society for the Palestinian Brothers simply to stand aside from it, as they had previously stood aside from the PLO's 'armed struggle'.

Yassin and his associates Abdel Aziz al-Rantisi and Salah Shehade originally formed Hamas in December 1987 in response to this emerging movement, as a 'paramilitary wing' of the Muslim Brotherhood in Palestine. In its August 1988 Covenant, Hamas moved away from the Palestinian Brothers' prior emphasis on pan-Islamic concerns towards more specifically Palestinian objectives, while continuing to assert its role as part of the universal Muslim Brotherhood.

The Hamas Covenant thus sought to tie together the Brotherhood's universalistic Islamism with Palestinian nationalism. It argued that 'nationalism, from the point of view of the Islamic Resistance Movement, is part of the religious creed' and that 'the Palestinian problem is a religious problem'. In the same vein, Hamas simultaneously made the claims that 'the liberation of Palestine is the personal duty of every Palestinian' and that 'the day that enemies usurp part of Muslim land, Jihad becomes the individual duty of every Muslim'.

This same Covenant also made reference to that notorious antisemitic Tsarist forgery *The Protocols of the Elders of Zion*. It repeated the tropes of European antisemitism about Jewish 'control of the world media' and the role of 'Jewish money' in stirring up revolutions in France, Russia and elsewhere. It also promoted a global conspiracy theory of its own that bizarrely included not only Jews and Freemasons, but also Western charitable organisations like the Rotarians and the Lions Clubs.

In the world outlook of Hamas, Israel was not an outpost of Western imperialism serving the latter's strategic purposes in the Middle East. Rather, the Jews 'with their money ... were able to control imperialistic countries and instigate them to colonise many countries in order to enable them [the Jews] to exploit their resources and spread corruption there'. Hamas promoted antisemitic themes that were common in the propaganda of both nationalist and conservative Arab regimes, but that had long since disappeared from the ideology of most other Palestinian organisations, especially in the years immediately before and during the First Intifada.

Having been regarded previously almost as collaborators by most PLO-supporting Palestinians, the Palestinian Brothers now tried to outbid them in their support for the Intifada. Hamas did not join the UNLU but called (smaller) mass actions of its own, although the pressure of its mass base would force it to coordinate these actions with the UNLU's most of the time. Hamas's network of institutions would complement the work of Palestinian 'civil society' in providing practical assistance to the uprising's mass base, although their prior legal and public status made them vulnerable to Israeli shutdowns.

Almost all of the PLO-aligned and other secular Palestinian factions supported the UNLU's call for an immediate end to the 1967 occupation, even those like the PFLP that continued to advocate a single 'democratic secular state' in Palestine. However, Hamas, at that time, denounced this limited immediate objective as a betrayal, and called instead for a struggle that 'strives to raise the banner of Allah over every inch of Palestine'.

Its programme was not for an independent Palestinian state nor even for a 'democratic secular state', but for an Islamic state resembling Iran's post-1979 Islamic Republic.

Hamas rejected all negotiations with Israel, even for tactical objectives, while asserting that 'jihad' was 'the only answer'. It formed its own separate armed wing, the Izz ad-Din al-Qassam Brigades in mid-1991, partly with a view to disrupting the 'diplomatic process' that was then taking shape with the preparations for the Madrid Conference. This diplomatic process then had the support of the UNLU and of most other Palestinian factions, almost all of whom would have been ignorant of Arafat's subsequent secret negotiations with Israel in Oslo.

However, the Brigades' armed campaign did not begin in earnest until April 1993, by which time the uprising was already in the final stages of its defeat. This campaign targeted Israeli soldiers, settlers and civilians alike, and pioneered the use of the suicide bombings that became Hamas's trademark. Hamas in effect had adopted much of the programme and strategy of its smaller but longer-established rival, Islamic Jihad, albeit from within the centre ground of Brotherhood-derived Islamism rather than its Qutbist extremes.

The frequent claim, made at the time and since, that Israel had 'created Hamas' is as ridiculous and as wide of the mark as claims by pro-Assad conspiracy theorists today that the USA's Central Intelligence Agency or the Israeli Mossad 'created' Islamic State. However, the disruptive and divisive character of Hamas's involvement in the First Intifada, and the provocative character of its subsequent armed actions, did give rise to what for some was plausible speculation that Israel's secret police, the Shin Bet, had 'infiltrated' its leadership, or at least had some influence over its decisions.

It was the collapse of the USSR that ultimately gave Hamas a uniquely influential role. Like the PFLP, most of the Palestinian left and many of the smaller PLO factions, Hamas rightly opposed the Oslo Accords of 1993, and joined the boycott of the Palestinian Authority and other Oslo institutions. Unlike these other organisations, however, Hamas was affected neither materially nor ideologically by the demise of the

USSR. On the contrary, it was able to position itself as the main organised Palestinian opponent of Oslo, while Fatah became hegemonic over secular Palestinian nationalism.

Hamas's armed actions in the 1990s occasionally gave voice to Palestinian frustration with the slow progress of the 'peace process' and with Israel's constant double-dealing, especially during Benjamin Netanyahu's first prime ministerial term in 1996–99. They also provided Netanyahu, who had opposed Oslo from the opposite direction, with a convenient occasional pretext for suspending negotiations, although this was also true of Rabin in 1993–95 and of his successor Shimon Peres in 1995–96.

The armed campaign also created bad blood between Fatah and Hamas, with the Palestinian Authority's security forces frequently engaging in the imprisonment, torture and occasional extrajudicial killings of Hamas militants. However, while this campaign brought Hamas notoriety, it did not at this stage bring it much popularity.

The prevailing mood under Oslo was one of waiting patiently for 'final status' negotiations that were supposed to deliver a comprehensive agreement: on the status of Jerusalem, the Jewish settlements, the Palestinian refugees, borders, the end of the occupation and a Palestinian state. In the meantime, Fatah claimed to be engaged in a 'state-building project' of its own through the Palestinian Authority's quasi-state institutions, a project that was supposed to make the end of the occupation an inevitability, if a painfully slow one.

The Second Intifada and the Crisis of Leadership

The bubble of optimistic patience with the 'peace process' that Oslo had encouraged was burst most spectacularly in September 2000. In May of that year, Israel's unilateral military withdrawal from Lebanon had sent many Palestinians the optimistic message that Israel could be forced to withdraw from occupied land without any formal agreement, if placed under sufficient pressure. Then, in July, Labor prime minister Ehud Barak's insulting 'generous offers' to Yasser Arafat at the Camp David Summit added to Palestinian unrest, by making it clear that Israel had no intention of allowing the Oslo peace process to bring about any meaningful Palestinian state.

Like the First Intifada, the Second Intifada began as an unarmed mass protest movement, albeit in very different new conditions. The spark for it was an intentionally provocative visit on 28 September by the Likud opposition leader, Ariel Sharon, and his right-wing supporters, protected by hundreds of Israeli riot police, to the Temple Mount compound in Jerusalem's Old City.

Sharon's stated purpose was to assert the right of 'all Israelis' to visit the Temple Mount, a right that was available only to a small number of Palestinians. Only ten days before, Palestinians had commemorated the 1982 Sabra and Shatila massacre that Sharon had overseen.

Known to Muslims as Haram al-Sharif, the 'Noble Sanctuary', the compound is home to al-Aqsa Mosque, the third-holiest site in Islam, and to the Wailing Wall, the single holiest site in Judaism. Disputes over the eventual status of the compound and of the Old City in general had been a sticking point in 'final status' negotiations. Sharon clearly intended to embarrass Barak in order to forestall any Israeli concessions on this question.

Riots broke out the following day in Jerusalem after Friday prayers, and spread within days to the rest of the 1967 territories. Dozens of Palestinians were killed and around 2,000 wounded in the first week, as Israel responded far more immediately and ferociously than it had in 1987. Israeli forces used both live and rubber-coated ammunition against protesters. On the second day, Israeli troops were filmed by a French television news crew shooting dead 12 year-old Muhammad al-Durrah as he sheltered behind his father while Israeli troops confronted protesters in the Gaza Strip.

The movement even spread into Israel itself, where thirteen of Israel's Arab minority citizens were killed during rioting in the Galilee region in the north of the country in October. Some 141 Palestinians were killed and around 6,000 wounded in the first month of the uprising, making it much bloodier than its predecessor.

The militarisation of the Second Intifada

Israel's tactics this time were very different. After the lynching in Ramallah of two Israeli reservists, who had been arrested while out of uniform, by civilians who stormed the police station in which they were being held, Israel began targeting the Palestinian Authority's own security forces, who it accused of tolerating, encouraging or even of taking part in 'terrorism'. Barak's final meeting as prime minister with Arafat in Egypt in January 2001 then failed to produce any concessions that could bring an end either to the uprising or to Israel's repression of it.

Sharon's subsequent election as prime minister in February 2001 brought an intensification of Israel's repression and its attacks on the Palestinian Authority's security apparatus, as well as on its civilian institutions and infrastructure. Sharon, like Netanyahu, had opposed the Oslo Accords and Israel needed a Palestinian Authority that could repress Palestinians, not one that could pose as a state-in-waiting while its people were engaged in revolt. In many ways, however, the Second Intifada was as much a revolt against the Palestinian Authority and the empty legacy of Oslo as it was a revolt against Israel's continued occupation.

Sharon instigated the 'targeted killing' of the militants and even of the civilian leaders of Palestinian factions. In defence of this policy, he argued that Israel was punishing those already guilty of planning to kill its soldiers and citizens, or that it was acting pre-emptively in self-defence.

Among the first of these extrajudicial executions was the killing of Hamas's Mahmoud Adani in the month that Sharon was elected, and of the PFLP's Abu Ali Mustafa six months later in August 2001. Among the most notorious were the killings of Hamas leader Sheikh Ahmed Yassin in March 2004 and his successor Abdel Aziz al-Rantisi a month later. Both were killed by missiles fired from Israeli helicopters, with nine civilian bystanders killed alongside Yassin in the first operation. In the July 2002 killing of the Izz ad-Din al-Qassam Brigades' leader, Salah Shehade, an Israeli jet dropped a one ton bomb onto Shehade's family home, destroying it and killing 15 people and wounding up to 150 others.

Israel specifically targeted figures from the one Palestinian faction, Hamas, that was practically guaranteed to respond with unrestrained armed actions of its own, in particular with the now notorious suicide bombings. This allowed Israel to continue its military escalations, encouraging further armed Palestinian actions in response, and thus 'militarising' the uprising.

This was accompanied by regular Israeli incursions into the 'Area A' parts of the 1967 territories that were supposed to be under the Palestinian Authority's exclusive control, often allegedly in pursuit of armed militants. In the most notorious of these incursions, for ten days in April 2002, Israeli bulldozers levelled much of Jenin's refugee camp. The siege of the Church of the Nativity in Bethlehem that started on the same day lasted for over a month, and ended only with an internationally-brokered deal in which 39 Palestinian militants were deported to

Spain, Italy and Gaza.

When set against the Palestinian Authority's increasingly pathetic appeals to Western and Arab states to place pressure on Israel to end its violence and to resume 'negotiations' in good faith, it should be little wonder that Hamas were able to seize from Arafat, and from his successor Mahmoud Abbas, the mantle of representing the principle of 'resistance' that Arafat himself had once personified.

In any case, the USA, Britain and their allies had by then already invaded Afghanistan as part of the 'Global War on Terror' that US President George W Bush had proclaimed after the al-Qaeda terrorist attacks on New York and Washington on 11 September 2001. The USA and Britain in particular were also preparing the way for the invasion and occupation of Iraq. Israel's war on the Palestinians, like these two wars, was understood to be a part of this 'War on Terror'. Arafat's pleas thus fell on deaf ears.

What had begun as a popular rising was now an extremely one-sided war that pitted one of the world's most militarised states against a few hundred, or at most a few thousand militants armed only with their own bodies and with improvised or smuggled light weapons. The lesson of Barak's 'mistake' in encouraging Palestinian aspirations by withdrawing from Lebanon was not subsequently lost on Ariel Sharon. Hence the siege of Gaza after Israel's 'disengagement' from it in 2005 and hence Sharon's repeated promises that Israel's withdrawal from Gaza would prove to be a 'punishment' and not a 'reward' for the Palestinians.

The rest, as they say, is history, and is recounted in far greater detail elsewhere.

The class character of the crisis of leadership

It is worth emphasising at this point that our purpose here is not merely to point to the 'bad ideas', the flawed strategies or even the insincere intentions of any number of Palestinian organisations, or even of their individual leaders. As much as any of these things may have been a factor in the Palestinian national movement's failure so far to secure any lasting victories for the Palestinian people, they are simply an expression at the level of ideology of a far more fundamental problem, that of the matrix of clashing material interests within which the Palestinians have been imprisoned ever since the 1948 Nakba.

In the capitalist epoch, the great wave of revolutions and wars for national liberation in the eighteenth and nineteenth centuries saw the rising bourgeois class assume the leadership of 'the nation' and of its struggles for independence, sovereignty and political freedom. The bourgeoisie were able to do this because, as a class, they were the owners and the representatives of an economic system that was vastly more productive than what it was replacing, but that still required systematic changes in law and government before it could realise its full potential.

The English, Dutch, French and American revolutions developed the prototype for these struggles. This then provided a model for much of Latin America in the early nineteenth century, and for Germany, Italy and much of central Europe in the 1840s, albeit with varying degrees of success. However, capitalism fulfilled its historically progressive role of revolutionising production and establishing a global economy over a century ago. Today, the bourgeoisie and its system is merely an obstacle to further progress.

On the one hand, capitalism's internal contradictions repeatedly create global economic crises and the threat of war. On the other hand, capitalism's pursuit of profit at all costs threatens humanity with the consequences of climate change. Moreover, capitalism's development has divided the world between a handful of imperialist powers that dominate the global economy, and a host of weaker powers condemned to stunted economic development and social disintegration. Today's capitalist class is thus a reactionary class on a global scale.

In the Arab bourgeoisie, this finds its most obscene expression in the conspicuous wealth and the barely-disguised parasitism of the ruling dynasties of the Arab Gulf states, in the habitual preference for dictatorship of regimes like Egypt's and

Algeria's, in the vile and deadly sectarian divisions of the Iraqi and Lebanese ruling classes, in the willingness to make war on its own people on the part of Syria's capitalist class, and in the abject dependence of all of these ruling elites on the protection of outside powers. The Palestinian bourgeoisie in particular is one incapable of providing any leadership to its own people.

In this world, the bourgeoisies of the smaller and less favoured nations are incapable of accumulating the capital and the resources necessary to impose their will even on their own countries' territory, let alone the rest of the world. Yet, the development of an independent capitalist Palestine has been the goal, whether stated explicitly or not, of all of the different factions that have sought to lead the Palestinians towards national liberation.

This goal has unavoidable implications for the Palestinian national struggle. It means seeking out agreements and alliances with the existing capitalist states in the region and, most importantly, with the imperialist powers. It also means reserving a role as Palestine's future ruling class for a Palestinian bourgeoisie that is inherently fragmented and weak.

A weak bourgeoisie in an imperialist world

The single largest component of the Palestinian bourgeoisie today is based in Jordan, where displaced Palestinians and their descendants form a majority of the population. This bourgeoisie has long accepted its second class position in the Jordanian state as the price of its own continued class rule, and it needs no other state for that purpose.

However, the wealthiest part of the Palestinian bourgeoisie (to some extent overlapping with this former group) has the bulk of its fortunes not in Palestine, but in the Arab Gulf states, in Europe, in North America and elsewhere. However sincerely held the 'nationalism' of any of its individual members, all that this class actually needs in material terms from a Palestinian state is an internationally-recognised legal vehicle for the registration and protection of its property, and possibly a low-wage offshore location for joint venture investments.

However, the bulk of the Palestinian people under occupation, and the refugees outside of Palestine for that matter, clearly need far more than this. They need the restoration of their rights and dignity, the ability to lead a normal life not blighted by war and occupation, a country that can welcome them from their exile as full citizens of the state and the ability to rise out of enforced economic subordination and backwardness.

The smaller and less wealthy part of the Palestinian bourgeoisie that still lives in Palestine clearly does suffer under the Israeli occupation in a way that its richer cousins elsewhere do not, even if its members do not suffer to the same extent as the ordinary people. Its property and even the lives of its individual members are repeatedly held hostage to Israel's military and economic aggressions.

This component of the Palestinian bourgeoisie can and does dream of a future 'Palestinian state' in which its members can be the ordinary ruling class of an ordinary capitalist country, exploiting its own working class and politically dominating all other classes of society, whether through the ideology of nationalism, of Islam or of democracy. But history has handed to this bourgeoisie the unfortunate role of being the economic, social and political subcontractors of Israeli, Arab, Western and expatriate Palestinian capital. It can no more declare its independence from these masters than it can eat its own head.

Into this gap has stepped the petty bourgeoisie, the middle class of educated professionals, of men and women of letters and of small property owners. Under a series of different banners, with a series of different ideologies, programmes and strategies, the Palestinian petty bourgeoisie has displayed initiative, determination and even a degree of heroic self-sacrifice in its leadership of the movement for national liberation.

Moreover, its material conditions of life are not so far removed from those of 'the people' at large. Many of its individual members have risen into their current position from far less privileged backgrounds. Many others, regardless of social origin, are periodically plunged back into the even more deprived and degrading conditions of life of those less privileged and more exploited, by the vicissitudes of war, conflict and capitalist crisis.

The Palestinian petty bourgeoisie, however, has acquired its 'independence' of the politically bankrupt big bourgeoisie only to the extent that it has been able to draw upon the support of the exploited classes: the workers and farmers, the refugees and the urban and rural poor. This state of affairs has lasted only as long as the leaderships developed by it have remained loyal to the demands and to the material interests of their mass base.

Yet, as a class, the petty bourgeoisie is tied to the continuation of capitalism, in a capitalist world that is now dominated by a small number of imperialist powers that exploit and terrorise the globe in competition with each other. Ultimately, by its very nature, the petty bourgeoisie also cannot satisfy the demands and the material interests of the masses. It therefore cannot generate and lead a political movement that expresses the needs and aspirations of the great majority of the Palestinian people.

Placed within arm's reach of political power and the trappings of state by imperialist capital, the petty bourgeoisie will split into opposed factions. One, even if it is only a minority, will pragmatically accept what appears to be on offer, inflicting a defeat on the national movement in the process. The other will continue a hopeless resistance with a diminished mass base, on the basis of methods of struggle whose defeats have already paved the way for the betrayals of its less principled counterparts.

The Irish republican movement has suffered from precisely this same class dynamic for a century and more; and the backward-looking piety of Hamas will no more save it from this fate than the heroism of the PLO's fedayeen prevented Arafat and Abbas from travelling down the same route.

The working class and the role of solidarity

It therefore falls to the working class, the principal exploited class of capitalist society, to step in where the bourgeoisie and the petty bourgeoisie have failed. Its spontaneously collective methods of struggle, used to good effect in the First Intifada, are the only methods that can mobilise 'the people' behind the leadership of capitalist society's only consistently revolutionary class.

This is not to say that 'armed struggle' is entirely redundant. All progressive mass struggles will have a tendency to develop into armed struggles once the question of power is posed; all will require some form of armed self-defence once subjected to the repression of a state. Rather, it is merely to observe on the basis of the historic experience of the PLO's 'armed struggle' and of the fate of the Second Intifada that 'armed struggle' conducted in isolation from mass struggles has natural limitations that cannot be overcome simply through the sincere intentions of those leading or conducting it, or through their willingness to embrace martyrdom.

On its own terms, 'armed struggle' leads ultimately only in the direction of negotiations, in which it will almost invariably be the weaker party that has to make the most concessions. The weaker party can seek to offset its weakness through external alliances, which in today's world primarily means alliances with more powerful states. But this in turn holds the tempo and the objectives of its struggle hostage to the machinations of those states and of their ruling classes. The Syrian revolution, as much as the Palestinian struggle for national liberation, has faced defeat after defeat for much the same reason.

Palestine's working class, however, is in a special bind. Unlike South Africa's working class under apartheid, the exploitation of its labour is a secondary or even a superfluous feature of Zionism's project of colonisation. Israel can manage without Palestinian labour, but not without Palestinian land. Working-class methods of struggle can therefore throw bourgeois society and the Israeli occupation into crisis; but in Palestine, their real strength is primarily in their ability to provoke and inspire similar struggles in other countries.

This therefore makes the Palestinian struggle even more dependent on the solidarity of the struggles of the oppressed and the exploited elsewhere. This applies most obviously within its own immediate sphere; Arab regimes whose containment and whose protection is the principal service that Israel performs for the Western imperialist powers, and whose peoples are instinctively hostile to those powers and sympathetic to the Palestinian people. This makes it all the more significant therefore that Palestinians by and large have demonstrated their support and sympathy for the 'Arab Spring' revolutions of 2011, including for the much-maligned Syrian revolution.

George Habash and his comrades were not wrong to advocate an 'Arab revolution', even if this national labelling implicitly restricted their practical horizons to the Arabic-speaking world alone. Here we should add that Turkey and Iran are clearly vital arenas in the struggle to oust imperialism from the region, and with it the struggle to end the Israeli apartheid state's oppression of the Arab Palestinians. The Kurds, anti-Zionist Israelis and the region's other oppressed minorities should also be understood as important allies in this struggle.

They were, however, wrong to seek to restrict this revolution's social scope within the confines of achieving capitalist modernity. They were wrong to have imagined for as long as they did that the Palestinians would have to wait until after an 'Arab revolution' before they could take serious steps forward in their own immediate struggles. They were most spectacularly wrong to have made an exception for the nationalist Arab regimes that have proved to be as deadly an enemy of the Palestinian cause as their conservative pro-Western counterparts have been.

'Solidarity', however, cannot stop at the boundaries of the twenty-odd Arab states. Those of us who live in the imperialist countries in whose service Israel exists, and whose governments provide Israel with the means to continue its oppression of the Palestinian people have a special duty to provide effective solidarity with them.

A new political programme

The development in detail of any future revolutionary socialist programme for the liberation of Palestine is a task that must rightly involve those who are already immersed in its struggles, and who will have to be accountable for their programmatic prescriptions to those who they seek to lead not in pages of written polemic, but in their own sphere of material existence. However, bearing in mind the history of the region, it is still possible to make some predictions of this programme's broad features in advance from a Marxist perspective.

First of all, this programme will fetishise neither 'armed struggle' nor 'nonviolent resistance', but will rely on a strategy of mobilising the masses of the exploited and oppressed. The demands that it will have to raise in the course of this mobilisation will therefore not only have to include demands for national and political freedom, but also social demands that address the burning material needs of society's most exploited. This will mobilise a struggle whose realisation cannot simply stop at national liberation, but that will embrace the social liberation of the working class and of the other exploited classes from capitalist exploitation.

It will take an interest in the struggles and in the democratic and national demands of the one-fifth to one-quarter of Israel's citizens who themselves are Arab Palestinians, and who today are second-class citizens of an ethnic exclusivist Jewish state. This constituency, neglected by almost all of the major Palestinian movements so far except in an auxiliary role, has aspirations that quite naturally give rise to demands that, however limited they might seem today, still pose a direct threat to the legitimacy of the Zionist project.

It will take a serious attitude towards the internal class contradictions of the Zionist state, in a way that prepares the ground for a rupture within Jewish Israeli society along class lines that undermines the Zionist project from within. This will neither take the form of 'concessions' to the existing ethnic privileges of Israel's less socially privileged Jewish citizens, nor of an appeal to the self-interest disguised as idealism of Israel's more socially privileged Jewish citizens. Rather, it will involve patient propaganda that will expose the deadly trap that Zionism has prepared for both, and that will offer them a more attractive future than the present.

Most importantly of all, this programme will have to embrace an internationalist outlook. It will place no faith in the 'support' of any capitalist state, whether in the Arab world or elsewhere. Nor will it involve any reliance on the 'democratic credentials' of any of the Western imperialist democracies, or the rhetoric of 'national sovereignty' of their Russian and Chinese rivals. Rather, its alliances will be with the mass struggles for democracy, for national liberation and against capitalism across the world, including within all of these states themselves.

In a subsequent chapter of this book we outline the key elements of a proposed programme for resolving this crisis of Palestinian leadership. Our central argument is that it will only be in the course of a global struggle for a classless, socialist society that the Palestinians, or any other oppressed nation, will be able to make permanent any temporary victories in their struggles for national liberation. This programme therefore seeks to link the ongoing struggles for national and democratic rights, like the right of return and the end of the occupation, to the struggle against capitalism itself, and for a socialist economy that provides for all its citizens both equally and sufficiently.

Peace and Ethnic Cleansing

The fifteen years since the defeat of the second Intifada have witnessed important changes in both the Israeli and the Palestinian political scenes; changes which took place in the context of wider events stemming from the US-led invasion of Iraq in that same year.

Centrally, these changes included the conflict between Fatah and Hamas which led to the Palestinians under occupation being divided between two rival administrations. Another factor since then has been the impact of the 'Arab Spring' revolutions of 2011, whose defeat produced new pressures on Hamas to join its rival Fatah in the charade of a never-ending 'peace process'. These are both dealt with in the next chapter.

The first development that we should account for, affecting both the settlements issue and an understanding of Israel's Zionist left, is that the 'peace camp' has acquired what might seem a most unlikely set of recruits. Ariel Sharon, the 'Butcher of Beirut', the hammer of the second Palestinian uprising, a man who for decades was almost the personification of Israeli state brutality, concluded after his defeat of the Intifada that a lasting Israeli victory would require an effective 'separation of populations', a demand long raised by the 'peace camp'.

The apartheid wall and 'separation'

The most notorious concrete expression of this policy has been Israel's construction of a 'separation barrier' in the West Bank, dubbed the 'apartheid wall' by Palestine solidarity activists. Winding some 708 kilometres though the West Bank, with only about 15 per cent of it running along the pre-1967 'Green

Line', this barrier's construction began in June 2002, with 180 kilometres completed by 2003 and 362 kilometres by 2006. A further 135 kilometres had either been built or were still under construction by as late as 2012.

Cutting deep into the West Bank along much of its route, it effectively annexes some 9.4 per cent of the West Bank to Israel, albeit physically rather than politically, containing about a hundred illegal Jewish settlements and around 400,000 settlers. Roughly half of these settlers are in occupied East Jerusalem and its satellite West Bank settlements like Ma'ale Adumim, Har Homa, Gilo and the sprawling Gush Etzion settlement bloc to the west of Bethlehem.

The wall also surrounds the town of Qalqilya from three sides, and pokes four large, and numerous smaller, 'fingers' into the West Bank: the 'Ariel finger' near Salfit, the 'Kedumim finger' west of Nablus, and another two near the village of Bil'in and the town of Ya'bad. Some 60,000 or so Palestinians live in the 'Seam Zone' between the wall and the Green Line, which has been designated a 'closed area' by the Israeli military.

These residents, and anyone else wishing to travel to or from this zone, must apply for permits to be allowed to do so. This effectively cuts off scores of thousands of people from jobs, businesses, farms and family, while adding yet another layer of cruel restrictions on Palestinian freedom of movement to those already imposed under the occupation.

Needless to say, Israeli citizens are not subject to such restrictions, and nor is 'anyone who is eligible to emigrate to Israel in accordance with the Law of Return', the Israeli state's standard euphemism for Jewish settlers who have not yet obtained Israeli citizenship. These settlers are treated as if they were Israeli citizens, while the surrounding populations are treated as suspect foreigners in their own country.

The apartheid wall's supposed justification was to protect Israeli citizens from Palestinian suicide bombers, but its patently obvious purpose is actually to annexe a majority of the illegal Jewish settlements to Israel, and to make a contiguous and viable Palestinian state an impossibility.

The International Court of Justice issued an advisory opinion in July 2004 that, on this basis, the wall was in violation of international law. The USA vetoed an October 2003 United Nations Security Council resolution that would have called upon Israel to dismantle those parts of the wall that lie beyond the Green Line. Protests against the wall, appropriately enough, have become part of the standard fare of anti-occupation activism. However, only a minority of the Israeli 'peace camp' have supported such protests, unsurprisingly given that Sharon's projected 'separation of populations' had been a major part of their programme long before it became part of his.

Bitter fruits of disengagement

So far, so predictable. What was less predictable was that this would be accompanied by a unilateral Israeli military withdrawal from the Gaza Strip or, rather, Israel's 'disengagement' from Gaza, to use an official designation that for once is somewhat more accurate than the more optimistic descriptions used by Western media desperate to point to some 'progress' towards 'peace'.

First proposed in December 2003, Sharon's disengagement plan was eventually approved in the Knesset in February 2005, following a series of defections from Sharon's coalition government by right-wing parties opposed to it. It was then implemented in August and September of that year.

Some 8,000 or so Gaza settlers, plus others in four isolated settlements in the northern West Bank, were 'evacuated', each receiving over $200,000 in compensation. A minority of the settlers held out to resist their eviction but they received much less public support in Israel than they had anticipated. Given Sharon's record as a vocal defender of the settlement programme overall, and his government's continued support for the much larger settlements elsewhere, this was not entirely surprising.

Sharon repeatedly made clear that this 'disengagement' was meant as a 'punishment' and not as a 'reward' for 'Palestinian terror'. Gaza was singled out for this attention partly because it was a stronghold of Hamas during the second Intifada but also because its Palestinian population was far too large and compact to allow for the strategy of creeping annexation conducted in the West Bank.

The political logic of this was spelt out by Sharon's senior adviser, Dov Weisglass. He described the disengagement plan in an October 2004 interview with Haaretz as 'freezing the peace process' and putting it 'in formaldehyde', in a way that would prevent the establishment of a Palestinian state. It would also 'prevent a discussion on the refugees, the borders and Jerusalem', indefinitely removing them from Israel's agenda 'with a [US] presidential blessing and the ratification of both houses of Congress'.

US President George W Bush hailed the plan as enabling progress on his own much-vaunted June 2002 'road map for peace'. Previously, somewhere between a fifth and a quarter of the Gaza Strip, with its more than two million residents, had been under the control of a few thousand settlers and the Israeli forces protecting them. Henceforth, Gaza would be placed under a tight economic siege and subjected to periodic Israeli bombardments from the air and from the sea.

This siege, and Israel's attacks on Gaza's civilians and infrastructure, would worsen still further after the election of a Hamas-led Palestinian Authority administration in January 2006, setting the stage for the last decade of conflict and rivalry between Fatah and Hamas.

The decline of Israel's 'peace camp'

All the same, Israel under Sharon had indeed 'pulled out' of one, albeit only one, of the territories occupied by Israel in 1967, removing all of the illegal Jewish settlements there in the process. These had been key demands of the Zionist 'peace camp', or at least of its most radical wing, for decades. The irony is that Sharon had beaten the Labor party's leader, Amram Mitzna, in a landslide election victory in January 2003, on a platform that opposed an almost identical plan from Labor.

More to the point, Sharon had to split his own ruling Likud party in order to bring this plan about. The disengagement plan's main opponent in the Likud, Benjamin Netanyahu, made a failed bid in September 2005 to oust Sharon from Likud's leadership, having previously resigned as finance minister. Two months later, however, the Labor party removed Sharon's coalition ally, Shimon Peres, from its own leadership, replacing him with the apparently more 'left-wing' leader Amir Peretz, who demanded the withdrawal of Labor's ministers from Sharon's coalition government.

Less than two weeks later, Sharon announced his departure from the Likud, abandoning its leadership to his predecessor and longtime rival Netanyahu, and founded a new party called Kadima. Peres, a longtime darling of the 'peace camp', joined Kadima a week later, and was briefly considered a possible successor for its leadership following Sharon's debilitating strokes in the following two months. Kadima, however, had also won over senior Likud figures like Sharon's successor Ehud Olmert and Olmert's foreign minister and deputy Tzipi Livni.

Kadima beat Likud by a landslide in Israel's March 2006 elections, albeit with the lowest voter turnout ever, and formed a coalition with Labor and two minor parties. Notwithstanding the hopes of Dov Weisglass, Kadima's ministers now did begin to talk about a 'Palestinian state', the resumption of the 'peace process', and negotiations to agree 'final borders' with the Palestinians.

Previously, 'peace camp' voters could choose from one 'left-wing' party, Meretz, one 'centre-left' party, Labor, and numerous small and fractious 'centrist' parties like Shinui. Now, they also had a new 'centre-right' party that had apparently come over to the peace camp's strategic vision of negotiations towards a 'two-state solution'.

Sharon and his successors were hailed by Western liberals as visionaries in the mould of Charles de Gaulle, the right-wing French president who accepted Algeria's independence in 1962. For others, it was proof of the old adage that 'only Nixon could go to China', in a reference to the right-wing US President Richard Nixon's meeting and subsequent detente with China's Mao Zedong in 1972.

It should, however, surprise no-one that Kadima in power behaved little differently from Labor in power under Yitzhak

Rabin, Shimon Peres or Ehud Barak. It was during Olmert's tenure that Israel conducted its infamous 'Operation Cast Lead' in December 2008 and January 2009, during which its forces killed some 1,500 Palestinians, wounded around 5,300, displaced 51,000 and destroyed about 4,000 homes, in one of the largest of its post-2006 attacks on Hamas-ruled Gaza.

Kadima's much-predicted potential for reshaping Israel's political scene, by creating a new consensus between left, right and centre in favour of a renewed 'peace process' based on unilateral 'disengagement', proved to be equally short-lived. Israel's February 2009 election produced a Labor-supported coalition, without Kadima, led by Likud under Netanyahu, and supported by Avigdor Lieberman's far-right Yisrael Beiteinu party, although Kadima was narrowly the largest single party, with 22.5 per cent of the vote to Likud's 21.6 per cent.

Elections in January 2013 and March 2015 also returned Netanyahu to power, this time in coalition with Lieberman and with the Religious Zionist Jewish Home party, with Kadima losing nine-tenths of its 2009 vote in 2013. Kadima then more or less disintegrated, with a split from it called Hatnuah led by Tzipi Livni taking shelter under the umbrella of a Labor-led electoral bloc called the Zionist Union in 2015.

Far from the 'broadening' of Israel's peace camp leading to any revival of the power of the 'Labor Zionist' establishment that dominated Israeli politics in the state's first three decades, it has merely seen the right-wing defectors to it share in the peace camp's long-term decline.

Some purists, keen to preserve the Zionist peace camp's 'left-wing' credentials, may object at this point that Sharon, Olmert, Livni and company were never true converts to their cause. In particular, they never committed themselves fully either to a Palestinian state, to a complete withdrawal from the 1967 occupied territories, or even to a complete removal of the settlements. But then again, neither did Peres, Rabin or Barak.

Every single Israeli government since 1967, including those supported by the 'peace camp', has expanded the settlements.

Only the most radical minority elements of the 'peace camp' have ever advocated a 'two-state solution' based on a full Israeli withdrawal to the Green Line and the abandonment of the settlements.

The love-hate relationship between the peace camp's mainstream 'electoral' wing and its more militant and idealistic 'activist' wing has always foundered on the basic class contradictions within Israel society. It is precisely these contradictions that actually inform the competition between the 'peace camp' and the 'settler camp' in Israeli politics.

Nor is the long-term decline of the peace camp any surprise, given Israel's long-term demographic trends. The peace camp's principal social base is among Israel's European Jewish Ashkenazi-origin middle class and labour aristocracy. Its core consists of the descendants of the 'Pioneers', the pre-1948 immigrants who dominated Zionist politics in Palestine under the British Mandate, and who consider Israel to be their own collective creation.

In other words, the peace camp's base is primarily amongst the more privileged sectors of Jewish Israeli society, those for whom the 'Zionist dream' has already paid off. For them, precipitous further territorial expansion risks undermining their social and ethnic privileges, through continued war and through the gradual erosion of Israel's legal fiction of a Jewish majority.

By contrast, Likud under Menachem Begin was able to overturn three decades of Labor hegemony in the late 1970s by relying on the votes of the less privileged layers of Jewish Israeli society, in particular the 'Oriental' Jewish immigrants from the Arab countries. They and their descendants occupy a much less favoured place in Israel's class structure. For them, the occupation, the settlements and Israel's continued expansion all offer a means of climbing the social ladder that would not be available otherwise. The peace camp has no social programme that could offer them any alternative.

Olmert's cloud of demographics

Begin's successors, from Yitzhak Shamir in the 1980s, to

Netanyahu in the 1990s, Sharon during the Second Intifada and Netanyahu again over the last decade, have similarly been able to rely on the votes of the wave of disadvantaged 'Russian' Jewish immigrants from the former Soviet republics, or on the support of racist parties like Lieberman's for which these immigrants vote. For any Marxist, the idea that the subjective 'idealism', and the obscured self-interest, of Israel's more privileged layers might be capable of producing progressive results, when set against the material needs of Israel's less privileged layers is, quite obviously, an illusion.

Breaking up the hegemonic cross-class Zionist bloc in Israeli politics, which repeatedly confronts the Palestinians as a seemingly undifferentiated mass, will require not the 'idealism' of the satisfied middle classes, but an appeal to the real class interests of those less privileged; for jobs, for housing, for decent living standards, for freedom from unemployment and insecurity. This will only be possible once serious defeats for the Zionist project impose restrictions on Israel's freedom of action that deprive its ruling class of the ability to 'buy off' the social discontent of its less privileged Jewish citizens at the expense of the Palestinians.

Yet it is precisely this struggle that the Zionist 'peace camp' has no interest in supporting, let alone in joining. In a settler-colony with an uncompleted project of colonisation, 'left' and 'right' simply do not have the same meanings that they have in more 'normal' and established capitalist societies. In any case, the single biggest factor in Sharon's 'conversion', and even more so in Olmert's, towards 'two states' and a 'separation of peoples' has been precisely one of the peace camp's longstanding shibboleths—the 'demographic argument'. This was set out most clearly by Olmert in an interview in December 2003, in which he argued as follows:

'Above all hovers the cloud of demographics. It [an Arab majority in Israel-Palestine] will come down on us not in the end of days, but in just another few years. We are approaching a point where more and more Palestinians will say: "There is no place for two states between Jordan and the sea. All we want is the right to vote." The day they get it, we will lose everything. I shudder to think that liberal Jewish organisations that shouldered the burden of the struggle against apartheid in South Africa will lead the struggle against us.'

He would later clarify his position in February 2004:

'The strategy is comprehensive and it will relate to all of the territories. Disengagement will have to take place equally in the West Bank.... As long as we talk about unilateral moves, I think the basic parameter has to be minimum Arabs under the jurisdiction and administration of the State of Israel, and maximum Jews.'

However, the objective of having 'minimum Arabs' and 'maximum Jews', in a defensible piece of land capable of satisfying the material expectations of the latter, can be achieved in more than one way. The racist Lieberman's proposed solution to the same 'problem' involves handing over some of the Arab-majority regions in pre-1967 Israel to the Palestinian Authority in a unilateral 'exchange' with the West Bank settlements, thereby depriving a large part of Israel's Arab minority of citizenship without abandoning continued expansion. In the longer term, Lieberman and others dream of removing both Israel's Arab citizens and the Palestinians under occupation from the country altogether. This in turn takes us back to the central problem of the Zionist project in the present day, and with it the question of the Palestinian refugees.

The right of return

It would not be an exaggeration to say that the Palestinian refugees outside of Palestine have been the single most neglected component of the Palestinian people, at least since the PLO under Yasser Arafat signed the Oslo accords with Israel in September 1993.

In the 1960s and 1970s, the Palestinian refugees had been the principal actors in the PLO's armed struggle with Israel. They have since been reduced to much the same abject and quiescent state that the Arab regimes tried to impose on them between their expulsion by Israel in 1948 and the beginning of their 'armed struggle' in 1965. Today's PLO towers over the refugees as a bloated bureaucracy financed by the Gulf Arab states. It polices them on behalf of Lebanon's sectarian-confessional nightmare state and the dictatorship of Syria's Bashar al-Assad, while dispensing grants and favours to those who behave themselves.

In Jordan, Palestinians form a majority of the population and have an organic relationship with their kith and kin in the West Bank, many of whom still hold Jordanian passports. The Palestinian-Jordanian bourgeoisie have long accepted their second-class position in the Jordanian state, in relation to the militarised Bedouin-origin elites that were placed in power under British rule.

In its youth, this bourgeoisie toyed with Palestinian nationalism and with the PLO's armed struggle, but the events of 'Black September' in 1970, when King Hussein crushed the Palestinian resistance in Jordan with the support of the conservative Arab states, and the acquiescence of Nasser's Egypt and Baathist Syria, put an end to that. The revolutionary turmoil of that period convinced the Palestinian-Jordanian bourgeoisie that their second-class political status was a price worth paying for the preservation of their property rights and political order. The Palestinians in Jordan, including the refugees, will therefore have to look elsewhere for leadership and it will probably take a revolution in Jordan to produce one.

Syria, in turn, was once regarded as the 'last bastion' of the Palestinian resistance, and was a refuge for most of the anti-Oslo Palestinian factions after 1993. Since then, however, a clear majority of Syria's Palestinians have supported and participated in the March 2011 revolution against the Assad regime. This has led Assad's regime to impose the same brutality on them as it has imposed on most of the rest of the Syrian people.

Yarmouk refugee camp, near Damascus, was a cultural and political icon of the Palestinian national movement in the 1970s, but Assad's regime has subjected it to a starvation siege and periodic bombardment that make Israel's siege of Gaza look positively amateurish and humane by comparison. Palestinians have joined Syrians in fleeing from what has become a vicious, foreign-backed, minority dictatorship, merging their own 'refugee question' into the now much larger Syrian one.

On this basis, some might conclude that the Palestinian 'right of return' is much further away now than it has ever been, although the events in Syria serve to underline its continuing relevance. Yet the Palestinian people as a whole still cling most tenaciously to the demand for the right of the Palestinian refugees to return to the lands from which they were expelled in 1948.

This includes the overwhelming majority of Palestinians in the 1967 territories, many of whom are refugees themselves, and most of whom today accept the programme of 'two states' as a pragmatic and apparently achievable objective. Not even the most craven and supine Palestinian leaders dare to talk in public of any abandonment of the 'right of return'.

Nor, realistically, can they. As we explain elsewhere, what is at stake in the debate around the Palestinian 'right of return' is not merely the economic rehabilitation or resettlement of however large or small a number of stateless and displaced people, but a key component of the entire Palestinian people's collective national right of self-determination.

It is certainly possible to imagine 'pragmatic' solutions to the refugee question that, while falling short of delivering 'absolute justice', nevertheless resolve the problem to the satisfaction of both peoples. But any abandonment of the principle of the 'right of return' is unthinkable for as long as Israel is still a Zionist state; for as long as Israel's need to maintain a Jewish majority requires it to attract new Jewish immigrants with the prospect of Western-style living standards; for as long as this in turn obliges Israel to engage in constant expansion; and for as long as this expansion is slowly squeezing what remains of the Palestinian people in Palestine into an ever-shrinking part of their own country.

Even if the Palestinians are granted all the trappings of 'statehood', with a 'government', passports, embassies, 'borders' and international recognition, no Palestinian can possibly feel entirely confident that they will not be displaced from their homes and lands again at some point in the future, for as long as Israel has not yet abandoned Zionism's project of a 'state for the Jews'; that is, until Israel itself has become merely 'a state of its citizens'.

The threat of ethnic cleansing

The two most commonly advocated 'solutions' to the Israeli-Palestinian conflict today are 'two states for two peoples', on the one side, and a single democratic state with equal citizenship for both, on the other. In reality, as Olmert and others have realised, Israel's continued expansion already leads it by degrees towards a 'one state solution', albeit a most undemocratic one, the longer that the alternative of 'two states' appears to be a fading prospect.

In the two and a half decades since Oslo, the charade of the 'peace process' has allowed Israel to avoid making up its mind either way, and thus has allowed it to preserve the current pernicious situation indefinitely. Netanyahu's near-indefinite suspension of the 'peace process' has effectively made this present apartheid-style reality into an official long-term policy, although how long Israel can sustain it is a different question.

There is, however, a third option. Israel could always 'complete the job' that it began in 1948. It could expel all of the remaining Arab Palestinian population from the land under its control. Even failing that, it could still expel so many Palestinians that a new Jewish majority within an expanded 'Greater Israel' becomes as unassailable as Israel's Jewish majority within the Green Line appears to be today.

This would resolve the concerns both of the social base of the 'settler camp' for continued expansion, and of the social base of the 'peace camp' for the preservation of Israel's Jewish majority and its Zionist political character. However much squeamishness the implementation of such a plan might provoke amongst some in the 'peace camp', the more likely reaction for most would simply be denial or evasion. After all, both Israel's 1948 and 1967 wars of conquest took place under the leadership of Labor Zionists.

Today, only a small minority of Israeli politicians openly advocate such a mass expulsion, but this minority does include people like Lieberman, who are at the centre of the right-wing bloc that has been in government under Netanyahu for almost a decade. It would probably require a generalised regional war to allow Israel to get away with it. Support for an 'ethnic cleansing' of the West Bank (and even of Israel itself) has far wider currency in Israeli public opinion, however, than one might suspect from the votes received by those parties and politicians who openly advocate it in public.

No less a personality than Benny Morris, a liberal professor often regarded as a stalwart of the 'peace camp', has expressed the view that Israel might be 'justified' in carrying out a mass expulsion, in the appropriately 'apocalyptic conditions' of, say, a war with Iran. The repeated references made by right-wing Israeli politicians to Israel's Arab citizens as a potential 'Kosovo in the Galilee' are equally ominous.

Worse still, the precedents are already there. First, the US-led occupation of Iraq and then the Syrian dictator's war against his own people have both brought about huge forced migrations on a scale much larger than what Israel would need to effect this particular 'solution' to the 'Palestinian problem'. These forced migrations have taken place either with the complicity or the indifference of the major global and regional powers.

We live in an age of Trump and Putin, of Assad and Erdogan, of Sisi and Netanyahu, of Modi and Duterte. This is an age in which the world has already turned a blind eye to the suffering of the Syrian and Iraqi peoples, and is today turning a blind eye to the sufferings of the Rohingyas. Equally, this is an age in which the threat of major wars is not such a far-off prospect. No-one should be complacent about the risk that Israel will one day seek to achieve 'normality' and 'stability' via the same route that has been travelled by so many other states in our bloodstained capitalist world.

Antisemitism, anti-Zionism, and anti-Imperialism

There are few international questions that generate such heated public controversy as the Israeli-Palestinian conflict. In terms of sordid economic advantage and strategic geopolitical interests, the State of Israel is one of the most valuable assets globally for both US imperialism and its British junior partner-in-crime.

However, support for the self-defined 'Jewish State' also performs a valuable ideological function. The capitalist class in the West uses a highly selective account of its conduct during the Second World War to impress upon us its 'democratic credentials' and, with those credentials, its present-day right to rule.

This war, after all, was fought principally against Nazi Germany under Adolf Hitler, whose absolute and incomparable evil is proven by the unique horror of the Holocaust. The mere mention of other genocides or massacres in the same context as Nazi Germany's attempted extermination of the European Jews, undermining as it does this claim of 'uniqueness', is thus regarded as virtual blasphemy.

If the USA and its Western allies are credited with having 'saved' Europe's Jews from extermination, then Israel is justified as a necessary fortress for preserving the survivors of the Holocaust and their descendants, and for preventing its future repetition. In this scenario, the sufferings of the Palestinian people are simply collateral damage in the struggle for this higher purpose. Anyone who challenges this narrative is accused of antisemitism and, in some sense, of Holocaust denial.

'Denying Israel's right to exist' is portrayed as being motivated by an intention to repeat the Nazi genocide, or at least to enable its repetition by others.

On the other hand, for those who oppose the Zionist movement's colonisation of Palestine and its consequent repeated displacements of its indigenous Arab population, a state built on these foundations is necessarily a racist state. It is a state that can achieve 'normality' and 'stability' only through the destruction of the Palestinians as a people or, at best, through their confinement to non-contiguous Bantustans like South Africa's under apartheid, or to US-style 'native reservations'.

Naturally, the debate between these opposed positions is ferocious, since what is involved on both sides are charges of national oppression, of racism and even of a will to genocide. Added to this explosive mix is the fact that our rulers, the British and US capitalist classes, see Israel as a vital guardian of their interests in the Middle East, and in particular of its immense oil wealth.

Israel divides the states of the Arab world like a wedge driven between them, and plays a key role in keeping those states friendly or at least compliant. Hence the enormous amounts of financial aid, economic investment and hi-tech weaponry that Israel has received from the USA and Europe over seven decades. In short, since its foundation, Israel has been the lynchpin of imperialist control of the Middle East, and, therefore, to oppose Israel is to threaten that control.

For our ruling classes, support for Israel is thus an acid test of loyalty to them. For the same reasons, opposition to Israel and support for the Palestinian people should also be an acid test for the organised socialist left.

The 'acceptable limits' of criticism

Every mainstream politician, whether of right, left or centre, who wants to be taken seriously must at some point make the appropriate and obligatory declarations of support for Israel's existence 'as a Jewish state', and in particular for Israel's 'safety and security'. This, for example, is what former Labour Party leader Ed Miliband did in June 2014, when he argued against the attempted 'isolation of Israel' by the global movement for Boycott, Divestment and Sanctions, BDS, and when he asserted that no-one in the Labour party should question 'Israel's right to exist'.

Politicians who fail to engage in this ritual of fealty are typically subjected to calumnies, denounced by the leaderships of their own political parties, and excluded or at least relegated to the margins of their parties where they can do no harm. The former Liberal Democrat MP Jenny Tonge discovered this to her cost after her repeated statements concerning Israel's siege of Gaza and its atrocities against Palestinian civilians.

It is not, one must understand, that people are not allowed to 'sympathise' with the Palestinians: as the helpless victims of war and conflict; as the deserving recipients of aid and charity; or as the inexplicably ungrateful beneficiaries of the high-minded and disinterested diplomacy of Western governments. It is not even that people are not allowed to 'criticise Israel', so long as this criticism observes certain limits and is tempered by a denunciation of 'Palestinian terrorism', or at least of 'violence on both sides'.

Indeed, a certain mode of criticism of former Israeli prime minister Ariel Sharon, of current prime minister Benjamin Netanyahu and of Likud and the other parties of the Israeli right is de rigeur amongst left-liberal media apologists for Israel, like Jonathan Freedland, a regular columnist for *The Guardian* newspaper on the subject. This criticism amounts to a lament that the Israeli right's policies in government (of aggressive settlement expansion and of an 'excessively' heavy-handed use of military force) have undermined the 'peace process' and confidence in the possibility of a 'two-state solution', and in so doing have fostered 'Palestinian terror' and a 'cycle of violence'.

However, to show solidarity with the Palestinian people, to take their side morally and politically in their struggle against the Israeli state, and above all to assert their inalienable right of armed resistance to an armed occupation, however ethically, advisably or counterproductively this right might be exercised in any given instance—all of these things are forbidden. The biggest red line of all is opposition to Zionism, to the idea of Israel as a 'Jewish state', a state that exists not as a 'state of all of its citizens' but as a permanent emergency homeland-in-waiting for Jewish people across the world, regardless of their current location, citizenship, familial origin or current familial ties.

The changing debate

The last few years, however, have seen a significant shift on this issue, at least as far as public debate in Britain is concerned. Nor has pro-Israel opinion in Britain been merely the product of a right-wing media. After all, it was Clement Attlee's much-mythologised Labour government of 1945–51 that presided over the events that led to the Partition of Palestine in 1947–49, the creation of Israel and the expulsion of three quarters of the Palestinian people from their homes and lands.

For decades afterwards, a kneejerk position of support for Israel as a supposedly 'progressive' state threatened by the surrounding Arab regimes, as 'the only democracy in the Middle East', was fairly mainstream in the Labour party and in the labour movement at large, even, and indeed especially, on the party's left. The fact that 'Labor Zionism' played a central role in establishing the State of Israel, that Israel's Labor Party was in government for three decades after that, and that it was and remains a member of the Socialist International all meant that it had deep and lasting links with the British Labour Party.

At that time, it was often enough mavericks on the party's right, like former Foreign Secretary Ernest Bevin, and more than a few Tories like Ian Gilmour, who affected a 'pro-Arab' position: 'pro-Arab', that is, in the sense of favouring a policy less antagonistic towards and less domestically problematic for the reactionary pro-Western Arab regimes. Stalwarts of the Labour left like Tony Benn, Ian Mikardo and former party leader Michael Foot were all ardent, if occasionally critical, sympathisers with Zionism during this period.

There had always been anti-Zionists both inside and outside of the Labour party, associated mainly with the revolutionary Marxist left. But these remained a vocal minority until

Israel's expansion gave them a wider hearing. Israel's occupation of the West Bank, East Jerusalem and the Gaza Strip in 1967, its invasion and occupation of Lebanon in 1982 and the first Palestinian Intifada of 1987–91 forced first the organised left and then the wider Labour left to reassess their views, most noteable amongst them being Tony Benn.

This, however, was not accompanied by any perceptible shift in the positions of the Labour party as a whole. If anything, the witch-hunting of the party's left under Neil Kinnock in the 1980s, and their mass exodus under Tony Blair and Gordon Brown after 1997, saw the Labour party's official stance move even further towards near-uncritical support for Israel. This came as part of an overall package that included support for, and participation in, US President George W Bush's 'Global War on Terror', with its invasions and occupations of Iraq and Afghanistan and Israel's bombardments of Lebanon and the Palestinian Gaza Strip.

The 'new' antisemitism

However, in the person of Jeremy Corbyn, the Labour Party aquired a leader with a long track record of solidarity with Palestine, and a similarly long track record of opposing Western wars and military interventions in the Middle East. This has predictably seen attempts to smear Corbyn himself, and his base of support in the party, as 'terrorist sympathisers' and as 'antisemites'. While both of these themes were present in the media campaign against him during Corbyn's first leadership election in 2015, it was not until Labour's first local government elections under his leadership, in May 2016, that this reached a crescendo of often bogus and almost invariably exaggerated accusations of 'antisemitism' levelled at the Labour left.

This notably failed to remove Corbyn from the party's leadership. But even after his second leadership election victory in the summer of 2016, the bogus 'antisemitism' witch-hunt has been allowed to simmer on. It serves as an occasional pretext for suspending or expelling individual party members, and for allowing anti-Corbyn Labour MPs periodically to express their dissatisfaction with their party's elected leader in public.

Corbyn's opponents in the media, on the right of the Labour party and in the openly capitalist parties, no doubt calculated that this was one of his weakest points. It was an issue on which they assumed that public opinion was so obviously on their side that merely raising it would be completely fatal to Corbyn and his supporters.

Their failure has revealed something else altogether. Public opinion on Israel-Palestine is now actually well to the left of what is considered acceptable in the mainstream media. In particular, labour movement opinion, as measured by the views of individual activists and by votes at union conferences in support of BDS, is well to the left of what is considered acceptable by Labour MPs and by the party's officialdom.

On this score, it must be stated clearly that antisemitism, real antisemitism, that is, should have no place in the politics of those committed to solidarity with the Palestinians. Indeed, insofar as Europe's long history of antisemitism plays a key role in Zionism's ideological self-justification, it should be said that antisemites are the enemies of Palestine solidarity, even where they pose as its friends.

The Nick Griffins and David Dukes of this world are no more the 'friends' of Arabs and Muslims in the Middle East than they are the friends of Muslims, Jews, black people or ethnic minorities in general at home. Here it might be added, however, that the modern-day far right is often quite vocally pro-Israel. Nor is this without reason, given Israel's role in the Islamophobic ideology that has largely taken the place of antisemitism in the West as a tool for demonising racially oppressed minorities, and for dividing the working class.

This Islamophobic pro-Zionism was a notable feature of the politics of the English Defence League and its various offshoots in the period immediately after the global financial crisis of 2008. It has since however achieved international notoriety with the rise of the Donald Trump-supporting 'alt-right' in the USA.

This movement's antisemitic ideologues, like Richard Spencer and Steve Bannon, support and admire Israel precisely because it is a state that is as racist in its foundational basis as the state that they would like to see for themselves at home. Spencer has even described himself as being a 'White Zionist' in the course of exchanges with the alt-right's liberal Jewish opponents.

Moreover, given the privileged role of Ashkenazi, that is, European, Jews within Israel itself, there is also an element of shared white supremacism. Last but not least, these pro-Israel antisemites see in Israel a destination to which they can ship off Jewish people from 'their own' countries in the future.

Antisemitism, the hatred of Jews as Jews, is something that exists in society at large. For this reason alone it would be surprising if it were completely absent from the labour movement, the organised left or even the Palestine solidarity movement. Even so, there are few movements that are as self-conscious about identifying and combating real antisemitism within their own ranks as the global Palestine solidarity movement. The movement's antisemitic false friends like Israel Shamir, Gilad Atzmon and Paul Eisen are invariably treated as personae non gratae, at least once their real political positions have been exposed.

The presence in the movement of a significant, visible and often quite vocal number of Jewish opponents of Zionism has often been the source of the necessary corrective to this antisemitic trend. This does not mean, however, that opposition either to Zionism or to antisemitism is primarily their responsibility. On the contrary, it is as much the responsibility of all socialists as is opposition to any other form of racist nationalism.

However, as with the subject of antisemitism in general, Jewish origin alone, no more than any other origin, is no guarantee of superior politics on this score. Both Shamir and Atzmon are themselves Jewish by origin, if not by present self-identification.

Indeed, anyone familiar with the Palestine solidarity movement will be more than aware of examples of a one-sided, un-nuanced, ill-informed, clumsily-expressed or otherwise hyperbolic 'anti-Zionism', which can, and sometimes does, shade over into antisemitic themes that can be taken up by conscious antisemites as cover for their own nefarious agendas. Much of it revolves around the much-debated role of an 'Israel lobby' in shaping Western policy towards the Middle East.

Genuine supporters of the Palestinian cause however should be the first to reject and contradict conspiracy theories that see the hand of Israel or of 'Zionism' behind what are actually the crimes or machinations of US, British or French imperialism. Similar things could be said of the suggestion that Washington or other Western capitals are themselves under some sort of 'Zionist occupation', a suggestion that is an insult to those Palestinians who are suffering under an actual Israeli occupation.

In promoting a fantastic worldview that distorts material reality, such theories hinder rather than aid a correct understanding of the real dynamics of both Zionism and imperialism. Moreover, by suggesting that our own ruling classes would not or could not have committed certain such crimes of their own volition, were it not for the 'power' or the manipulations of you-know-who, such theories both let our own rulers off the hook and discredit the Palestinian cause by echoing the classical themes of European antisemitism.

Combating this tendency effectively, however, is a task that requires patient political education and the promotion of a consistently socialist and internationalist worldview. This is a task that is not helped in the least by mendacious accusations conducted in a witch-hunt atmosphere with a view to demonising and delegitimising anti-Zionist, anti-war and anti-imperialist politics in general.

A test of loyalty to empire

At this point, it might legitimately be asked: why all the fuss? Why does a country the size of Wales, whose atrocities are easily matched by the atrocities of any number of oppressive states and regimes worldwide, receive so much attention? For Zionism's apologists, the answer once again is 'antisemitism'. Their argument is that Israel, 'the Jew amongst nations' is somehow being 'singled out' for criticism.

However, as we attempt to explain in this book, Israel is

unique enough in the present-day world that the charge of 'singling out' is utterly misplaced. At the very least, the fact that Israel enjoys such consistent global impunity, that it is 'singled out' for political and diplomatic protection from what might otherwise be the consequences of its actions, and by our own governments at that, is reason enough for the attention it receives.

However, if Israel's 'safety and security' are a 'red line' for our ruling classes in the West, then this is not because 'Zionists', or even just some Jewish people, for that matter, 'control US foreign policy'. Rather it is because Israel occupies such a central place in the system of alliances of the world's richest and most powerful states, ours included. As a result, loyalty to its security and to its regional interests is almost equivalent to loyalty to those states themselves.

As an outpost of empire, support for Israel is practically equivalent to loyalty to the principle of empire itself, including to the informal but nevertheless very real post-colonial empires of the USA, Britain, France, the European Union, Nato and the entire 'Western bloc' of which Israel is an integral component. This has been a feature of the Zionist project from the outset.

Theodor Herzl, the founder of political Zionism, understood that it would be possible to create a 'Jewish state' on a piece of land that had barely any Jewish people living on it only if this project received the support of one or other of the principal imperialist powers of the day. As a proposed new European settler-colony, a Jewish state needed a 'mother country', preferably European, to protect and oversee the process of colonisation that would give it political and demographic viability.

In his famous 1896 pamphlet *The State of the Jews*, Herzl argued, 'should the Powers declare themselves willing to admit our sovereignty over a neutral piece of land, then the Society [for Jewish colonisation] will enter into negotiations for the possession of this land'.

After examining the 'important experiments in colonisation' in Palestine and in Argentina, he drew the conclusion that these had been conducted 'on the mistaken principle of a gradual infiltration of Jews'. He continued:

> 'An infiltration is bound to end badly. It continues till the inevitable moment when the native population feels itself threatened, and forces the Government to stop a further influx of Jews. Immigration is consequently futile unless we have the sovereign right to continue such immigration.'

Focusing on Palestine, Herzl went on to argue that a Jewish colony there would 'form a portion of a rampart of Europe against Asia, an outpost of civilisation as opposed to barbarism. We should as a neutral State remain in contact with all Europe, which would have to guarantee our existence'.

A rampart of 'European civilisation'

The Zionist movement as a whole would eventually abandon Argentina in favour of Palestine as the location for its proposed Jewish state. Herzl himself personally approached almost all of the available candidates for the role of a 'mother country': Tsarist Russia, the German Kaiser, Ottoman Turkey and, of course, Britain.

But it would eventually be Chaim Weizmann, then president of the Zionist Federation of Great Britain and Ireland, who managed to translate Herzl's vision into a reality. This took the form of the 1917 Balfour Declaration, in which Britain's antisemitic Foreign Secretary, Arthur Balfour, the architect of racist immigration laws designed to keep out Jewish refugees from Tsarist Russia, agreed to 'the establishment in Palestine of a national home for the Jewish people'.

The terms of this deal were well understood by both sides. Sir Ronald Storrs, the first British governor of Jerusalem, argued that Jewish colonisation in Palestine would 'form for England a little loyal Jewish Ulster in a sea of potentially hostile Arabism'. It would be a base for British control of Egypt, of Iraq with its oilfields and of the all-important route to British-ruled India. In return, Britain would facilitate Jewish immigration, land purchases and the building of quasi-state institutions that excluded the native Arab majority from a say in the future of their own country.

Palestinian resistance to British rule and Zionist colonisation eventually made British imperialism reticent about completing the job of transforming Palestine from a British-ruled colony for European Jews into the 'Jewish State' of Zionism's dreams. As a result, the British-Zionist alliance ended quite badly. An armed insurgency against British rule by the Zionist movement's Revisionist right wing eventually forced the Attlee government to disclaim responsibility for Palestine's future, and to hand it over to a United Nations in which the European powers' numerous African and Asian colonies still had no representation.

However, the post-1945 world order into which Israel subsequently came into existence was one in which it was not British but US imperialism that ruled the roost globally. US support for Israel certainly played a role in radicalising the Arab nationalist movement in the 1950s and 1960s, and in turning it against a USA towards which Arab nationalists had up until then not been especially hostile. But it also played a key role in the new system of regional alliances; with Turkey, with Iran under the Shah, with the sectarian Maronite ascendancy in Lebanon, with Saudi Arabia and so forth, that allowed US imperialism to supplant its British and French rivals, the former colonial powers in the region.

The Six Day War of June 1967 subsequently gave Israel an opportunity to demonstrate its indispensability as a frontline state in the long Cold War with the USSR. This set the stage for the enduring alliance between Israel and the Western imperialist bloc that has continued to the present day.

The old deal with Britain was therefore recast in new terms. In return for a guarantee of impunity in its dealings with the Palestinians, Israel would become a 'watchdog state' for the Western powers. Its role would be that of occasionally punishing Arab regimes 'whose discourtesy to the West went beyond the bounds of the permissible', as Gershom Schocken, editor of Israel's *Haaretz* newspaper famously put it in September 1951.

In today's increasingly 'multipolar' post-Cold War order,

with US imperialism no longer the unchallengeable world power that it was immediately after the collapse of the USSR, Israel's relationship with the Western bloc is no longer quite so straightforward. This is partly because of the effect of Israel's oppression of the Palestinian people on public opinion in Arab states that the West needs as allies. But it is also because of its increasingly poor reception by public opinion in the Western world itself.

This latter point can legitimately be claimed as a partial victory for the decades of patient and often difficult work done by the global Palestine solidarity movement in changing public opinion in the West. It may, however, still be a long time before this alone leads to any serious limitations on the impunity that Israel has enjoyed from the Western powers so far.

Even so, the shifting alliances of this increasingly unpredictable global order have created a real fear on the part of Israel's ruling class that the Western world, and the USA in particular, may not be able or willing to act as Israel's military, political and diplomatic guarantor in perpetuity. US President Barack Obama's nuclear deal with Iran, which effectively brought to an end decades of sanctions that had been in place since the overthrow of the pro-US Shah in 1979, alarmed many in Israel, effectively conceding to Iran a new role in 'maintaining regional security' on behalf of the Western powers, in Iraq in particular.

These fears so far have only partly been assuaged by the anti-Iranian rhetoric and machinations of Obama's successor Donald Trump. In any case, Trump's unpredictability and domestic weakness, and the possibility that he might not serve out his full term, make his rhetoric no special guarantee of anything.

Netanyahu, like Trump a mercurial and aggressively nationalistic tub-thumper, seems to have responded to Obama's Iran policy, and to the changing shape of the new global order, by trying to diversify Israel's international points of support, with Russia under Vladimir Putin competing with the USA for Israel's favours and attention.

Like Egypt's dictator Abdel Fattah el-Sisi, Turkey's strongman Recep Tayyip Erdogan, India's Hindu-nationalist premier Narendra Modi and the Philippines' reactionary president Rodrigo Duterte, Netanyahu appears to be preparing for a world in which he can play off the USA, Russia and China against each other, seeking support for Israel's crimes from one or another of this trio of global imperialist powers whenever any of the others appear to be reticent about granting it.

The 'Israel lobby' and the 'national interest'

In this context, of the shifting, occasionally colliding and occasionally converging strategic interests of major states on a world scale, the so-called 'Israel lobby' should be seen not as a cause but a byproduct of Israel's decades-long alliance with Western imperialism.

As significant a role as 'the lobby' plays in influencing US electoral politics and the overall ideological outlook of the Executive branch, it is neither 'the lobby' nor any more secretive 'conspiracy' that dictates US support for Israel. That is far better explained by the more mundane considerations of the need to maintain control of an unstable and strategically-located region with invaluable energy resources.

In Britain, where Jewish opinion by and large is probably still more liberal and left-leaning than in the USA, the role of 'the lobby' is performed not by major pressure groups like the American Israel Public Affairs Committee, AIPAC, but by the self-appointed representatives of 'the Jewish community': *The Jewish Chronicle*, the Board of Deputies of British Jews, the Chief Rabbi, the Jewish Leadership Council and so on. But these bodies and individuals are finding themselves increasingly out of touch with their own communities' younger generations.

The Israeli embassy, most notoriously in the form of the current Israeli Ambassador, Mark Regev, might occasionally be called upon in the media to comment on 'antisemitism' and on 'anti-Israel sentiment' in Britain whenever Israel is at war, or whenever else public controversies over Israel come to the surface in mainstream British politics. But in the grand scheme of things, this 'hasbara' is no different in principle to the information wars and public relations exercises that all states engage in.

What is perhaps surprising is the degree of credibility it is given. Even more remarkable is the fact that the diplomatic representative of a foreign state is effectively allowed to pose as a representative of the opinions of a domestic constituency. It is as if Jewish people in Britain were really just displaced Israelis only temporarily resident in the country, in need of a foreign power to 'protect' them in a country in which they are actually full citizens—a foreign power moreover that makes an explicit ideological claim to their loyalty and support.

Within the Labour party, organisations like Labour Friends of Israel and the badly-misnamed Jewish Labour Movement quite visibly play an organised role in setting the terms of the debate at party conferences and in Constituency Labour Parties. This, however, should be seen in context. Much the same is true of Progress (the home of the party's increasingly isolated Blairite holdouts), of Blue Labour and indeed of the Corbyn-supporting Momentum tendency, albeit far less effectively.

That there exists an 'Israel lobby' and that it plays an organised role in political life is indisputable. But it is necessary neither to exaggerate its real power nor its practical role in order to understand the resilience of pro-Israel opinion in mainstream British politics. A clear understanding of the ideology and strategic interests of empire is enough for that purpose.

The danger of an excessive focus on the role of 'the lobby' is not just the risk of shading off into conspiratorial themes about 'Jewish power' that have always been a feature of antisemitic ideology. It could also promote the illusion that politicians and media figures are not promoting their own country's 'national interests' in defending Israel, but another country's altogether; that is to say, that they are insufficiently 'patriotic'.

By contrast, we should make exactly the opposite case: that, in a class-divided society, the 'national interests' of our rulers are a million miles removed from the interests of those who they rule over; that the interests of the working class are international; that these international interests should dictate our support for the struggles of all of the oppressed across the world; and that it is precisely the 'national interests' of the nation-states within which oppressed and exploited humanity is imprisoned that are part of the problem.

Equally though, if Israel does not 'control' the foreign policy of its imperial patrons, then neither are its imperial patrons fully able to control or restrain Israel's own actions. Like any state, Israel has interests of its own that do not always fully accord with those of its Western protectors, and interests in particular that create repeated problems for the Western powers' client Arab regimes.

Like the ruling class of any settler-colony in a sea of actually or potentially hostile natives, Israel's ruling class is compelled always to think in terms of its own survival and possible expansion. Hence the constant concern over the ethnic demography of the territory under Israel's control, over the deterrent power of its military capacity, over the rise of regional powers like Iran, and over its access to land, water and other resources that it needs to continue and complete the project of colonisation on which it was founded.

Most of all, Israel's ruling class fears popular revolutions in the Arab world that might bring to power regimes prepared to practice the support for the Palestinian cause that previous Arab regimes have only ever preached. This was made clear by Israeli official society's fearful reaction to the 'Arab Spring' uprisings of 2011.

By contrast, the ruling classes of the dominant imperialist powers can afford to think in terms of their global interests on a timescale of decades, in a way that allows them to sacrifice some clients and allies in order to preserve their strategic interests overall. The inherent risk of a divergence between the interests of Israel and those of its imperial patrons, and with that the loss of impunity and Western support, is therefore real enough that it creates an objective need for constant propaganda to offset it. The 'Israel lobby' is therefore likely to stay in business for some time to come.

Zionism and antisemitism

In any case, 'the lobby', to the extent that it exists, is neither wholly nor even predominantly Jewish in its composition. In the USA in particular, the single largest component of the 'Israel lobby' is not Jewish at all but Evangelical Christian, and often deeply antisemitic in its politics concerning Jewish people at home. US neo-Nazi Richard Spencer's outlook on this question therefore has quite a long pedigree.

Nor, incidentally, is this collusion between Zionists and antisemites anything new. Dating back to Herzl himself, the Zionist movement has always recognised antisemitism as a force and as a movement with objectives that were at least in part compatible with its own, albeit objectives inspired by hatred for the Jews rather than by nationalistic self-identification with them.

Indeed, Herzl once commented in his diaries that 'the anti-Semites will become our most dependable friends, the anti-Semitic countries our allies' once Zionism came within reach of achieving a Jewish state. What Herzl probably could not have imagined when he wrote those words was that there would one day be an antisemitic regime whose dictatorial leading figure would not be content merely with driving the Jews out of Europe, but who instead would attempt to annihilate them altogether; and that he would succeed in liquidating six million of them.

Both Zionism and antisemitism based themselves on the assumptions that the Jews were an 'alien presence' in Europe; that they were a people 'in exile' from their 'real' homeland; and that they were an evidently unassimilable people with an alien culture, whose continued presence in this 'exile' was harmful both to them and to their 'host communities'. The parallels with the themes of today's anti-Muslim bigotry are striking.

Where antisemites typically did not care where the Jews went, so long as it was somewhere else, Zionism offered the practical solution of creating a new country to which Jewish people could be made to emigrate en masse. While not all antisemites were Zionists, more than a few antisemites, indeed very likely a majority of antisemites depending on time and place, were positively enthusiastic about Zionism's proposed solution to Europe's so-called 'Jewish question'.

To do full justice to the issues raised by the relationship between Zionism and antisemitism is beyond the scope of this present work. Anyone interested in exploring them in greater detail would be well advised to read Lenni Brenner's *Zionism in the Age of the Dictators*, as well as Francis R Nicosia's *Zionism and Anti-Semitism in Nazi Germany* and Edwin Black's *The Transfer Agreement*.

The most basic thing to bear in mind however is that Zionists, then as now, saw in antisemitism not only a justification for their own project but also a possible tool for achieving their goals. Conversely, Jewish socialists and communists alongside their non-Jewish co-thinkers were at the forefront of the struggles against fascism and antisemitism. They quite rightly saw Zionism as advocating a withdrawal from the battlefield against these evils, as well as supporting imperialism's oppression and exploitation of the peoples of the Middle East.

The crimes and ideology of empire

However, the squeamishness with which respectable society treats this subject reveals something else worthy of note. Our ruling classes in the West, since the end of the Second World War and the creation of Israel, have more or less incorporated the major themes of Zionist ideology wholesale into their own. This is particularly true of Zionism's narrative of the history of European antisemitism and of the Nazi genocide of the European Jews.

In their own rendering of it, this takes the form of a solemn and sincere atonement for their own past antisemitism. In their own eyes and in the historic outlook that they promote to the rest of us, their support for Israel in the present day demonstrates that they have redeemed themselves for their own past misdeeds.

The fact that Marxian socialists before 1914, and revolutionary communists after the First World War, loathed and denounced antisemitism and were in the vanguard of the fight against fascism is hushed up completely. So, too, is the fact that, until after the Holocaust, most politically active Jewish people were socialists, communists or liberal assimilationists rather than Zionists.

That is to say that capitalist Europe, the same racist and antisemitic Europe that gave us both the transatlantic slave trade and the Nazi Holocaust, considers that its bloody debt to the Jews has been discharged by having provided them with a homeland in another people's country. But this 'homeland' is one that the majority of Jewish people alive today will almost certainly never live in, whether or not they identify with it.

The ruling classes in the imperialist West, appropriately enough, have thereby arrived at a 'colonial solution' to the so-called 'Jewish question'. This material fact, however, has to be justified by means of ideology; and ideology is something that can take on a life of its own.

Their problem is that 'colonialism' and 'colonisation' are now dirty words, at least in the world since the bloody rise and fall of Hitler's short-lived Nazi empire and the 'decolonisation' and formal independence of Europe's former colonial subjects. Israel is unique in the present day primarily in the sense that it is the last surviving settler-colonising state of any significance whose founding project of colonisation is still ongoing and as yet not fully completed.

For this reason it should not be too surprising that two of the countries with the most visible levels of public support for and sympathy with Israel are the USA and Australia. Both of them are former settler-colonies themselves, that more or less completed the task of destroying their indigenous peoples only a century ago. Both too are countries where the legacy of this history still informs the dominant ideology and the dominant view of their states' foundations.

The inhabitants of these countries, to the extent that they have not yet broken with the outlook of their own ruling classes, can look at Israel today and see in it their own countries about a hundred and fifty years ago; and this is a picture of which they are not particularly ashamed.

In other countries, and especially in European countries whose colonising wars largely took place 'elsewhere', safely out of sight and out of mind as far as the inhabitants of the metropolis were concerned, this history is an embarrassment. So, too, is the ideology that was developed to justify it, at least when its themes are stated explicitly.

This ideology sought to legitimise separation walls to keep the natives in reservations, and away from the 'civilised' world represented by the settlers. It was explicitly racist and provoked obsessive demographic fears about the higher birthrates of the indigenous colonised peoples. It developed elaborate legal systems to classify the 'natives' and to control their movements.

Inherent within it was the ominous talk of 'surplus populations', and a lack of shame concerning war, conquest, slaughter and forced displacement. But this is recognisably the same ideology that Nazi Germany distilled into its most concentrated and poisonous form, and that it deployed to such destructive and murderous effect in the course of justifying its own empire-building project in Europe, including against the European Jews.

Any serious examination of the Holocaust would have to recognise this family resemblance to the crimes of the other imperialist powers, who occupy their privileged place in today's world primarily on account of the consequences of these crimes. Likewise, any serious examination of Zionism's own project of colonisation would have to recognise it as the younger cousin of these same predecessors. This remains true even though a substantial part of the beneficiaries of Zionist colonisation today are themselves the descendants of past victims of racist genocide.

Seen in this context, the Nazi Holocaust is no longer an apparently inexplicable event, elevated from the sphere of history into the realm of metaphysics. Rather it becomes one, albeit certainly one of the most horrific, of a litany of crimes against humanity for which our ruling classes bear full responsibility and from which they still derive numerous benefits: the genocidal conquest of the Americas, the slave plantations of the US Deep South and the Caribbean, the scramble for Africa, the plundering of the Indian subcontinent and southeast Asia, the forcing of the opium trade on China, the colonial rape of Algeria and the Congo, the Bengal famine, the Irish famine, the Vietnam War and the occupation of Iraq. The list could be extended at will.

Israel's attempted destruction of the Palestinian people might not be on the same scale as some of these crimes, although it easily matches and surpasses many of them. But it is one that is still taking place, and it is one in which our own ruling classes are entirely complicit. For this reason alone, it should be as much an 'acid test' for us as it is for them.

Towards a Programme for Palestinian Liberation

A century after the Balfour Declaration, in which Britain first promised a national home for the world's Jews in Palestine, promising at the same time that 'nothing shall be done which may prejudice the civil and religious rights of existing non-Jewish communities in Palestine', these communities—the Palestinian people—have had their rights massively violated. Now numbering twelve million, less than half of whom still live in their historic homeland, either in the state of Israel or the Occupied Territories of the West Bank and Gaza. The remaining six-to-seven million are refugees, still living in squalid camps into which they and their families were driven in 1948 and 1967.

Despite this, Palestinians not only still exist as a people but continue to resist their national annihilation, as determinedly as ever. They face an enemy with one of the world's most technologically advanced militaries, armed with nuclear weapons; the misnamed Israel Defence Force, IDF. It has the formidable surveillance and special services apparatus of Mossad, Shabak and Shin Bet, the envy of repressive regimes the world over. Its cyber warfare capacity is reckoned to be amongst the top five or six in the world. To cap it all, it has the unlimited backing, logistical and financial, of the world's sole superpower.

Zionist settler colonisation required the transfer of Jewish refugees from European antisemitism to Palestine and a political and economic regime there that enabled them to displace its indigenous inhabitants. This was only achieved by an alliance with British imperialism, victorious in the First World

War over the Ottoman Empire, through its subsequent twenty years rule in Palestine. This alone enabled a sizeable (but still not majority) settler population to establish and arm itself. This movement, especially its so-called Labour element, strove to dispossess the indigenous poor peasants and operated a Jewish labour only policy in the factories, shops and offices.

However, the Zionist project would never have succeeded in creating a majority were it not for the enormous historic tragedy for Jewish people in Europe; the culmination of anti-semitic persecution in the Holocaust (Shoah). Six million perished, nearly five million of them from the Yiddish-speaking communities of Poland and the Soviet Union, a further half a million from Hungary. Yet Zionism was not the main instrument of resistance to this, nor did it provide an effective refuge for most of its victims until this was too late. Its sponsors, Britain and the USA, did not open their borders to the mass of Jewish refugees either before or after the war. Nor did they attempt to hinder the Holocaust by bombing its infrastructure even when they knew it was underway. The Palestinians, despite the actions of some of their leaders, were not responsible for the Holocaust, yet they were compelled to pay its cost. The Zionist project did not prevent the slaughter of Europe's Jews, and the foundation of Israel was not justified by it.

Thus, one immense historic tragedy led to another, the occupation of 78 per cent of the Palestine Mandate and the wholesale ethnic cleansing of at least 750,000 Palestinians from their homes and lands; this was the Nakba, the Catastrophe. Palestinian citizens of Israel are to this day legally forbidden to commemorate it. But this catastrophe did not come to an end in 1949. In 1967, Israel completed its occupation of all that remained of Palestine, taking the entire West Bank and Gaza Strip and expelling a further 300,000 from their homes. Since then, Israel has remorselessly 'made facts on the ground' seizing the best land on the West Bank, available to them after their conquests. Despite the Oslo agreements with the Palestine Liberation Organisation, 61 per cent of the West Bank remains under the direct control of the IDF. Settlement goes on today, aided by the construction of the Apartheid

Wall, fortified townships, military zones and roads and countless checkpoints. 2018 Israeli statistics reveal that the number of Jewish settlers living in the occupied West Bank reached 435,708 a figure that rises to 700,000 if East Jerusalem is included. The aim of successive Israeli governments, open or concealed, is to make the situation permanent and irreversible and in the process make it impossible for any politically sovereign and economically viable Palestinian state to come into existence.

Israel repeatedly demands recognition of its right to exist from the Palestinians and condemns those who refuse to do so as antisemites. But a state founded on the denial to another people of their right to self-determination cannot claim this right for itself. The Palestinian leadership has recognised such a right; in 1988, in the Oslo Accords of September 1993, and since, but Israel has never recognised Palestine's right to exist as a sovereign state. The British Labour Party leader, Jeremy Corbyn, promised that a Labour government, led by him, would do so. He condemned the siege of Gaza; the slaughter of unarmed demonstrators there in 2018, and threatened to cut off arms sales and military cooperation if this continued.

This unleashed an unprecedented campaign of slander and defamation against him and the left wing in his party. The Boycott, Divestment and Sanctions movement, BDS, in which anti-Zionist Jews in Israel and abroad play a prominent role, has sent the right wing governments of Israel into a frenzy of campaigning against the friends of the Palestinians. This in turn indicates that Palestine is not lost, that its exiled people will return and live in a single state that respects the two nations that now live in Palestine. In no way does this mean 'driving the Jews into the sea', a 'second Holocaust' or all the other horror stories designed to deny the Palestinians their rights.

Palestinian resistance

Up to 1967, the Palestinian leadership placed their hopes for liberation on the Arab states, especially those ruled by nationalist regimes like Egypt, hoping they could one day defeat Israel. But, after the Six Day War and Egypt's reconciliation with the USA, it became clear that the Palestinians themselves would have to be the principal agency of their own liberation. Fatah under Yasser Arafat, plus the Popular Front for the Liberation of Palestine (PFLP) under George Habash, the Democratic Front for the Liberation of Palestine (DFLP), and other groupings, turned to armed struggle, that is, a strategy of guerrilla warfare. However, this also failed.

It did, however, shift the focus of resistance to the population of the Occupied Territories. In December 1987, the First Intifada began in Gaza; young Palestinians, armed only with rocks and petrol bombs, faced the full might of the IDF. Israeli Defence Minister Yitzhak Rabin infamously ordered his forces to 'break the bones' of captured demonstrators. Five years of heroic mass civil disobedience ensued: strikes, demonstrations, refusal to pay taxes, and boycotts of Israeli products led to increasing worldwide hostility to Israel and became such an embarrassment to its American backers that negotiations between Israel and the PLO led to the Oslo Accords in 1993. These were supposed to culminate in agreements on 'permanent status' issues including Jerusalem, water rights, border delineation, settlements, and refugees.

The rest of the decade was spent in fruitless negotiations over these. Worse than that, the conditions of the inhabitants of the West Bank, Gaza and the Palestinian citizens of Israel itself, deteriorated, with the checkpoint regime making economic and family life exhausting and humiliating. But the best on offer at the Camp David summit in July 2000 was a Palestinian statelet divided into four non-contiguous cantons surrounded by Israeli territory and IDF forces. These South African style Bantustans would have no control over their own borders, airspace or water resources. The establishment of such a 'state', moreover, would have legitimised illegal settlements on its territory and further territorial demands within the 1967 borders.

Although the so-called 'two state solution' has been repeatedly accepted by the PLO/PNA and paid lip service by succeeding Israeli governments and US administrations, and is supported de facto by Hamas, it has proved to be a mirage;

one that is ever-receding thanks to Israeli encroachments. This false solution has as it main purpose to deceive world public opinion. With the collapse of the Camp David agreement, the outbreak of the Second Intifada and the construction of the Separation Barrier, better known as the Apartheid Wall, it became as clear as day that Israel would never accept a viable two state solution. Israel will never willingly accept a sovereign and equal Palestinian state or allow the return of those it expelled.

The liberation of the Palestinian people, and the freedom of the peoples of the Middle East from Western domination and exploitation, requires Israel's revolutionary dismantling as a racist state and its replacement by a single state for both its peoples, Palestinian and Israeli-Jewish. This does not mean either the expulsion of the Israeli population or its destruction as a nation.

Strategy and leadership

Pan-Arab nationalism, whether based on the Palestinian bourgeoisie in the Diaspora or on the ruling classes in the surrounding states, has failed to liberate Palestine or even substantially improve the lot of its people. Petty bourgeois guerrilla forces, whether influenced by Nasserist or Baathist regimes in the 1960s, or by radical Stalinists in the 1970s and 80s, have also failed to do this. Fatah, first under Yasser Arafat and then under Mahmoud Abbas, turned to the reactionary utopia of an imperialist-brokered peace process with Israel. In the process it became a craven agency of the Zionist state and the imperialist powers, despite repeated perfidies and humiliations practiced on it by Tel Aviv-Jerusalem and Washington.

After 25 years of 'Oslo' the Palestine National Authority 'controls' only 39 per cent of the West Bank with the rest still under IDF occupation. Large numbers of Palestinians turned against Fatah because of its prostration before the Zionists and its leaders' manifest corruption and greed. In the 2006 Legislative Council elections, Hamas took 44.45 per cent of the vote, whilst Fatah received 41.43 per cent. With Israeli and US collusion, Fatah sabotaged the Hamas government and kept power on the West Bank, but lost Gaza.

Hamas, with its reactionary Islamist ideology, continued to resist Israel, and thus drew the remorseless hatred of both Israel and the West. Gaza was placed under a fearful siege where nearly two million people have been collectively punished for this resistance. But the Hamas strategy of rockets fired into Israel and suicide attacks on Israeli soldiers and civilians proved totally ineffective in breaking the will of such a powerful adversary and gave it a pretext to wreak destruction and terror on the inhabitants of Gaza a hundred times greater than anything Hamas could inflict. It is plain that neither the Fatah nor the Hamas regimes in the West Bank and Gaza can liberate Palestine.

In short, neither relying on Arab monarchs or nationalist dictators, nor on guerrilla warfare, no matter how courageous, nor political Islamist martyrs, can liberate the people of Palestine. Only mass struggle, by workers, peasants and youth, as seen in the Intifadas and the demonstrations in Gaza and the West Bank, can be a launchpad for effective struggle. The general strike and workplace occupation too will heighten the struggle and call forth actions of solidarity from progressive Israelis, in the surrounding region and around the world.

The leadership needed for such a strategy must be a revolutionary party which wins the vanguard fighters, women, men, youth of the Palestinian communities both in Israel and beyond its borders, as well as courageous anti-Zionist Israeli Jews. By the very character of the struggle, this needs to be internationally based as well as internationalist in its politics and thus able to bring the maximum forces to bear against oppression. Such an organisation needs to formulate a programme, a strategy for victory. It must be one that starts from the ongoing struggles on all fronts.

End the siege of Gaza

In the Gaza Strip 1.9 million people are kept in what is in effect a ghetto. They are besieged by land and sea, subjected to regular bombing of their homes, schools, hospitals, and workplaces. Materials for repairing the destruction are restricted. Gaza is dependent for its water, electricity, food and medical supplies on the Israelis, who regularly cut them off as collective punishment for acts of resistance, which they insolently call terrorism. In fact, it is the IDF who terrorise the population of this enclave. Half the working age population is unemployed and the United Nations says its economy is on the verge of collapse.

Since Israel's unilateral withdrawal of its forces and settlers from the Strip in 2005 and since Hamas won the 2006 elections, Israel has repeatedly launched major attacks on Gaza. Operation Hot Winter in 2008, Operation Cast Lead in 2008–09, Operation Pillar of Defence in 2012 and, in July 2014, Operation Protective Edge. These attacks have led to mass protests in many countries. When, in May 2010, the international solidarity movement organised the Gaza Flotilla in an attempt to run the naval blockade with vital supplies, Israeli commandos boarded the boats and forced them to turn back. On one, the Mavi Marmara, they killed nine people and injured many others.

In March 2018, when a united front of many organisations and youth organised the Great March of Return to the Gaza fence, murderous sniper fire from the IDF killed over 160, most of them unarmed and those that were only with slingshots and incendiary balloons. To celebrate 70 years since Israel's foundation, Donald Trump declared Jerusalem the site of the US embassy, thus recognising it as Israel's, not Palestine's, capital. To add injury to insult, he also froze $300 million in US contributions to Unrwa, the UN agency for Palestine refugees. With Trump and Netanyahu having won the Egyptian dictator and the Saudi Crown Prince into a de facto alliance, some new Israeli aggression, against Lebanon, Gaza or Iran, is in the offing under the disguise of an outrageous peace plan that will be rejected.

In the years ahead, the international movement of solidarity with Palestine needs to step up its actions around the demands:

• Put an end Israel's land, sea and air blockade of Gaza, opening its port to aid, trade and economic supplies

• Allow completely free movement to and from the West

Bank and Egypt.
- For international recognition of Gaza's inhabitants as citizens of a sovereign state of Palestine.
- Massive aid to reconstruct and equip the schools, hospitals and houses and workplaces, paid for by the 'great powers' that have looted the region.

International solidarity

The BDS movement seeks to persuade institutions of all kinds to withdraw funding and support for Israeli and international agencies or companies involved in the violation of Palestinian rights. Certainly, BDS on its own will not stop Israeli atrocities like those perpetrated in Gaza, nor the settlement and fragmentation of Palestinian areas in the West Bank. Changing public opinion in the imperialist democracies alone will not change their rulers' support for Israel. Only radical and fundamental political change in those countries, allied to the overthrow of the puppet regimes in the Middle East, whose countries they exploit and dominate, will achieve this.

Nevertheless, BDS is a step in this direction and that is why the Israeli state and its embassies around the world, why the Zionist movement, move heaven and earth to stop it and to stop the rise of mass sympathy for the Palestinian cause. The Boycott of South Africa did not of itself lead to the downfall of Apartheid. That was a result of the mass action of the township youth and black workers' movement of the 1970s and 1980s. In the same manner, the BDS movement must expose the crimes of Israel and encourage and give support to the struggle of the Palestinian masses and their supporters in Israeli society. Equally important is support for the democratic and workers' movement in surrounding countries, like those that occurred in the Arab Spring of 2011.

The response, orchestrated by Israeli embassies, has been to force parties, academic institutions and governments to accept the definition and examples of antisemitism of the International Holocaust Remembrance Alliance, IHRA. This includes the proposition that, 'denying the Jewish people their right to self-determination, e.g., by claiming that the existence of a State of Israel is a racist endeavour' and 'requiring of it a behaviour not expected or demanded of any other democratic nation' is inherently antisemitic. As we have said, the former assertion ignores the fact that if Israeli-Jewish self determination meant in 1948, and means today, denying the same right to the non-Jewish majority inhabitants, indeed driving them out, keeping those who remain in degrading and inhuman conditions, then yes it is indeed a racist endeavour and Israel's right to do this is no democratic right whatsoever. The Zionist claims that anti-Israel/anti-Zionist views are, ipso facto, antisemitic, devalue and defocus from fighting real and genuine antisemitism, which still looms large in the arsenal of racist populists and outright fascists, and will re-emerge with virulence whenever capitalist societies enter into crisis. Israel's actions do not protect the interests of the world's Jewish communities, they isolate and harm them. It is the people who defend the Palestinians and fight Islamophobia, who will be the strongest fighters against the antisemites, too.

First and foremost the working class movement in Europe and North America must be won to declare its support for Palestinian liberation, seeing it as an integral part of its own struggle for socialism. As steps towards this we must win the parties and unions of the international labour movement to the following demands:

• Boycott factories and scientific and academic institutions, which produce materials for Israeli aggression and repression.

• Transport workers on the roads, railways, docks and airports should refuse to handle exports and imports, starting with weapons and high tech used in repression, goods produced in Israeli settlements in occupied territory, etc.

• Resist the attempts to stigmatise and illegalise criticism and boycott of Israel as antisemitism.

Equal rights for Israel's Palestinian citizens

Israel's latest Basic Law defines Israel as 'the Nation-State of the Jewish people', who alone have the right to self-determination in it and whose language, Hebrew, is the state language. Thereby, Israel confesses to the justice of the charge that it is an apartheid, that is, a racist, enterprise. There is nothing antisemitic in saying this since Israel and the Zionist project are not synonymous with Jewish identity or the world's Jewish communities, increasing numbers of whom, despite intimidation, declare against Israel's treatment of the Palestinians. To this day, millions of Palestinians are denied access to their homeland; their lands and properties remain expropriated, purely because they are not Jewish. Since its establishment, Israel has systematically discriminated against its own citizens on this basis, and, subjected the non-citizen Palestinians in the West Bank and Gaza Strip to a military regime characterised by freedom of colonisation but continued destruction of Palestinian homes, and strict segregation.

In 1973, the United Nations General Assembly adopted the International Convention on the Suppression and Punishment of the Crime of Apartheid, which included in its definition 'the right to leave and to return to their country, the right to a nationality, the right to freedom of movement and residence'. The definition also includes 'the expropriation of landed property belonging to a racial group'. In fact, 'non-Jews' are not allowed to buy or rent land on the 93 per cent of land controlled by the Israeli state, expropriated from their forbears. The legal rights centre, Adala, calculates that more than 50 laws discriminate against Palestinian Israeli citizens on land ownership, housing rights, the right to a family life, education, and more. Though Palestinian Israeli citizens can vote in parliamentary elections, and become Members of Knesset, in 2016 this assembly explicitly rejected a bill which would have made equality a Basic, that is, a constitutional, Law.

Palestinian village communities and urban areas are regularly declared 'unrecognised' and bulldozed. Israeli non-Jewish citizens with spouses from the West Bank or Gaza Strip cannot bring them to Israel and the High Court, which admitted this was a violation of human rights, added 'human rights are not a prescription for national suicide' and rejected the appeal. Living areas are racially segregated and the school system conspicuously privileges Jewish-Israelis. Housing too is effectively segregated. 70 per cent of Israeli communities have Admission

Committees which filter residents and are systematically used to exclude Palestinians.

The state controls 93 per cent of the land in Israel, and a government agency, the Israel Land Administration, ILA, manages and allocates this land. The ILA lacks any mandate to disburse land in a fair and just fashion, and members of the Jewish National Fund, JNF, constitute almost half of the ILA's governing council. The JNF has functions normally performed by a state. In 2005 its chair, Yehiel Leket, asserted that it 'is not obliged to act for the good of all its citizens (but) for the good of the Jewish people only'. The JNF also directly owns 13 per cent of all public land, some of the most fertile and productive in the country. An especially vicious campaign has been waged against the Bedouin community in the Negev and in Galilee, some 250,000 people at least. Traditionally nomadic herders, they are regarded as blocking Zionist settlement projects and violating Israel's stolen sovereignty over these areas. Their communities are regularly 'unrecognised' and their dwellings demolished. Their medical and educational facilities stand in horrific contrast to those available to Jewish Israelis.

Against these gross violations of democracy and rampant racism we demand:

• A regime of full freedom of movement between all the components of historic Palestine for all Arab Palestinians and all Jewish Israelis.

• For the institution of a common citizenship for all Arab Palestinians and all Jewish Israelis, with appropriate provisions made for the acquisition of this citizenship by Palestinian refugees outside of the country.

• For the abolition of Israel's Law of Return and all other laws that provide privileged access to immigration, residence or citizenship on the basis of Jewish ethnicity or religion.

• For the abolition of all Israeli laws that restrict the right of Arab citizens of Israel to transmit their citizenship to spouses or offspring.

• For the abolition of all Israeli laws that discriminate against Arab citizens of Israel in the sphere of property ownership or other civil rights, for full individual civil equality between Jews and Arabs in the whole of historic Palestine.

- For the prohibition and annulment of 'private' and other 'non-state' legal provisions, contracts or covenants that restrict the rights of residence of non-Jews.
- Nationalise and deracialise the Jewish National Fund, ending all privileges for Jews, and making access to the use of state land available to all.
- Recognise the right of the Bedouin to the lands on which they live and manage their animals.

Free the West Bank from Israeli occupation

The Occupied Territories, called Judaea and Samaria by the Israeli state and commonly called the West Bank, are in fact an archipelago of Palestinian administered islands. The western bank of the Jordan, a zone around 20km wide is occupied by the military with the exception of a zone around Jericho. On the other hand, a strip of land along the Green Line, now marked and transgressed by the security barrier, is heavily settled in contravention of UN resolutions. Whereas there were 260,000 Israeli settlers in the West Bank and East Jerusalem in 1993 when the Oslo Accords were signed, today they number more than 600,000, grouped in about 140 colonies. Here, above all, Israel has created an apartheid situation where Israelis occupy the best land and have first access to resources, where Palestinians are hemmed in by walls, military roads and checkpoints, their villages and towns often dominated by hilltop settlements of armed and aggressive settlers.

The 'security barrier', now known internationally as 'the Apartheid wall', contravenes international law, though of course no international authority, no state power, can or will punish Israel for this. Likewise, the 2018 declaration of Jerusalem as the 'undivided' and eternal capital of Israel, and its recognition by the United States with its embassy, are yet more measures to prevent the city ever becoming the capital of Palestine. Israel blatantly obstructs Palestinian political activities which are normal in a democracy; checkpoints and separation walls hinder movement, making the proper functioning of the Legislative Council difficult if not impossible. Its members and party representatives are often subject to lengthy detentions or imprisonment by Israel, whose state forces have even assassinated some, particularly Hamas, members.

We demand:

• Demolish the apartheid wall, for freedom of movement for all Palestinians throughout the Gaza strip, the West Bank and into Israel.

• Oppose Israel's right to oppress and expel Palestinians from historic Palestine and reject the blackmail of 'recognising Israel's right to exist' which is used to justify this.

• We call for the abolition of the racially exclusive West Bank settlements and their transformation into multi-ethnic municipalities under the control of democratically elected assemblies.

• No international recognition of Jerusalem as Israel's capital. Recognition of it as the capital of a future Palestinian state.

• At the end of June 2018, there were 5,667 Palestinian security detainees and political prisoners, including several hundred children, being held by the Israel Prison Service, IPS. We demand their immediate and unconditional release.

• A vital step in the liberation struggle is to replace the corrupt and collaborationist Fatah leadership. We should fight for free and fair elections to a Palestinian Constituent Assembly.

For women's liberation

Women have been active in the Palestinian struggle since the 1920s, when they protested with men against British occupation. They suffered cruelly in the Nakba, including brutal rapes, aimed at humiliating and demoralising the population and speeding the ethnic cleansing. Nevertheless, in the refugee camps and in exile, women preserved their communities, and passed on their identification with their homeland to subsequent generations. In the period of guerrilla struggle, Leila Khaled became an international symbol of the entire struggle.

Today, women still face deliberate humiliation and harassment at Israeli checkpoints. Israeli bombs do not discriminate according to sex. Though traditional Palestinian society is socially conservative, 'shielding' women and girls from what is considered 'dishonourable' activity, many women found freedom through political education and mobilisation. During the two Intifadas, women became organisers of the communities, forming street committees and other organisations.

Yet, while women's role has been recognised as crucial, they are still rarely involved in political decision-making. The Palestinian Authority, PA, limited women's employment to being secretaries, or teachers in public schools. Women are still underrepresented in the leadership of the main Palestinian political parties.

The victory of Hamas in Gaza represented a backward step for women's rights because of their push to replace Palestinian law with Sharia law. Women are obliged to adopt Islamic dress and restrictions on culture. Often they can't even leave home without the permission of a male relative. Nevertheless, Palestinian women activists campaign for laws to protect women from honour killings and male domestic violence. Recently, the Great March of Return, in which as many as 40 per cent of the participants were women, showed like the Intifadas before them, that the struggle against Israeli domination interacts with, and strengthens, the struggle for women's liberation.

We must fight for:

• An end to the harassment of women by Israeli soldiers and of the checkpoint searches.

• Full educational and legal equality for women, equal property rights, equal pay for equal work.

• Positive discrimination in choosing women members to all political and state bodies and services.

• No impunity for those who murder, rape and beat women, whether they are relatives or strangers.

• For women's support centres, medical care, the right to decide over having a child.

• End all patriarchal restrictions on women's freedom of movement, dress, choice of partners.

• For an autonomous and democratic national Palestinian Women's movement.

For a one state, socialist solution

In reality the 'two state solution' is dead. Acceptance of it in words exists as a fig leaf for Israeli encroachments. For the US and Western European states, it excuses continued support for Israel, and for reformist parties like British Labour it enables it to evade recognition that the existence of the state of Israel as a Jewish state, intrinsically means national annihilation for the Palestinians.

Overthrowing the present Zionist state does not mean annihilating the Israeli nation. No serious Palestinian organisation demands this. All Islamist movements, kings and dictators in the Arab world who have in the past, or do today, issue impotent antisemitic threats to 'drive the Jews into the sea' should be utterly condemned. They are enemies, not friends, of the Palestinians as well as the Israeli people.

Only the working classes of these national, linguistic and religious-cultural communities, their youth, their women, can bring this about. At the present time, most Israeli-Jewish workers are tied to the oppressor state by the Histadrut, never a genuine class trade union but one of the principal agencies of expropriation and separation of workers from the two ethnicities. Progressive Israeli workers seeking the security of a free and equal society should break from the Histadrut and form united trade unions with their Palestinian sisters and brothers.

Palestinians as an oppressed people have no interest in reversing oppression as the Zionists did. We absolutely reject antisemitism and welcome all those Jews in Israel and worldwide who support Palestinian rights and the goal of building up a country without national, racial, religious or linguistic privileges for any one community.

True, the return of millions of Palestinian refugees would create serious social and economic problems if it were left to the capitalists and the market to provide the answer. However, there is a way that the historic land of Palestine can support both peoples. The only way to resolve the conflict over access to land, work, housing education, is social ownership of the means of production, land, factories, offices, and likewise of equal provision of health, education and housing etc., all coordinated by a democratic plan

Therefore, we fight for a socialist solution based on common ownership of the land and all the large scale means of production. This does not mean the expropriation of those actually working the land but on the contrary will enable them to improve and develop it, providing a good life for themselves and food and other agricultural products for the villages, towns and cities contributing to a democratically agreed plan.

• In the factories and other workplaces we fight for workers' control and management.

• Land to the tillers! We demand the nationalisation of the land so that those who originally tilled it, and wish to do so again, can return, and those Israelis who have worked the land for many years and wish to continue can do so alongside their Palestinian brothers and sisters in democratic cooperatives, providing food for the entire population.

• Complete nationalisation of all banks and financial institutions under the control of their workers.

• Nationalisation under workers' control of all large-scale industry and the establishment of cross-sectoral committees to begin a plan of production and distribution.

• For a massive programme of public works to build housing, schools and hospitals. Create integrated work groups, which allocate housing according to need.

• For a regional plan of energy production which shifts away from fossil fuel burning for electricity production towards renewable energies.

• Support for the struggles of other ethnic minorities within the Zionist state, for example, Chinese and east European migrant labourers.

• Support all the social and economic struggles of the Israeli-Jewish workers and youth so long as these are not directed at maintaining privileges against their class brothers and sisters.

Permanent revolution

The liberation of the Palestinians, in pre-1967 Israel, in the Occupied Territories, in the refugee camps, can only come about through a strategy of permanent revolution, that is, turning the democratic struggle against national oppression into a fight for social ownership, planning and control under a workers' and peasants' government. It also means the international extension of the revolution. Palestine is a small country and its advance to socialism will only be successful on the basis of the spread of combined democratic and socialist revolution throughout the whole regions.

Nearly two hundred years ago, the capitalist countries of Europe began to seize parts of the Middle East from the dying Ottoman Empire. For a century, the enormous oil wealth of the Middle East has been plundered by these powers, joined and to a large extent replaced by the United States after the Second World War. Its natural wealth flowed west and east to fuel the post war world's industrial and commercial development of Europe, America and Japan whilst the masses of the Arab countries and Iran have lived in poverty under corrupt and dictatorial regimes.

Israel is a wedge driven into the fractured Arab world. Billions of US dollars have built a militarily powerful agency capable of acting, if need arises, as their policeman. Israel is a high-tech military power with nuclear weapons and is one of the world's top weapons exporters with $6.5 billion in annual arms sales. It is under no serious threat from the much weaker Arab states or Iran. Yet Israel and the USA have attacked, or threatened to attack, them if they defy their wishes, no matter how ineffectually or symbolically.

Ousting these imperialist powers and their assorted regional gendarmes is thus integral to freedom for Palestine and the end of the racist settler state.

• We fight for the nationalisation without compensation of all the holdings of the imperialist multinationals, of the oil companies and their assets throughout the region.

• We demand that the imperialist states and the oil companies pay massive compensation for their super-exploitation of the region over the last century.

• For the driving out of all US bases, all 'Western' troops, the closing of all their bases and naval installations. Russia's ongoing murderous actions in Syria show that the same applies equally to their bases in that country.

A revolutionary party

The Israeli state can only be truly defeated and the possibility of a socialist state opened up, if it is smashed by a revolutionary struggle against the Zionist ruling class, led by Palestinians and the progressive forces within the Israeli community. We cannot be under the illusion that this will not require a mass insurrectionary movement that must plan and prepare for this final confrontation. Only a revolutionary party can prepare the vanguard workers and youth for this task. Therefore, the party must organise illegally where necessary, and also be a disciplined cadre party, operating under democratic centralism in order to ensure its effectiveness and ability to survive repression.

The revolutionary party would be open to all vanguard fighters who support its programme; it must reach out and draw in workers, women, youth and intellectuals. The party would seek to win progressive Israeli-Jewish workers and youth into its ranks.

It will set itself the goal of fighting for the overthrow not only of the Israeli government but also of the corrupt Palestine National Authority, replacing them with a constituent assembly, tasked with drawing up the constitution of a secular, democratic and socialist state. At the peak of this revolutionary struggle, we fight to bring to power a workers' and peasants' government. Its aim will be to take power into the hands of councils of delegates, arm the working people and smash the repressive bourgeois state in the process.

The following slogans sum up the strategy to be fought for in Palestine and by the international working class:

• Down with all the imperialist powers, exploiters and oppressors of the peoples of the Middle East!

• Smash the Zionist state, an instrument of imperialism!

• Victory to the national liberation of the Palestinian people!

• For permanent revolution in Palestine and the Middle East!

• For a socialist workers' republic of Palestine in a United Socialist States of the Middle East!

• For the Fifth International, a vital weapon of workers and all oppressed peoples fighting for their liberation!

Theses on Zionism, Israel, Palestine and Arab Nationalism*

Race, nation or 'people-class'?

The Jews are clearly not a race. The original Hebrew people and language belonged to the Semitic family, but two and a half millennia of residence amongst non-Semitic peoples, widespread proselytism to Judaism in earlier periods and intermarriage has made these communities, like most other peoples, a 'racial mixture'. Mass conversions to Judaism of entirely non-Semitic peoples—the Khazars in the Russian Steppes and the Falashas in Ethiopia are the most striking examples. But Jewish communities in the centuries before their medieval and modern persecution regularly proselytised on a similar scale among those gentiles performing the same economic functions as themselves. Only the malign fanatics of antisemitism and the extreme far right racist elements of the Zionist movement claim that the Jews are a 'race apart'.

Nor are the Jews a nation. Modern nations are the product of the bourgeois epoch, not eternal or millennia-long communities. Bourgeois nationalisms, however, usually claim to be re-founding ancient nations when they are in fact forming a new nation. This is equally true of the Jewish nationalism of the 19th and 20th centuries. It is incontrovertible that two ancient Hebrew

---

* Passed by the delegate conference of the Movement for a Revolutionary Communist International [predecessor of the League for the Fifth International] in September 1988.

states, Israel and Judah, existed in the millennium preceding the Christian era. These two states were, however, destroyed by the Assyrians and Babylonians (in 720 BC and 586 BC respectively).

The ruling and priestly classes (not the whole people) of Judah were exiled to Babylon, where their social function and the religious ideology that expressed it underwent a radical transformation. The monotheistic religion of Judaism was born. An exploiting class of priests and merchants developed, performing an economic function within the Persian, Macedonian and Roman Empires.

The Diaspora—the scattered Jewish communities of the Mediterranean basin, the Fertile Crescent and beyond—was the product, not of a forced exile, but of the functioning of merchant capital. The religious ideology, with its myth of the Exile and its retention of Hebrew as a sacred language, served to link these communities.

Priestly rabbinical authorities were allowed to exercise authority over these scattered communities—some quite large, as in Egypt, Babylonia and Palestine. After the Babylonian deportation however most Jews lived outside Palestine. The majority of the population of Palestine were not Jews, although they were undoubtedly descendants of the old Hebrew peasantry as well as Canaanites, Philistines etc.

The non-assimilation of these communities—vaunted as a unique expression of fidelity either to their religion by orthodox religious Jews or to their nationhood by Zionists—is no mystery. There was no world of nations in the ancient and medieval worlds to be assimilated into. The Jewish communities were not atypical of or in contradiction with the world in which they performed a vital role. Other 'exiled' or minority communities have played analogous roles—Armenians, Copts, and the Indian and Chinese communities in South East Asia and Africa.

This phenomenon has been analysed most systematically by the Trotskyist Abram Leon in his work *The Jewish Question* published in 1946. He terms this formation a 'people-class'. The essential axis of the Jewish communities was their functioning as merchant and usurers' capital in pre-capitalist modes of production. Around the big merchants and usurers oscillated strata of shipping workers, artisans, caravan traders, peddlers, shopkeepers etc., making up a Jewish community. Jews did move into other trades and occupations, but to the extent that they were estranged from the money economy they tended to be assimilated not into other 'nations' but into other religions.

This analysis explains the longevity of the Jewish communities and the preservation of their religion and sacred language. Leon shows that 'it is because the Jews have preserved themselves as a social class that they have likewise retained several of their religious ethnic and linguistic traits.' 'Judaism', he maintains 'mirrors the interests of a pre-capitalist merchant class'.

This people-class constituted a series of self-governing communities ruled by scribes, and later rabbis who related directly to the gentile rulers. The Law (Torah) and the teachings of the rabbis (Talmud) constituted a basis to link the far flung communities and keep them from dissolving into the peoples surrounding them. However, the flourishing of the communities of the people-class was only compatible with an economy otherwise dominated by subsistence agriculture. Thus the stable conditions of economic life of the Middle East and Mediterranean allowed for the survival into the modern period of these communities. In Europe, however, the Middle Ages saw the process of the destruction and expulsion of the Jewish communities.

With the development of merchant and then banking capital in the cities of Europe from the 13th to the 15th centuries, the Jews were restricted more and more to usury. The simultaneous emergence of debt bondage for the peasants and petty nobility as feudalism began to break down, motivated the vicious pogroms and expulsions of the Jews during these centuries.

The German Jews speaking a dialect of Middle High German (Yiddish as it came to be known) moved eastwards into, as yet, less developed Poland. Here, between the 15th and 17th centuries under the Polish monarchy they flourished, being allowed complete autonomy and self-government in their network of small towns (*stetls*).

However, economic development caught up with them. Their role as innkeepers, shopkeepers, pawnbrokers, but above all as bailiffs of the feudal lords and kings, meant that class hatred developed between them and the Ukrainian and Polish peasantry. Thus the great peasant revolts of the 17th and 18th century all saw massacres of the Jews. The dark age of the Eastern European Jews (Ashkenazim) began. At the other end of the continent, in 1492 the Spanish monarchy expelled or forcibly converted the old Jewish communities of Spain. Some 150,000 Jews moved into Europe, North Africa and the Ottoman Empire becoming the Sephardic communities, where they remained untroubled until the advent of Zionism.

Anti-Semitism and Zionism

The development of industrial capitalism in the 18th and 19th centuries in Western, then Central, and last of all in Eastern Europe began the dissolution of the people-class. Class differentiation—into big bourgeois financiers, petty bourgeois traders and proletarians—led to the rapid assimilation of large numbers of Jews and to the conversion of Judaism into merely one religion amongst others. Jews in Western and Central Europe adopted the culture and national identities of the countries where they lived.

Had the development of capitalism proceeded evenly and in the same way in Eastern Europe, a similar process of the dissolution of the people-class would undoubtedly have taken place. But while capitalism performed its destructive mission—the dissolution of pre-capitalist relationships, and the impoverishment of peasants and artisans—it did not absorb all of these classes into modern capitalist production.

This impoverishment hit the once prosperous Jewish communities particularly hard, since the Tsarist Empire—a Bonapartist dictatorship of late feudalism desperately resisting the disintegrative tendencies of capitalism and bourgeois democracy—blocked the absorption of the Jews into Russian and Polish economic, social and political life. While the Jews were no longer able to continue their old people-class role, nor could they assimilate. They became a pariah caste within the Tsarist Empire.

The bourgeois revolutions in England, Holland, the United States and, above all, France liberated the Jews from their late medieval discriminatory laws or allowed them to officially 're-turn' to countries from which they had been expelled. From the mid-18th to the mid-19th centuries a rapid process of modernisation and enlightenment developed within the Jewish communities, leading to powerful assimilationist tendencies. However, by the last quarter of the 19th century a counter-active tendency developed; namely, antisemitism.

This had its social roots in the decaying classes, the half-ruined aristocracy, the peasants, the artisans and small shopkeepers. In Central Europe, modern capitalist development was rapidly and ruthlessly ruining all these classes. Yet none could turn against the capitalist class as a whole. In addition, the spread of universal suffrage drove sections of ruling class politicians like the German Otto von Bismarck to create a reactionary electoral base.

The antisemitic pogroms of 1882–83 in Russia started a process of westward emigration towards Germany, France, England and the USA. A tiny group of Jews (calling themselves the Lovers of Zion) emigrated to Palestine, where they bought and cultivated land. In France and England, wealthy and respected leaders of the Jewish community were terrified that mass immigration by 'backward' (i.e. unassimilated), 'eastern' Jews would provoke a backlash. They started to fund and encourage colonisation schemes in North Africa and Palestine.

Zionism came together as a political movement under the inspiration of Theodor Herzl (1860–1904). Herzl became convinced that the antisemites were right about one thing: the Jews were a 'foreign body' in Europe. He conceived it their task to create a Jewish state as a colony outside Europe. Having considered Argentina and Uganda, the Zionist movement, founded in 1898, realised that only the 'ancient home' would appeal to religious Eastern European Jews, the only substantial numbers wishing to emigrate anywhere, and Palestine was a tempting prize to Russian, German, British and French imperialists, because of the mineral resources located in the region and its geostrategic location.

Zionism aimed to achieve its goal through approaches to a succession of imperialist powers in the years before the First World War. But with the defeat of Germany, Austria-Hungary and Ottoman Turkey in this war and the Russian Revolution, Zionism switched its attention to British imperialism, which was poised to gain from the dismemberment of the Ottoman Empire.

The Zionists, however, remained a tiny minority within the Jewish communities in Europe and America, which as a whole remained committed either to bourgeois liberalism (the upper classes and some petty bourgeois) or to the growing labour movement. Even in Eastern Europe it remained a minority within Jewish communities until the rise of fascism and the triumph of Stalinism.

Through the welter of small parties and their coalitions two fundamental traditions existed within Zionism, whose founding figures were, respectively, Ber Borochov (1881–1917) and Ze'ev (Vladimir) Jabotinsky (1880–1940). Jabotinsky started his political activity in Tsarist Russia as a leader and polemicist of the Union for Equal Rights, a Jewish bourgeois organisation with a mixed liberal and Zionist membership. He was a bitter enemy of the Bund (the General Jewish Labour Bund), a non-Zionist Jewish workers' organisation in Lithuania, Poland and Russia, and also of those Labour Zionists who looked to the working class.

In the early 1920s he became disillusioned both with official bourgeois Zionism and hostile to the ascendancy that Labour Zionism was establishing in Palestine. In addition, after having served in the British forces against the Turks in the First World War, he rapidly became disillusioned with British Mandate Authorities in Palestine, because they were limiting settlement to an annual quota. In 1924 he founded the Revisionist Party, whose tactics and strategy were to force the British to allow unlimited entry, to form Jewish military and police units and to seize the Arabs' land. His objective was an autonomous Jewish state on both sides of the Jordan. In 1935 Jabotinsky split from the World Zionist Organisation. His party, and especially its youth wing, flirted with Mussolini and Italian fascism. The Labour Zionists denounced it as fascist. By 1939 the Revisionists formed the terrorist Irgun Zvai Leumi as an alternative to the Labour-dominated Zionist army (Haganah).

Labour Zionism, on the other hand, has its roots in the period around the 1905 Revolution in Russia and its influence on the Jewish artisan, petty bourgeois and less class-conscious worker. Ber Borochov started his career as a convinced Zionist, although for a few months, in 1900–01, he was a member of the Russian Social Democratic Labour Party (RSDLP) before being expelled. He was also active in the local groups that called themselves *Poale Zion* (Workers of Zion). Before 1905 Borochov was moving rightwards, pouring scorn on the hopes that revolution in Russia would ease the plight of the Jews. At this stage he believed that the Palestinian *fellaheen* (peasants) would be absorbed into the Jewish nation.

However, the 1905–07 revolution had a powerful impact on him and in 1906–07 he altered his positions substantially. He became organiser and coordinator of the Poale Zion groups and helped centralise them into a party, founded in February 1906, with the name Jewish Social Democratic Labour Party (Poale Zion—Workers of Zion). While it demanded 'personal autonomy' and a Jewish parliament (*seymi*) as steps towards territorial independence, it placed most of its stress on participation in the Russian Revolution against Tsarism. Clearly it was being influenced by the Bund and, on tactical questions, stood closer to Bolshevism than Menshevism.

On Palestine Borochov believed it would 'naturally' develop as the centre for Jewish capital and labour, given the unwillingness of the western states to let in Jewish refugees. The Poale Zion movement should create labour exchanges and organise workers in Palestine, but 'it would be a great error to suggest that we call for emigration to Palestine. That we leave to the natural process', he said. Borochov's reason for clinging to the Palestine project was that the Jews, because of economic development, had not developed a large modern proletariat. To obtain this they would have to settle in their own territory. Thereby, the over-large bourgeoisie and petty bourgeoisie would disappear and then a 'normal' labour movement would move on to socialism. It was this latter idea that triumphed as Labour Zionism. During the 1920s Poale Zion developed branches in America, Western Europe and Palestine. In Russia Poale Zion took an anti-war stand in 1914 and rallied to the defence of the October Revolution after 1917.

The Mandate and colonisation

The project of a mass colonisation of Palestine by Jewish settlers from Eastern Europe would never have got beyond the literal state of a utopia, had it not been for the plans of the imperialist powers to dismember the Ottoman Empire, a process that had begun in the 1840s. As early as May 1916 French and British imperialism embodied this plan in the infamous Sykes-Picot Agreement.

They developed a scheme for dividing the Arabs by developing allies who would help them dominate the region. One of these was to be a project of colonial settlement of Palestine. Imperialism found ready to hand the project for the exploitation of Palestine by big British bourgeois like Baron Rothschild (1868–1937). In November 1917, the British Foreign Secretary and leader of the Conservative Party, Arthur Balfour (1848–1930) notified Rothschild that the British now publicly supported the setting up of a 'national home' for the Jews in Palestine. The Balfour Declaration was to have historic consequences for the Palestinian people—then 95 per cent of the population—since they were to be denied the right to self-determination in their own country during the three decades of British rule.

The main reasons of the British were military-strategic; control of the Suez Canal, the railway lines to the Persian Gulf and stopover points on the projected air links to India. In addition it would facilitate economic control of the enormous Iraqi and Persian oilfields. From 1918, under the protection of the British military authorities, Chaim Weizmann (1874–1952) and the Zionist Commission began to organise the settler community in Palestine. A quota of 16–17,000 immigrants a year was agreed. Between 1918 and 1939 this led to a rise of the Jewish population from 60,000 to 445,000 or nearly 30 per cent of the population. Land was purchased by the various Zionist agencies, usually from big absentee landlords resident in Beirut and Egypt. Arab peasant tenants were unceremoniously bundled off the land their forebears had worked for centuries.

Yet even in 1939 this only resulted in five per cent of the total land area of Palestine being in Jewish hands. Thus only by outright theft, mass expulsions and terror could the Palestinian peasantry be dispossessed. As well as settlers and land, only a massive influx of capital could have established the settlers. Jewish bourgeois immigrants from Germany, heavily restricted by racist immigration laws from entering Britain, France and the USA, brought in substantial quantities of capital between 1920–35.

To land, immigrants, and capital, had to be added the crucial element of Jewish Labour. Here the Labour or Socialist Zionists of Poale Zion played an indispensible role. Baron Rothschild and the big bourgeois Zionists were quite happy to super-exploit Arab labour in their settlements and factories. But the 'Marxist' Zionists realised at once that this would turn the Jewish settlers into a privileged petty bourgeois stratum, like the *colons* in French Algeria, dependent on the exploitation of Arab labour and, as history was to show in the latter case, ultimately doomed to be overthrown by them. Hence they campaigned and organised for Jewish labour only—i.e. the expulsion of Palestinian labour.

This led to the formation of the *Histadrut* (General Federation of Jewish Workers in the Land of Israel) in 1920. Its General Secretary and founding leader of Israel, David Ben-Gurion said 'without it, I doubt whether we would have had a state'. In the inter-war years the Histadrut was the Zionist state in embryo. Next to the government it was from the 1930s the largest single employer. It organised a systematic boycott and exclusion of Arab labour and, increasingly, of Arab farm produce.

Up to 1936 this process had the benevolent support and protection of the British Mandatory Authorities, who systematically refused to recognise the Arabs and Palestinians as a people or nation at all, recognising only religious communities. The Arabs were given no civil or political rights, whereas the Jewish Agency was consulted as a quasi-official body.

The Jewish settlers, coming from Europe (albeit a backward part of the continent), were used to and expected European wage rates. Palestinian Arabs were paid at a historically lower subsistence rate. Therefore in purely economic terms, Jewish labour would never be able to compete for employment by a neutral capitalist employer. Hence the necessity for an isolated separate Jewish economy. The Jewish workers were thus from the outset a labour aristocracy within Palestine. Average personal income was in a ratio of 2:1 for unskilled workers and, even with skilled workers, the Jewish settler earned 70 per cent more than his Arab equivalent.

Whereas the class profile of the *Yishuv* (Jewish settler community) showed a basically advanced capitalist structure, the Arab population showed a profile of 'backward' economic development. For the Arabs in 1943, 59 per cent worked in agriculture whereas for the Jews the figure was 19.1 per cent. In construction, industry and mining the figures were 11.9 per cent and 30.6 per cent respectively.

None of the left Zionist or Labour Zionist parties opposed this vicious, racist violation of class solidarity and internationalism. Indeed the Labour Zionists were the main proponents of this apartheid-like policy. The Histadrut was a Zionist-chauvinist labour front which tied the Jewish workers to the state and the employers, while impeding the class organisation of the Arab proletarians. It fought hard to split and destroy unions that united Arab and Jewish workers (e.g. the railway workers' union). Eventually in 1934 the Histadrut set up a pathetic and subordinate Arab section.

The Arabs in Palestine

Palestine was conquered by the Arabs in the seventh century AD from the Byzantine Empire. They neither found an empty country nor did they drive out the existing population and settle it en masse. They found living there a peasantry descended from the Canaanites, the Hebrews, the Philistines (from whom the country takes its name) and minorities of Greeks, Syrians etc. From these peoples as well as the Arab Bedouin tribes the modern Palestinians are descended. Gradually Arabic replaced the earlier related Semitic language, Aramaic, which the population (including the Judaeans) had spoken.

Palestine passed in the early 16th century into the hands of the Ottoman Turkish Empire. It remained a part of the Empire but its large landowners exercised considerable autonomy. Palestine did not constitute a single province or unit, nor did the Palestinians as a whole distinguish themselves from their surrounding fellow Arabic speakers. The country was in fact ruled by the head of a series of clans (*ashair*), each headed by a sheikh appointed by the most powerful households within the clan.

In 1858 a new land law greatly stimulated the breakup of clan property and the emergence of great landowners and impoverished landless peasants. The landlords became landowners more easily, shedding the traditional restrictions on the buying and selling of land. The sheikhs of the clans lost their power in favour of the newly 'enfranchised' landowners.

The losers in this 'land reform' were the peasants who, even as late as 1922, formed 81 per cent of the population. They lost their communal rights and having no written title to their lands were often evicted. Whereas before seed and tools had been advanced to the individual peasant family by the clan organisation, now the peasants had to turn to urban moneylenders for loans. Debt bondage, foreclosure and evictions followed on a massive scale.

Into this already class divided countryside dominated by rich landlords who lived in the cities—Jerusalem, Jaffa, Nablus, Beirut and even further afield—came the Zionist settlers. Well-funded, they found it relatively easy to buy land from the *effendis* (feudal landowners).

The other component of the ruling class was the urban merchants. Often they belonged to non-Muslim and sometimes non-Arab communities—Greeks, Italians, Armenians, and Jews. They held a privileged position because of the 'capitulations' the Ottoman government made to the western powers whereby extra-territorial rights were granted to various communities. Amongst these was freedom from paying customs dues.

The drawing of Palestine into the world economy dominated by European capitalism, as well as the development of capitalist agrarian relations, enormously increased trade and consequently the growth and importance of the ports of Gaza, Jaffa, and Haifa. Among the Arab population the Christians exercised a near monopoly of large- and small-scale trade and became a prosperous petty bourgeoisie.

However the Palestinian bourgeoisie proper was weak because of the under development of the country and, moreover, was made up largely of minority religious or ethnic communities. It therefore fell to the landowners to lead (or rather mislead) the resistance of the Palestinians to the Zionist settlement. The key figure between the wars was the Mufti of Jerusalem, Mohammed Amin al-Husseini (1895/7–1974). Against the al-Husseinis was ranged the other influential family, the Nashashibis, who held the mayoralty of Jerusalem. Both oscillated between opposition to the British and the Zionists and collaboration with them.

The Mufti and the landowners in general tried to divert hostility from the big landowners—who were themselves evicting peasants and selling land to the Zionist agencies—onto the settlers. This led to vicious attacks on the Jews by mobs of the urban and village poor, and the Mufti evinced strong antisemitic tendencies. Their resistance to the British—who paid their salaries and could dismiss them from office—was far more circumspect.

Only in 1936 did a truly national and popular uprising against the British develop. The world economic crisis and stagnation meant a rise in unemployment among Arab and Jewish workers after 1936. Since Hitler came to power three years before, immigration became a flood and with it increases in land purchase and evictions. Conflicts between Jewish settlers and evicted Arab villagers increased. In October 1936 Arab dockworkers struck and were replaced with Jewish strikebreakers.

Guerrilla warfare broke out in Galilee. Rioting in Egypt against the British and a general strike in Syria inspired the Arabs in Palestine. Local committees were formed from below, and a general strike proclaimed, which lasted for six months. Gradually the strike movement developed into an all-out rebellion aimed at the British and, to a lesser extent, the Zionist settlements. In 1936 at least 5,000 guerrillas were fighting in the hills. As a result of British repression, the Palestinian elite fled to surrounding states, and the movement in 1937 became a spontaneous, largely peasant movement.

The landowner-bourgeois leaders betrayed the peasant struggle—calling an armistice in 1936 and entering into secret negotiations with the Zionists and the British, but also coquetting with Nazi German imperialism. They were terrified of the peasant uprising, and indeed, most landowners fled the countryside. The rebellion was in the end crushed, but it did alert the British—with another war with Germany on the horizon—to the need to shift the axis of their Middle East policy, i.e., away from their dependence on the Zionists to courting Arab elites and nationalists in the region.

From fascism to founding Israel

Before 1945 Zionism had never become the majority ideology among the Jewish communities of Europe or North America. However, the Holocaust, with its murder of six million Jews, allowed Zionism to triumph decisively over socialist and liberal forces and the state of Israel to be founded.

Antisemitism was central to Nazi ideology. For them the Jews constituted the historic foe of the Aryan 'master race'. The attacks on Jewish world finance involved an attack on Germany's rivals—British, American and French imperialism—which were said to be in the service of Jewish bankers. However, Nazi antisemitism was not simply the most violent form of an all-pervasive antisemitism that contaminated the whole world, as the Zionists claimed.

This fails to recognise the specific class roots of German fascism, which was a product of a tremendously acute social crisis in a defeated imperialist country 'robbed' of its few colonies by rival imperialism. The failure of the Communist and Social Democratic parties (KPD and SPD) to take power in the revolutionary crisis of 1923 allowed fascism to grow among the petty bourgeoisie and lumpenproletariat.

However, before 1933 antisemitism was not the most central part of fascism's appeal to these layers. In the big cities, even after 1933, antisemitism was met with indifference and sometimes with outright hostility. Apart from the Stormtroopers (SA) there was little 'popular' participation in the pogroms. In Austria and southern Germany, however, there was a greater degree of spontaneously-occurring violent acts carried out against the Jews by the urban petty bourgeoisie and the peasantry; the latter often found themselves in debt to Jewish merchant capital and the former faced competition from a broader layer of Jewish traders and craft workers than elsewhere.

After 1933 antisemitism was a state policy. The first wave of anti-Jewish measures was a strictly limited concession to the petty bourgeois mass base of fascism. But it went alongside the destruction of this mass base's political influence (e.g. the Night of the Long Knives, June 1934) by Hitler at the behest of the big German monopolists and the army high command, who allowed Hitler to come to power but wanted their class and caste interests safeguarded from the outbursts by the 'rabble'.

The removal of German citizenship from most Jews in September 1934, the restrictions on the flight of Jewish capital and the setting up of emigration offices gave way to less intense discrimination between 1935 and 1937 as economic recovery took off and the SA was in large measure demobilised. However, the threat of another major recession and the threat of war in

1938 led to a renewed antisemitic campaign. From November 1938 Jewish property was confiscated wholesale, Jews were excluded from education and entertainment and were forced to wear the Star of David in public. At this, those wealthier Jews who could still emigrate did so, leaving the rest together with socialists, gays and gypsies to face imprisonment, ghettoisation and then extermination in the camps.

By 1939 the patent failure of German economic autarchy to provide a long-term solution for Germany posed the need to break out of the constricting frontiers to the east and south, and to plunder the industrial and agricultural riches of Austria, Czechoslovakia and later Poland and the Ukraine. But in these potential zones of plunder there was a major concentration of world Jewry.

That the Germans were able to wipe out nearly all these people was a uniquely horrible act of planned genocide—unique, that is, in the high proportion of a people wiped out in the extremely brief period it took. However, it was far from unique, if by this is meant that Nazi genocide applied only to the Jews. German imperialism, of which Nazism was, as Trotsky called it, a 'chemically pure distillation', wished to occupy and colonise the rich agricultural lands of Poland and the Ukraine and the oilfields of the Caucasus. Most of the populations of these areas were unwanted.

Thus the Germans slaughtered and starved to death millions of Slavs—more than the sum total of Jews. At first the Jews, too, were meant to be worked to death. But after the Blitzkrieg failed to achieve a lightning victory over the Soviet Union, food supplies dwindled and the liquidation of 'unnecessary mouths' in the rear was stepped up. The SS was charged from early 1942 with the 'final solution'. Between 1939 and 1941 Jews had already been herded into ghettos and specially-constructed concentration camps for forced labour. From 1942 death camps were constructed or converted, designed to liquidate 11 million Jews, either through forced labour or by wholesale extermination. By 1943 knowledge of all this was filtering abroad. By 1945 between five and six million Jews had been massacred—the most concentrated act of genocide so far attempted in human history.

Zionist accounts of the Holocaust present this genocide as an isolated fact in human history, linking it only to antisemitism. Yet this is clearly not the case. Millions of Native Americans from the sixteenth to the nineteenth centuries, and untold numbers of Africans in two centuries of slave trade, have been victims of genocide too. Modern imperialist racism arose to justify these horrors. Marxists have no wish to detract in any way from the special horror of the Holocaust—special in the concentrated and intense nature of the genocide—but we do insist that it was not unique and nor was its fundamental origin in antisemitic ideology. Rather, the latter and its practical fulfillment was a product of imperialism's extreme crisis. Thus, far from downplaying the significance of the Holocaust, it makes it of broader historic importance. For it could happen again for just as long as imperialism and its wars continue to exist, and not just to Jews but to many other oppressed minorities.

Much dispute has raged over the evidence of collusion between the Zionists and the Nazis. Zionists obviously deny or minimise it. For overzealous 'anti-Zionists' and some conservative Arab nationalists it is evidence of an absolute identity between evil genocidal Nazism and Zionism. The historical evidence confirms neither view. Zionism before 1933 played no significant role in Jewish resistance to the rise of Nazism. It looked on Nazism with a sanguine eye as Herzl had done with the French and Russian antisemites, seeing them as essential 'push' to get Jews to leave Europe. The Zionists too wanted a Germany 'cleansed of Jews' provided that these Jews could emigrate to Palestine and nowhere else. As a result while socialists, communists and even liberal Jews were courageous fighters against Hitler, the Zionists attempted to do a deal with him.

Thus the Zionist Federation of Germany was in direct negotiations with the SS for several years. The SS allowed Zionist periodicals and even a uniformed Zionist youth movement to exist when all other political organisations were persecuted.

Even during the war itself Rudolf Kastner (1906–1957), Secretary of the Zionist Committee in Budapest, negotiated with Adolf Eichmann for 1,000 wealthy Jews to escape to Switzerland in return for the Zionists' good offices in persuading Hungary's 800,000 Jews to be deported 'peacefully'.

As a result over 200,000 were deported to Auschwitz and other death camps. Yet this degree of collusion was special and, at heart, contradicted the project of Zionism which aimed to get as many Jews as possible to Palestine. In order to realise this, during the war the Zionists inside the USA and Europe were opposed to any relaxation of racist immigration controls operated by the imperialist democracies.

Zionism, in an attempt to negate antisemitism, ends up confirming the law of the unity of opposites. This is not to equate or identify the two but to insist that, firstly, Zionism is a product and a response to antisemitism, and that secondly, it is a response that cannot overcome it because it accepts antisemitism's definition of the widespread Jewish religious communities and their tendency to see their assimilation under capitalism as a problem.

Zionism sees Jewishness as unambiguously good whereas antisemitism sees it as an evil. But Zionism needs antisemitism, as part of its very raison d'etre. It believes it is the force that will continue to drive the Jewish communities towards Palestine. Thus Zionists have negotiated with antisemites to facilitate this process.

Does this mean that the Zionists colluded with the 'Final Solution'? No, but it does mean that that they did nothing to aid the plight of its victims, although Zionists could and did join in heroic uprisings such as in the Warsaw Ghetto. While it was being prepared and even after it was underway they did little beyond smuggling a relative handful of refugees into Palestine.

The creation of Israel

Zionism, as a colonial settler movement, had to be strategically allied to one imperialist power or another. Not only did these powers provide the funds for settlement but also more importantly they controlled the Middle East. British imperialism was hegemonic there from 1918 until 1947–53 when it was supplanted by the USA.

The conflict between Zionism and Britain was not an anti-imperialist struggle by the former. Rather, it was a conflict provoked by a switch of policy by Britain in 1939. By then, British imperialism accepted that in order to maintain control over strategic resources such as the Suez Canal, rail and air routes and the oil fields of Iraq and the Gulf, it would have to oversee the creation of pliant Arab semi-colonial regimes. This involved propping up the monarchies of Egypt, Iran, Transjordan, Iraq and the Gulf states. But this in turn meant scaling down Britain's commitment to the Zionists.

This change was evident from 1936, when the Palestinian uprising indicated the threat of Arab nationalism. But it was retarded by the outbreak of World War II and the support for Britain given by the Zionists. But during the war the Zionist right prepared for the eventual conflict with Britain. While the Irgun guerrilla group suspended operations against the British in the war, the 'Stern Gang' (Lehi) did not, and even tried to make contacts with the fascists.

While the Grand Mufti of Jerusalem helped the SS in the war, Irgun and Haganah fought with the British. This helped transform Haganah into a professional armed force. Meanwhile the British disarmed and crushed the organisations of the Arabs in Palestine.

With the end of the war the conflict between Britain and Zionism resumed. The Zionists lobbied hard with US imperialism to get immediate permission for 100,000 survivors of the Holocaust to be allowed into Palestine. But the dominant Arabist faction within the British ruling class aimed to block this and negotiate a partition of Palestine between the Zionists and Transjordan, which would allow a strategic military presence for Britain.

But Britain underestimated both the strength of the new US-Zionist alliance and the resistance of the Palestinians to this plan.

Three years of struggle to stop 'illegal' immigration, to suppress both Arab and Zionist 'terrorism' failed completely. In February 1947 Britain announced it would end its mandate by August 1948. In fact, they withdrew unilaterally in May 1948, in order to try and realise their plans by proxy, by coordinating an invasion of the so-called 'Arab armies'. In truth the only force capable of fighting the Haganah was the Arab Legion, led, trained and armed by Britain.

No serious threat was posed by the Arab forces (e.g. Egypt, Syria and Lebanon), partly because they were under-trained and under-armed as a result of previous British policy; partly because the Transjordan monarchy was only interested in a deal with the Zionists for partition around the borders proposed in the UN Plan, which would allow Britain a continued role. But the USA was opposed to any British presence and so rushed to aid the newly-founded state of Israel. Stalinism too rushed to exert political influence over the Zionists and so fill the vacuum created by the departure of British imperialism. In the face of this balance of forces, the Palestinians suffered a historic catastrophe (Nakba).

They were brutally driven out of their towns and villages throughout the area that the Zionists decided they could militarily occupy and hold. But such an area would bring with it a huge Palestinian population. Therefore this had to be driven out in the process of conquest. Jaffa was attacked by Haganah and Irgun, and its Arab population of 100,000 was reduced in days to 5,000. Atrocities such as Deir Yassin (107 murdered) were calculated acts of barbarity designed to spread panic and induce the Palestinians to flee.

Why did the Zionists not settle for the UN plan which the USA and Britain were happy to see implemented? In essence because even the undemocratic UN planned partition (which awarded 54 per cent of the area to 33 per cent of its population that was Jewish) still left the Arabs as a bare majority in the proposed Jewish state, where they would own three-quarters of the land.

The pogroms and 1948–49 'War of Independence' were conducted to carry out a radical extension of the area under the control of Israel and a much-reduced presence of Arabs within it. In the war the Arab states also cynically grabbed what they could (e.g. Egypt, the Gaza Strip, Transjordan, East Jerusalem and the West Bank) but the Palestinians were left with nothing. Israel finished with 73 per cent of the area (including the mineral-rich Negev desert). In the process 750,000 Palestinians were driven off their land and from their homes in the wretched refugee camps into the surrounding pro-British semi-colonial Arab states.

In the conflict between the Palestinian Arabs and the Zionists, for revolutionary socialists it was necessary to take a defeatist position in relation to the Zionists and militarily support the resistance of the Arabs. The 'War of Independence' was in fact a war to establish a pro-imperialist colonial-settler state in the Middle East, under the dominance of the USA. It was an objective that by its very nature denied the right of the Palestinian Arabs to self-determination.

It was correct to be defencist in relation to the struggle waged by Transjordan and later Egypt in the War of Independence. The defeat of Israel was a lesser evil, as it would have seriously disrupted the attempt of Israel to establish a stable pro-imperialist regime in the region, and one based on the expulsion of the mass of Palestinians from their land. However, revolutionaries should not have supported the war aims of the Arab League states which were annexationist. Indeed they should have fought the Arab League's attempt to enforce its own version of partition, exposed the attempted deals struck with Israel against the interests of the Palestinians and been intransigent foes of the Arab League's antisemitism.

Class and nation in Israel

Despite the political role that Israel plays in the Middle East, Israel itself cannot be considered an imperialist country in economic terms. Although it possesses many unique features, it should be understood as a special type of advanced, privileged, 'subsidised semi-colony'. The most decisive structural feature of Israel's economic subordination to imperialism has been its overwhelming dependence on capital imports for investment. Between 1952 and 1985 Israel has received some $40 billion of long-term capital imports in the form of grants, reparation payments from West Germany and donations from the Jewish diaspora, none of which have needed repaying. In addition, low interest long-term loans from the USA have furnished the means for capital investment in Israel. Since Israel's exports of goods and services have never been more than 65 per cent of the level of imports, including capital, Israel has run a permanent balance of payments deficit.

Over time the weight of reparations payments and donations from world Zionism has fallen and loans and grants from the USA have risen. Since 1973 the USA has contributed between 45 to 51 per cent of all capital imports on an annual basis and between 60 to 80 per cent of all long-term loans.

In the period between 1950 and 1973 Israel's economy grew at a rapid pace, suffering only one recession in 1965–66. The massive influx of immigrants together with the import of capital allowed expanded accumulation to take place in the context of a long boom for world imperialism. This period witnessed the displacement of citrus fruit production and diamond polishing industries by the growth of import-substitution manufacturing industry, especially in textiles, food processing and later in chemicals and mining. Despite this growth the main structural change in imports has been in consumer durables. In forty years of existence Israel has reduced its share of these in overall imports from 31 per cent to 8 per cent. But dependency on oil for energy has tripled and raw materials imports have grown, while the proportion of capital investment goods imports has only dropped from 22 per cent in 1949 to 18.7 per cent in 1984.

Throughout the transformation process there was negligible foreign ownership of fixed capital. This remains the case today with the virtual absence of exploitation in Israel by imperialism. Moreover, the export of capital from the USA and Europe was undertaken not in order to realise a 'surplus profit' but to sustain the state of Israel for political reasons.

The import of capital in such huge amounts allowed the rapid accumulation to take place without the super-exploitation of an internal section of the working class or through massive taxation, as in many of the less developed countries. On the contrary, the accumulation took place alongside an expansion of living standards for the majority of the population.

By the end of the 1960s Israel possessed a highly-monopolised and modern industrial economy, including a banking sector. Its internal market was saturated, its export-orientated industries growing. But, unlike South Africa these were not to provide sufficient preconditions for Israel to make the transition to a minor imperialist power. There are several reasons for this:

(a) The end of the long boom during 1971–73, the massive shock to Israel of the 1973–75 recession, and the curtailment in export markets.

(b) The inwardly-directed nature of investment by the Israeli state and private monopoly capital due to the very nature of the Zionist state. Finance capital had up until 1973 small amounts of capital abroad (petro-chemicals, loans) but these were insignificant in scope; since 1973 Israeli banks have persistently had net foreign liabilities. Between 1980–84 net total portfolio investments of Israeli finance capital abroad was a mere $1.2 billion; net direct fixed investments was negative for the same period.

Above all, the need to consolidate the whole Jewish population behind the state undermined the process of class differentiation and compelled investment to be internal to sustain jobs, welfare, housing, wages, rather than look for super-profits abroad by recycling externally the capital imports from the USA and elsewhere. On the other hand it has been impossible politically to mimic South Africa and rely upon a massive super-exploited working class within the nation. The contradiction of a 'closed Jewish economy' prevented the evolution of Israeli finance capital into an imperialist capital. Israel's development was frozen. There is no internal self-sustaining dynamic of capital accumulation and this leads to limited class polarisation.

(c) Finally, Israel cannot be considered an imperialist country even by virtue of its relationship with the occupied territories since 1967. The West Bank and Gaza do provide a constant source of surplus cheap labour for Israel and a captive market for the high productivity citrus fruit agribusiness of Israel. But this has to be set against the fact that as a result of the 1967 war Israel was cut off from its large natural hinterland in the rest of the Middle East. It has to be set against the fact that there is no industrial or infrastructural development in the Occupied Territories under the spur of Israeli finance capital. The parallel here is more the economic relationship that exists between the Philippines and the more developed LDCs in South East Asia or even Peru's dependency on Brazil. Finally, it has to be set against the huge costs to Israel of military occupation.

Israel then is not even a minor imperialist power, despite its pro-imperialist proxy role in the region (and in Latin America and South Asia etc.) Israel is a special type of semi-colony, one whose condition is masked by its relationship to imperialism rather than fundamentally altered. We can characterise its advanced or privileged semi-colonial status thus:

(a) Its semi-colonial dependency is not based on the repatriation of super-profits from fixed investments. Between 1952 and 1984 there was a mere total of $2 billion of foreign investment in Israel.

(b) The debt burden, while it is a channel for exploitation through interest repayments, is more a burden on its future than its present. On the one hand, as the size of the capital imports has grown in the 1970s and 1980s, as the weight of loans over grants has increased and as the Israeli economic growth has faltered badly in the post-1973 period, then the foreign indebtedness of Israel has grown apace. In the 1980s this has been exacerbated by an increasing tendency for Israel to rely on short-term loans. By 1986 Israel's foreign debt was $24 billion and growing. In 1985–86 debt repayments were $8 billion out of a government-spending total of $21 billion.

On the other hand, interest payments are a much smaller

proportion of export earnings (17 to 20 per cent) than in Brazil or Mexico and they are far outweighed by the inflow of new capital on favourable terms as well as grants. Since 1982 while there has been a heavy net drain of capital from Latin America, Israel continues to enjoy a net surplus (i.e. new loans exceed net repayments).

(c) The subordinate nature of Israel's economy flows from its dependency on continued privileged treatment over its debt and from the privileged access that Israeli exports have to many European and US markets, as well as access to markets that the major imperialists would prefer not to have, or have only through Israel. Like certain other semi-colonies in Africa, Israel is not an economically profitable semi-colony considered in isolation. But its presence and role in the Middle East helps to ensure the continued super-exploitation of other Arab semi-colonies in the region.

The political independence that Israel shows vis-à-vis the USA flows not from its own independent economic power but through the support that Zionism has among the sizable Jewish community in the USA itself and whose big bourgeoisie is an influential sector of the US ruling class.

Whereas Israel's growth rates were favourable in comparison with the OECD nations in the 1960s, in the 1970s and 1980s they have been lower than OECD and LDC (especially Newly Industrialised Countries) averages. In terms of material consumption levels, provision of social welfare, literacy etc., Israel is comparable to Spain, a level sustained only by massive external aid rather than any internal self-sustaining cycle of accumulation. In general falling immigration and rising emigration bear witness to the unfavourable development of Israel since 1973.

Since 1973 Israel's economy has lurched from crisis to crisis; massive inflation, spiralling indebtedness, and low growth. Unlike Brazil and others, Israel was not able to undertake accelerated industrial growth after the 1973–75 recession via recycled OPEC petro-dollars, partly due to political reasons and partly because of its already heavy debt burden. The internal structure of the manufacturing sector did change in the 1970s and 1980s with electronics and weapons coming more to prominence in the export sector. This has been mainly as a result of US and South African investment whose purpose is to sustain outlets for these goods to areas of the world which South Africa and the USA find it politically difficult to relate to directly.

The 1980s have brought the highest inflation in the world (1981), a disastrous and costly military adventure in Lebanon (1982), and a stock market collapse (1983) with growth hovering at an average below 2 per cent per annum for the decade.

It has taken an unprecedented national coalition since 1984 to be able to stabilise the economic situation to a degree, introduce monetary reform, get inflation down to low double figures and introduce austerity.

Hence we conclude that Israel is a capitalist state, a relatively well-developed one. But it is not an imperialist country; rather it is a type of semi-colony, one which is subordinate to US (and to a lesser extent European) imperialism. The majority of its workers in no way suffer exploitation or super-exploitation by imperialist capital. On the contrary, its non-Arab workers benefit from the import of imperialist capital.

The unique character of this state is to be understood in the colonial project of Zionism and imperialism to have a local gendarme in the Middle East. This coincidence of interests alone accounts for the materialisation and continuation of the reactionary-utopia that is Israel. Were imperialist finance capital to remove its support the Zionist state would collapse into economic chaos, class conflict and heightened struggle by the Palestinians for national liberation.

The structural features of ownership and control of Israeli capital in the post-1948 state were laid down in the Yishuv. The colonising project of Labour Zionism under the British Mandate was controlled by the Histadrut, founded in 1920 by the left Zionist parties. It sponsored and organised the growth of the Zionist agricultural settlements in Palestine—the *kibbutzim* and later the *moshavim* (rural settlements, mainly of oriental Jews using larger landed tracts based on individual ownership but marketing goods on a cooperative basis). Indeed, in the immediate post-foundation years the bulk of Israel's GDP and exports were products of the kibbutzim. Apologists for Zionism have long pointed to these settlements as evidence of Israel's social democratic nature or as islands of 'socialism' within Israel.

In origin they were the advanced guards of colonisation. After 1948 they were the border garrison posts of the new state. In reality their famous cooperativism and egalitarian self-denial was a product of economic necessity. Jewish labour came from an area with a higher historic cost of reproduction than Arab labour which would in Palestine mean that Arab labour would always undercut Jewish labour in a free market.

Jewish labour thus had to exclude Arab labour from competing and at the same time 'exploit itself' voluntarily to promote rapid accumulation. They have always been organised in order to create a surplus for profitable sale in the export market. The post-1948 formation of the moshavim was a further sacrifice of the 'cooperative' ideal to the laws of the market.

Today, the kibbutzim are more marginal to the economic life of Israel, more capitalistically run (capital intensive), are regarded by many Jews as a 'planter aristocracy' and are almost totally supporters of Labour Zionism. They only embrace 3 per cent of the Jewish population (almost exclusively Ashkenazi) and involve the super-exploitation of the oriental Jews who do not live on the kibbutz in the menial tasks.

As a result of its origins in the 'pioneer settlements' of the Mandate period the Histadrut in the early 1980s was responsible for nearly 80 per cent of the total employment in agriculture. It played a decisive military, economic and political role in the colonisation project of Zionism by driving Palestinians from their land. It did nothing to promote class based unity and solidarity among all workers of the region. Rather it deliberately sought to bar the Palestinian workers from the unions and denied them their democratic rights in general. In sum the Histadrut was never in its predominant character a trade union and has become less and less so in the forty years of the existence of the Israeli state. We must fight to break up the Histadrut and build new unions.

Since 1948 the Histadrut has diversified its capital ownership into construction, banking, some transport and manufacturing. Its industrial conglomerate, Koor, employs 20 per cent of the Histadrut membership; its construction monopoly, Soheh Boneh, employed 26 per cent of the membership in 1976. It owns Bank Hapoalim, one of the three big banking monopolies. In all the Histadrut-owned businesses account for some 23 per cent of GDP (1980).

Consequently, it is naive to portray the Histadrut as a trade union even though today some 60 per cent of all Israelis are members of this 'trade union' which embraces workers, housewives and employers of five or fewer workers, all of whom are eligible to join. In origin it was the main institution of colonial settlement, run by Labour Zionism. As its economic interests evolved beyond the petty bourgeois confines of the early kibbutzim into industry it developed a Labour Department to represent the interests of the employees that it in part employed! The top personnel of the Histadrut's companies, unions and the Labour Party are interlocking or even identical. In addition it organises the health insurance for the whole of Israel's population, which accounts for over 60 per cent of the membership's dues. Nevertheless, it is where the Jewish (and Israeli Arab) workers are organised as workers on the economic front, and it is necessary to work within it to accelerate the development of class consciousness, both trade union and political.

In its totality the Histadrut is one of the three pillars of Zionist capitalism, serving to retard and repress class differentiation and polarisation. Alongside the Histadrut, the state sector (a coalition of government, Jewish Agency, National Fund and United Jewish Appeal to the USA) controls up to 25 per cent of the economy (30 per cent of employment in 1982) and is the main conduit for capital imports. The state and Histadrut embrace the large modern plants in weaponry, chemicals and are heavily export-oriented and, with the exception of construction, are mainly employers of Jewish labour. Private sector business interests are overwhelmingly concentrated in small- and medium-sized manufacturing units with an emphasis on consumer-produced goods for the home market. Some two-thirds of the workforce in this sector are Arabs from inside and beyond the Green Line. As a result the weight of the private monopoly sector has grown in Israeli economic life as manufacturing has accounted for an increasing proportion of domestic production and exports.

Over the course of the last forty years the Israeli Jews have become a nation. They have revived an archaic language (Hebrew) to become a first language amongst a majority of Israelis; a national culture transcends the ethnic divisions.

The main bearers of this national culture and consciousness are the *Sabra* (i.e. Israeli-born Jews) of all ethnic groups. But an important element of the national consciousness of the Israeli Jews is its chauvinist and oppressive attitude to the Arabs. The Israeli Jews have forged a national consciousness over the last forty years that is distinct from their sense of themselves as part of world Jewry. But this identity has been formed only by a simultaneous denial of the legitimate rights of the Palestinians to self-determination. Consequently, Israel is an oppressor nation and as such we do not recognise its right to exist as a nation state.

Yet in considering the question of Israeli national identity account has to be taken of the enormously powerful disintegrative aspects of the ethnic and class contradictions both between the Israeli Arabs and the Jews and within the Jewish community itself.

To begin with, the state of Israel is in reality a creation of the Ashkenazi Jews, the half million or so refugees from Eastern and Central Europe who colonised it under the mandate and carved it out (arms in hand) in the period 1948–49. To a large extent it remains their state whichever party holds the governmental power. At every level they have the best jobs, hold the key levers of economic power, enjoy the best pay; their 'culture' is taken as dominant and they are the main channel to the economic reservoir of world Jewry which is predominantly Ashkanazi.

But the Ashkenazim found themselves in possession of a state with too few people and with a class structure that was top heavy to the privileged. The Zionists always recognised the need to draw in oriental Jews under the Mandate to provide a labour force for the unskilled and semi-skilled jobs. This became a burning necessity in 1949. Even then the Ashkenazi were 85 per cent urban, concentrated in administration and the service sector, together with a small rural elite in the kibbutzim. Today the Ashkenazi Jewish workers are a veritable labour aristocracy within the state or Histadrut-owned industrial sector and in the middle and upper echelons of the state bureaucracy.

From 1949 until 1951 in an unrestricted way and thereafter with some restrictions, the Labour Party government sucked in hundreds of thousands of Jews. In three years (after May 1948) the population of Israel jumped from 0.6 to 1.6 million. Only half the new arrivals could be considered survivors of the Holocaust, the rest were oriental Jews, drawn to Israel not because of any suffering as Jews in their previous countries but because of the promise of a better life. Despite the desire to do so, Zionism has been unable to attract significant numbers of Jews to Israel from Europe or the USA where life is for most at least as comfortable. They have not been much more successful with Soviet Jews, some 70 per cent preferring not to go to or not to stay in Israel after leaving the USSR.

The oriental Jews were used first to colonise the vast acres of land from which the Palestinians had been expelled; located in 'development towns' strategically placed behind the border kibbutzim. Secondly, they were to provide the vast reservoir of urban semi- and unskilled proletarians for Israeli capitalism. This need accelerated in the concentrated period of industrial growth after 1958.

The oriental Jews are discriminated against within Israeli society and are subject to an element of racial oppression from the European Jews. Through the mechanism of educational qualifications, among others, they are concentrated in manual, lower paid jobs within the state/Histadrut industrial sector, and to a lesser extent the lower rungs of clerical occupations. Today, the oriental Jews are the bulk of the industrial proletariat. Until recently they have rarely risen through the political administration to positions of prominence or power which have largely remained Ashkenazi/Labour Party controlled.

But since the 1967 war and the occupation of the West Bank and Gaza Strip the oriental Jews have experienced a degree of social/class mobility which has both further stratified them and consolidated the whole Jewish population of Israel into a shared common oppressive and exploitative relationship to the Palestinian Arabs.

The large absorption of Arab labour into the Israeli economy since 1967 has done several things. First, it has allowed large numbers of Jews to move out of the proletariat and become small employers of cheap Arab labour. Secondly, because cheap Arab labour undermined the wages of the oriental workers, minimum wages have benefited these workers in the mixed sector.

In the closed (Jewish only) sector labour has been scarce, acting as a forcing house for capital-intensive industry and creating demand for skilled labour, which has again benefited the Ashkenazi Jews. Everyone wins, so long as someone else (imperialism) foots the bill.

From these developments it is possible to discern a broad common attitude amongst all Jews in Israel to the continued occupation of the West Bank; no party wishes to end the cheap supply of labour across the Green Line. Without it most of the small Jewish capitalists will lose out, as will the workers. At the same time the extreme right is marginalised because its plans for a 'Greater Israel' free of Arabs would have the same effect.

In addition to the ethnic/class differentiation within the Israeli Jews there exists considerable ethnic differentiation within the camp of the oriental Jews. There are at least four religious groups: Sephardi (Spain), Bavli (Iraq), Roman (Italian) and Yemeni. Moreover, the first have their own language (Ladino, a Castillian dialect with Hebrew alphabet) while the rest speak dialects of

Arabic. Outside these groups there are also the Moroccans (the majority of oriental Jews), the Kurds, the Persians etc. Moreover, Yiddish is now spoken only by a minority.

There is hostility between these groups as well as a deep rooted ethnic and cultural diversity. It is well known that there is an economic stratification within the oriental Jews from Kurds at the bottom to the Sephardi at the top. All these distinctions are deliberately fostered by the Ashkenazi elite.

In addition, during the last two decades Israeli Arabs have become less Israeli and more Palestinian in their consciousness, as a consequence of the West Bank occupation. The Israeli Arabs form 18 per cent of the population and nearly 80 per cent of them are Muslim, with the rest being Christian or Druze. They are citizens in a Jewish state, people or descendants of people who were trapped inside Israel after the 'War of Independence' in 1949. Many of these have subsequently had their land taken away from them. Today they are among Israel's most super-exploited and oppressed citizens. They are denied access to many jobs, and are concentrated in the construction sector (over 40 per cent of all Arabs are employed here). Many also work in the small-scale establishments of the private service sector that grew up in the post-1967 period. Their wage levels are up to 30 per cent lower than those of the Ashkenazi and 10 to 20 per cent lower than for oriental Jews. In the 1970s their relative wages fell, under the impact of the flood of new labour across the Green Line as they found themselves in competition with their Palestinian brothers and sisters.

The oppression of the Israeli Arabs is justified by the most vicious anti-Arab racism which again confirms that Zionism, far from trancending antisemitism is parasitically dependent upon it. This unity of opposites reaches its most extreme form whenever both Labour and the Revisionists portray the Arabs as 'stupid', 'dirty', 'lazy', 'violent'—all of which is the stock in trade of western imperialist racism. Such racism can be used to justify atrocities from Deir Yassin to the 1982 massacre in the Palestinian refugee camps of Sabra and Shatila, carried out by Lebanese Phalangist militias, but in which Israel's forces were implicated.

Zionism is a national chauvinist ideology that justifies itself through the use of racism. Is Zionism therefore simply racism? No, this does not follow at all. No ideologies are without contradictions, even those which are predominantly reactionary. There are Zionists who do seek to extend rights, even land to the Palestinian Arabs. But this progressive, anti-racist, democratic element within Zionism forms a distinct minority.

Nor is this to deny that there are reactionary elements in the relatively progressive democratic and anti-imperialist movements. They can even change their whole character when the progressive struggle against national oppression is concluded. Arab nationalism can and does contain anti-communist, anti-working class and even antisemitic elements. But because the Palestinian struggle is a progressive one, these components have a limited and subordinate impact. They draw their roots from economic backwardness in the Arab world (even feudal and semi-feudal forces), from the impact of imperialist exploitation on the urban poor and from an unthinking reaction to Zionist racism.

All this imposes a twin duty on revolutionary communists. On the one side, to fight alongside Palestinian nationalists while at the same time combatting religious obscurantism and any anti-Jewish outburst. On the other, while fighting against Zionism and for the destruction of a state that fosters national and racist oppression of the Palestinians, it is essential to strike tactical alliances with left Zionists (such as the Progressive List for Peace, Stalinists, Peace Now) in defence of democratic rights for the Palestinians, the better to break them from Zionism completely.

Broadly, there have been three major parties or blocs since 1948. The least significant has been the New Religious Party (NRP), which existed in fragmented form before 1956. The small support for it (about 10 per cent at its peak and declining thereafter) is a reflection of the overall weakness of religious parties in Israel. This at first surprising fact, in a state that is obliged to embody religion in the self-definition of its citizenship, is due to the orthodox religious parties being firmly opposed to the Zionist project in establishing the state of Israel. While they were the first to organise politically within the diaspora they were adamant that the diaspora was a punishment on the Jews that could not be righted by the work of man. Hence the generally secular nature of the main Zionist parties. Only the Holocaust forced them to reconsider and adopt a pragmatic attitude to Israel. The NRP formally advocates a policy of establishing Israel in the whole of Greater Israel, but its pragmatism has led several smaller rightist, orthodox parties to split or form independently since 1973 and especially since the treaty with Egypt was signed at Camp David in 1979.

For the first thirty years of its existence, Israel was governed by Mapai (Israeli Labour Party (ILP) after 1967). This was founded in 1930 and was (and remains) the main party of the Ashkenazi Jews and hence the state bureaucracy, Histadrut and the kibbutzim. It has commanded the vote of a third or more of the population since 1949, up until 1961 standing alone and afterwards in various blocs. Today it is mainly a party of the privileged Ashkenazi labour aristocracy; the allegiance of the bulk of the (majority) oriental industrial proletariat do not see it as their party and in the main do not vote for it. This is also the case for the Arab workers.

It cannot be considered a bourgeois workers' party of the Israeli working class because as a party tied to the Histadrut (and its corporate capital) and the main national institutions of the state, the ILP does not rest on the organisations of the working class. Revolutionaries cannot call for a vote for it.

The smaller Mapam Party was the party of the kibbutzim 'pioneers' whose ideology was a mix of petty bourgeois socialism and Zionism. It used to be able to command some 14 per cent of the vote. But as the kibbutzim have declined in importance and changed their nature, their allegiance has shifted towards the ILP and Mapam has been forced to shelter under its wing.

The third political bloc is that of the open parties of the nationalist bourgeoisie. One side has its roots in the Revisionists who split into differing factions in the 1920s and 1930s over their attitude to the mandate and the future state's boundaries. But by 1951 they had found their home in the Herut Party. The Liberal Party was a more respectable party (i.e. free of the stigma of terrorism) at the service of the growing private bourgeoisie of the new state. The formation of Likud in 1973 as a coalition of both Herud and the Liberals was a result of the growing weight of the private sector bourgeoisie and the rise of the hawks after 'winning' the 1967 and 1973 wars. This coalition made a successful challenge to the hegemony of Labour possible. The growth of the oriental Jewish population, with its alienation from Labour and the Ashkenazim, made possible the successful demagogic manipulation of their hopes for a better deal. Election success followed in 1977 and 1981, which returned the two Likud governments of Begin/Shamir.

In essence very little divides the Labour and Likud blocs in the field of domestic economic policy. Rhetoric, demagogy and naked buying of votes are routinely directed at their respective 'constituencies' at election time. This flows from the need of all Zionist parties to keep together the Jewish bloc and retard class differentiation. It is evidenced by the record of the National Coalition 1984–88.

The main differences are to be found in perspectives for dealing with the Arab states and the Palestinians' fight for self-determination. On the one hand both Labour and Likud are united in their resistance to the desire of the extreme right (Kach, Shass, Tami, Tehya—products of the disgust at Camp David Accords of 1978) for more restrictive measures against the Arabs, and against those like Peace Now who would give the Palestinians their own state. This is because both proposals would undermine the Arabs' essential function in the Zionist economy.

On the other hand they are divided over whether this function should be preserved by continuing the occupation of the West Bank (with all the consequent political instability, and especially the deepening polarising effect it has within Zionism since the failure of the Lebanon war of 1982), which is Likud's strategy. Likud also favours increased settlements in the West Bank because in recent years this has consolidated its base amongst the oriental Jews who are now the bulk of the new 'settlers'.

Labour, on the other hand, would prefer to seek a negotiated settlement with US imperialism and the conservative Arab regimes (especially Egypt and Jordan) who could then police a Bantustan 'Palestinian' state on the West Bank while preserving its function as supplier of cheap labour and captive market for Israeli agriculture.

Arab nationalism

At the heart of pan-Arab nationalism is the belief that behind the fragmentation of the Middle East into many diverse nation states lies one Arab nation, united by a common language and culture, capable of economic unity or integration. Today over 100 million people speak the same language (Arabic) across 15 countries stretching from Morocco to the Gulf, from the Mediterranean to the Upper Nile.

Yet the Arab world is evidently divided too. Asked, 'what is your nationality?' an Arab will likely answer 'Egyptian', 'Moroccan' etc. Nor is the Arab world congruent with the Muslim world—the semi-arid area occupied by the Arabs, Turks, Persians, and Indo-Afghans, including parts of tropical Asia and even Black Africa. Some parts of the Arab world are not Muslim (e.g. parts of Lebanon and Sudan). Nor are all the Arabs of one racial origin.

Nevertheless, it is said that imperialism and before that colonialism disrupted an organic evolving unity of the Arab nation; its defeat and removal will allow for the unification of the Arab nation. What is the material basis of the Arab nation and should the Arab working class seek to incorporate it into its programme of permanent revolution in the Middle East?

The original Arabs were an ancient people of the Gulf peninsula. From early times, quite different paths of evolution were taken by northern and southern Arabia. The latter, the present day Yemen, was a settled civilisation with extensive irrigation systems and an important role in trade between Egypt, Africa and India. In the north the desert was scattered with oases and crossed by caravan routes carrying long distance trade from the Persian Gulf and bringing India and China into connection with Syria, Egypt and Europe.

The nomads and merchants of the northern and western part of the peninsular welded the area into a state for the first time under the merchant prophet-ruler Mohammed (AD 571–632). The subsequent Arab conquests resulted in a vast Arab empire or Caliphate, which reached its maximum extent about 732 AD. This did not involve a mass settlement of Arabs within these countries but their conquest by a small military-religious elite. Throughout most of these areas both the Christian and Jewish population welcomed them as deliverers from Byzantine Orthodoxy. They did not 'convert by the sword' as their western detractors claimed. Instead they imposed a tax on non-Muslims, which over centuries converted ever-larger numbers to Islam.

The spread of the Arabic language was via the great trading cities, Damascus and Baghdad. Here Arabic gradually absorbed or replaced previous closely related Semitic languages (Aramaic in Syria). The pre-existing populations were Arabised and Islamicised while of course transmitting to the erstwhile nomads all the riches of the Persian, Syrian, Hellenistic and Egyptian civilisations.

The unification of the southern Mediterranean world, the Levant and the whole Fertile Crescent with Persia greatly stimulated mercantile activity, and with it luxury goods production in the great trading cities. Within this system were also included the river irrigation societies of Mesopotamia and Egypt (Asiatic mode of production). The Caliphate rapidly took on the fundamental features of Asiatic despotism.

The united Caliphate lasted for scarce a century before the Spanish and North African portions split away. Oriental despotism based on the tribute of the peasants of Egypt and Mesopotamia replaced the Arab-merchant class. The relative weakening of the mercantile basis of the empire led to its subdivision. Yet Arabic as a language and a culture continued to spread. In fact it was only from the 12th century that it became the majority language in countries like Egypt. Whilst an Arab culture—embracing poetry, philosophy, music, art, architecture and mathematics, far more developed than that of medieval Europe existed—it did not mean that an Arab nation with national consciousness (nationalism) had come into being. This explains why the submission of the Caliphate, its repeated fragmentation and its rule by Turks, Kurds, Berbers, Mongols, and Circassians, in no case provoked a national or Arab uprising.

By the sixteenth century feudal Europe was pregnant with capitalism. Merchant capital was developing apace in Italy, Portugal, Holland, England and Spain. Consequent naval developments displaced the overland caravan routes and the Mediterranean by round-Africa routes. The Arab east, robbed of its mercantile prosperity, sank into backwardness and economic decline. The Ottoman Empire, after two centuries of glory, also declined and fragmented under the strain. By the early nineteenth century the new capitalist states, France and Britain, had begun to penetrate the Arab world, seeking to control the trade routes for their capitalist goods to pass eastwards and seeking areas for colonial settlement.

It can be seen from the above that though there was a linguistically Arab Caliphate from the mid-seventh century, by the mid-tenth century the Caliph was Persian and a hundred years later a Turkish sultan ruled the 'Arab' world, which was in any case fragmenting. The less than three hundred years of a unified Arab state clearly has enormous historic importance for modern twentieth century Arab nationalism, but it does not follow that it actually was an Arab nation state subsequently divided by foreign oppressors or by 'western imperialists'.

It was in fact the irruption of the forces of French and British capitalism, spearheaded by Napoleon's armies and Nelson's fleet at the turn of the 19th century, that announced a new phase of development for the Middle East. British rule in Egypt in the 19th century was aimed at restricting its independence from the Ottoman Empire (which needed to be preserved as a bulwark against Russia) and at penetrating its economy in the first place through control over the Suez Canal.

Pushing the government into debt led to resistance. But this was crushed in the 1880s and Egypt became a disguised colony of Britain and was essential to her communications with India and East Africa. While the 'Uprising of 1919' made the British declare Egypt 'independent' it included the reservation that British troops continue to be stationed in Egypt, that Sudan remain in British hands, and that Europeans retain their extra-territorial rights. In short, Egypt's independence was nominal.

Economically, Egypt served as a market for British manufactured goods and a cotton plantation to serve the mills of Lancashire. A colonial bourgeoisie developed, but one heavily tied to the large landowners which were the product of earlier land reforms. The Wafd became the party of this bourgeoisie. Saad Zaghloul founded the Wafd Party at the end of the First World War. Ideologically, it represented a nationalist modernist response of this most developed Arab country. It strove by constitutional means to persuade the British and the King to admit them to office and to make political and economic concessions. Wartime economic prosperity had stimulated the growth of an urban middle class—lawyers, doctors, academics, journalists and civil servants—which formed the basis of radical opposition to the British.

The other mass force was the Society of Muslim Brothers founded in 1928 by Hassan al-Banna (1906–1949). It demanded the expulsion of the British by mass action and individual terrorism. It wanted a totally Islamic society and was fiercely anti-communist. At its peak it had nearly half a million members. Thus Egypt remained until the 1950s a country dominated by either Egyptian nationalism or Islamic fundamentalism.

Despite deceitful promises to Arab leaders from Britain following the 1914–18 war, Britain and France carved up the region under the cover of the League of Nations Mandates. The al-Husseini family were bought off with Faisal being made King of Iraq; Abdullah was made Emir of Transjordan and Hussein recognised as King of the Hejaz. Thus the feudal Bedouin chieftains proved their complete inability to lead an Arab national movement or to create an Arab state even of the *Mashreq* (the eastern half of the Arab lands). They proved themselves over the following decades complete tools of British imperialism. The dialectic of development was such that pre-imperialist domination could not produce the political cement for nationhood, whereas imperialist domination integrated the Arab world into the world economy at the cost of Balkanisation and division.

The imperialists' carve up of the Arab world was now complete. The Balkanisation of the Middle East after the First World War as a result of the defeat and collapse of the Ottoman Empire created artificial nation states as political entities; the forced development of subordinate colonial and semi-colonial capitalism, however, gave these nation states an economic content, eventually creating (weak) national bourgeoisies. Imperialism inserted the separate nation states into the system of world economy differently and separately, further dislocating their ties with each other.

The speed, brutality and deceitfulness of this process and the impact of harsh and arrogant occupation, plus the Zionist project in Palestine, all stimulated anti-imperialist sentiment and struggle. The origins of secular Arab nationalism lie in Syria. Disillusionment with the Turkish revolution of 1908 and repulsion from its consciously Turkish nationalism inspired the first groups of Arab nationalists in Syria. In 1913 an Arab National Congress was held in Paris. When the First World War broke out the British set about engineering an 'Arab revolt' against the Ottomans who were allied to Germany. This involved stimulating Arab nationalism. It also involved deceiving the Arab forces as to Anglo-French (and Russian) designs on the Middle East.

Arab nationalism as an ideology of the urban petty bourgeoisie linked to these struggles really developed in the 1920s and 1930s. Its main representatives were Amin al Rihani (1876–1940), Edmond Rabbath (1902–1991), Sami Shawkat, and Sati' al-Husri (1880–1968). Insurrectionary struggle wracked Syria from 1925 to 1927 and Palestine from 1936 to 1938. Previously vague feelings of identity based on language and religious culture developed into a shared experience of exploitation, and domination and revolt against them. Economic development and the creation of modern state machines created a new and educated middle class. The role of the radio, newspapers and books helped to activate the common bond of the Arabic language and spread modern ideas—secular nationalism, socialism, communism and fascism in these classes.

But before the foundation of the Zionist state, pan-Arabist nationalism remained a distinctly minority current, outpaced by Islamic fundamentalism/pan-Islamism on the right, by regional nationalism (Egyptian or Greater Syrian) and by Stalinism on the left. It was the catastrophe of the first Arab-Israeli war and the humiliation it involved for all the adjacent Arab states that launched Arab nationalism into a mass force—one that was to dominate the Arab world from the early 1950s to the end of the 1960s.

Nasserism and the 'Arab Revolution'

The loss of the 1948–49 war discredited all the bourgeois politicians of Egypt. It is not surprising that it was in the army that this humiliation was most keenly felt. In Egypt a coup came in 1952. Its organising force was the Free Officers' movement, within which the leading figure was Gamal Abdel Nasser (1918-1970). From a lower petty bourgeois background, Nasser was an undogmatic nationalist, determined to rid Egypt of the British and help his country on the road to development. Over the next decade he pragmatically and eclectically espoused pan-Arabism and the statified economy as the road to development. The only major immediate social measure was a sweeping land reform creating a sizeable kulak class—a solid social basis for Egyptian Bonapartism.

In 1954 Nasser forced the British to agree to a two-year evacuation plan from the Suez Canal. In addition he refused to join a US-organised cold war alliance of Arab states against the USSR. He wanted to stand between the two blocs but took advantage of the willingness of the USSR to give aid to 'non-aligned' countries. US and British resistance to the Aswan Dam project forced Nasser to nationalise the Suez Canal to use its revenues to pay for the dam. Britain, France and Israel attacked Egypt but Arab resistance, USSR support and the hostility of US imperialism to Britain's unilateral actions (which threatened to bring down the USA's system of alliances) led to France and Britain's defeat and withdrawal. In this conflict it was correct for revolutionaries to have pursued a defeatist policy in France and Britain, to have demanded unconditional arms from the USSR for Egypt and no reliance on or support for US imperialism.

Nasser's triumph was such as no Arab statesman had ever achieved. A hundred years of humiliation for the Egyptian and Arab peoples was signally avenged. For the next 11 years Nasserism was the overwhelming influence in the Arab world. Nasser's prestige as the leader of the Egyptian revolution spread to the whole Arab world. For over a decade, Nasser was to seem to millions the embodiment of the Arab revolution. Egypt under his leadership seemed fated to achieve the united Arab state and break the influence not only of the weakened and humbled British but also the new hegemonic influence, the USA.

Arab nationalism rapidly developed in the most important Arab states. In Syria after fusing with the Socialist Party of Akram al-Hawrani (1912–1996), the Ba'athists became the most dynamic political force. Once the predominant force within the government, the Ba'athists proposed a union between Egypt and Syria. Nasser hesitated, but as leader of the 'Arab revolution' he could hardly refuse. The United Arab Republic (UAR) came into being (1958) with a new Bonapartist constitution and Nasser as president. Arab nationalism was at its zenith.

But the conditions that created Egyptian Bonapartism—a land reform that wiped out the big landlords and benefitted the rich peasant (fellaheen), the discredited and split forces of opposition whether Islamic, Stalinist or conservative bourgeois—did not exist in Syria. The Syrian Ba'athists had expected Nasser to rule Syria through them. Speedily undeceived they passed into opposition. Also a bitter feud erupted between the UAR and Iraq, which struck a damaging blow to the hopes of expanding the union of Arab States.

Meanwhile, faced by imperialist hostility and economic boycott Nasser resorted to a series of far-reaching nationalisations and state capitalist measures totally in keeping with his Bonapartist regime. He wished to stimulate (capitalist) development but not to strengthen the hostile bourgeoisie with its many links to British, French and US imperialism. He nationalised cotton export firms, banks and finance institutions and 275 major industrial firms. A further land reform broadened his base in the peasantry.

The application of these measures to Syria, a country with a stronger urban and rural bourgeoisie, alienated the right. The communists were already hostile so Nasser succeeded in setting all the possessing and politically influential classes against him. In September 1961 a coup toppled the Egyptian satraps and the first experiment in Arab unity collapsed.

In the aftermath of this fiasco Nasser was obliged to resort to socialist demagogy to cloak his Bonapartist-state capitalist regime. He declared Arab socialism to be the embodiment of social democracy. He created the Arab Socialist Union as a mass organisation. From September 1962 he threw his efforts into supporting the struggle in the Yemen against reactionary forces and in Aden against the British. In 1963 the Syrian and Iraqi Ba'athists came to hold sole power and, albeit cautiously, declared their support for Egypt's campaign against the reactionary regimes of the Arabian peninsular. Once more, as in 1958–61 the Arab revolution seemed on the move, headed by military officers professing nationalist and socialist ideologies. Unity discussions started again. This time they broke down in bitter mutual recriminations.

After this failure Nasser had to return to the framework of the Arab League and to talks with the pro-imperialist conservative regimes. In August 1965 he even made his peace directly with King Faisal. Soon he was being outflanked by the Syrian

Ba'athists whose radical wing had seized power and was supporting a new Palestinian guerilla organisation, Fatah, which began a campaign against Israel in 1965. Israeli counter-attacks drove Syria and Egypt into a joint military command in case of war, and the latter promised assistance to Syria in case of attack.

Israeli reprisals against Jordan for harbouring Fatah led to Hussein demanding that mighty Egypt cease hiding behind UN troops and close the straits to the Israeli port of Eylat. Nasser did so to avoid losing face. Jordan signed a joint defence pact with Egypt. The Arab world was in a state of great excitement. United action against Israel by both 'revolutionary nationalist' and traditionalist states seemed imminent. The unity of the Arab nation would perhaps soon be forged in the heat of a victorious war against the Zionist intruder. But despite all the rhetorical threats no attack was planned. Instead it was Israel who struck first.

The Six Day War against Egypt in 1967 was aimed as a double blow against the Palestinian resistance and Nasser's refusal to subordinate Egypt to the wishes of US imperialism. In this it had the same essential features as the 1973 war. In both conflicts it was necessary to be defeatist inside Israel and critically support Egypt, Syria and Jordan in the military conflict, while at the same time struggling for the right of the Palestinians to self-determination, even against the wishes of the Arab states.

The war in early June was a total, humiliating and crushing blow for Nasserism and Arab nationalism as the ideology of the military-Bonapartist regimes of the major Arab states. In 1948–49 Arabs had been able to blame the incompetent corrupt semi-feudal regimes in hock to imperialism as the cause of their defeat. All the political achievements of Nasserism and Ba'athism suddenly proved hollow, and the impotence of these forces to unite the Arab world and confront Zionism, let alone imperialism, were cruelly demonstrated. Henceforth attention would turn to a different quarter, to the Palestinians and the Palestine Liberation Organisation (PLO).

Palestinian nationalism and the PLO

The soil from which a specifically Palestinian nationalism could grow existed in the mandate period among the intelligentsia within the merchant (mainly Christian) Arab population. It developed a highly westernised outlook with their newspapers and periodicals playing a leading role in the campaign to resist Zionism and in the development of a Palestinian and Arab national consciousness.

Among the key external factors in developing this was the British imperialists' refusal to grant Palestine's inhabitants self-determination or self government, and the separation in 1918 of Palestine from Syria (a French Mandate) and from Transjordan (a British puppet monarchy). Trade routes were disrupted as a result and the economy decisively reoriented by the Mandate government. Cash crops for export came to dominate the most fertile area—the coastal plain. Citrus fruit exports, largely to Britain, increased enormously.

No less important was the effect of the Zionist colonisation. By 1935 Jewish organisations and individuals owned 12 per cent of the total arable land. Given the impoverished *minifundia* of the Arab population, burdened with debt and unable to afford irrigation, machinery and fertiliser to increase productivity, the Arab peasantry's land hunger became ever more intense.

These external pressures, allied to the destruction of pre-capitalist social relations, created the basis for the birth of a national consciousness among the Arab Palestinian population. Until the unmasking of pan-Arabist movements such as Nasserism, however, a specifically Palestinian nationalism was muted.

Today, the PLO has become the umbrella organisation including all the major forces in struggle against Zionism for Palestinian national self-determination. As an alliance of mass political, cultural and military organisations, it has become the centre for national resistance, performing the role of a surrogate state throughout the Palestinian diaspora.

It has armed forces, a parliament and a 'government' but it is sovereign in no definite territorial area: and in the last analysis it depends on the support or toleration of the other Arab states. Set up by Nasser and the Arab regimes in 1964, the 'official' PLO under Ahmad Shiqueiry was unable even to establish its hegemony over the Palestinian masses, and remained a pliant tool of the neighbouring bourgeois Arab states. In fact Shiqueiry was rapidly outflanked by the growth of Fatah (the Palestinian National Liberation Movement), which gained in popularity after launching its first guerrilla strike on Israel in 1965. Fatah under Yasser Arafat (1929–2004) eventually took control of the PLO in 1969.

Fatah was founded with financial backing from the exiled Palestinian bourgeoisie. It reversed the previous strategic schema—first pan-Arab liberation, then Palestinian freedom. Given the manifest failure of Egypt and Syria in 1967 and given the successful guerrilla struggles of the 1960s—the FLN in Algeria, the NLF in Vietnam, the July 26th Movement in Cuba, Fatah proposed a similar struggle to destabilise and internally disrupt the Zionist state. Attacks were to be launched from the neighbouring states—Jordan, Lebanon and Syria.

Revolutionary communists (Trotskyists) are opposed to a strategy of guerrilla warfare for the following reasons. Our strategy is the mobilisation of the urban and rural masses under the leadership of the working class. To withdraw from production, from the towns and cities and even from the most densely populated agricultural districts the most fearless fighters, to concentrate their activity solely on military combat training is to deprive an oppressed people and exploited classes of their cadres for direct mass action. It denudes and weakens economic and political struggle in favour of military action, which by and large is episodic and desultory. Thus while the PLO factions set up armed militias based on the camps for twenty years or more, they neglected the organisation and mobilisation of the Palestinians within the Zionist state. The result was to create an elite of trained fighters not a vanguard of mass struggle.

In fact the PLO and Fatah were never able to develop guerrilla warfare on a mass scale or penetrate the Zionist state except on daring, but always suicidal, missions. The one victory Fatah won, in 1968, was fought on Jordanian soil (Karameh) where they repulsed an attack by Israeli raiding forces against a refugee camp. Moreover since the guerrilla groups depend for their finance and their base of operations on bourgeois Arab regimes, both conservative and 'radical', it has repeatedly been restricted, disciplined and indeed expelled and disarmed by these regimes. In addition it has been pressured into repeated attempts at diplomatic solutions. Fatah, with the closest links to its Saudi and Gulf backers, has repeatedly proved amenable to these projects.

The limitations of this bourgeois nationalist strategy were tragically revealed in Jordan during 1970. The strength of the PLO having extended beyond the Palestinian camps into the very institutions of the Jordanian state, ended with ferocious attacks by the Hashemite regime. Despite a general strike and widespread calls for the overthrow of the monarchy, Fatah's policy of 'non-interference' and express support for the Jordanian-Palestinian bourgeoisie of the Kingdom caused them to attempt the demobilisation of the Palestinian and Jordanian masses in the face of Hussein's assault. The resultant massacre of 2–3,000 Palestinian fighters (Black September) must be seen as a direct result of this strategy of dependence on and alliance with the Arab regimes.

One organisation within the PLO, which at least in words, rejects the principle of non-interference is the Popular Front for the Liberation of Palestine (PFLP). Founded by former leaders of the Arab National Movement, most prominent among them being George Habash (1926–2008), the PFLP evolved quickly in the direction of Stalinism. Though it argued for the resistance itself to seize power in Jordan in 1970, given the political leadership of the movement this could only be taken as a call for the establishment of a democratic bourgeois regime. Indeed the PFLP is totally committed to the Stalinist 'stages' theory, which limits the immediate goal of the national struggle to the realisation of democratic demands in a capitalist economy. No established tendency in the Palestinian movement was fighting in 1970 for a revolution in Jordan which would have required councils of worker, peasant and soldier delegates to take power. Thus a decisive opportunity was missed in striking a real blow at imperialism and its local agents.

Despite inclusion in its programme of the need for a 'revolutionary Marxist-Leninist party', the PFLP has not adopted a strategy of organising the Palestinian workers for mass struggle against Zionism. Indeed it sank, after Black September, into a despairing petty bourgeois strategy of individual terror, initiating a wave of hijackings and hostage taking. While unconditionally defending from state repression those militants who adopt such methods, Trotskyists reject and fight against the adoption of these forms of struggle, because they are completely ineffective for promoting the victory of the national liberation struggle and because they condemn the masses to the role of passive bystander rather than the instrument of their own liberation.

The failure of the PLO's strategy to yield results, together with the Israeli occupation of the West Bank and Gaza following the 1967 war, spurred the growth within the PLO of support for the formation of a Palestinian state on the newly occupied territories; such a 'mini-state' was to exist alongside the Zionist state itself.

Between 1967 and 1973 the Popular Democratic Front For the Liberation of Palestine (PDFLP)—later known simply as DFLP—which was a split from the PFLP and led by Naif Hawatmeh (b. 1938), argued for the West Bank to become a liberated zone, free of Israeli troops and no longer under Jordanian tutelage. Under the impact of the defeat in the 1973 war the idea was transformed by Fatah into that of a 'mini-state'. Despite the opposition of the DFLP to Fatah's increasing reliance on the Arab regimes, the mini-state policy has led directly to manoeuvres with 'democratic' imperialism, the Arab bourgeoisie, the United Nations and the USSR—all in an attempt to persuade the Zionists to grant limited autonomy to the West Bank and Gaza.

All consistent advocates of self-determination for the Palestinians must reject this slogan as a reactionary dead end for the struggle for national liberation. A quasi-Bantustan, economically and militarily dominated by Israel, is an attractive prospect for those powers seeking to 'stabilise' the situation in the region by diverting and undermining the prospects for any sustained anti-imperialist revolt.

Support for this within the PLO stems to a large extent from layers keen to appropriate the power and the material benefits of office. For the Palestinian masses such a solution would be a betrayal of their just aspiration to return to their homeland as free and equal citizens of a non-confessional and democratic state. To date only the Palestinian Communist Party has taken the line of compromise and retreat to its logical conclusion and recognised the state of Israel's right to exist. Since the decision of Hussein of Jordan to renounce his claim to the West Bank the PLO has signaled further preparedness to recognise the state of Israel and seek a political settlement based on a West Bank state. Any future election of a Labour Party government in Israel may well accelerate the PLO's abandonment and betrayal of the Palestinians' legitimate goal of a state in the whole of Palestine.

Opposition to the mini-state has in the past been led by a 'Rejection Front' of Palestinian organisations, most prominent among them being the PFLP. Yet this attitude remains only slightly more progressive than the position of Fatah and the DFLP. All Palestinian organisations (except for the Islamic Jihad) whether 'realist' or 'rejectionist' support the PLO's central slogan of a 'Democratic Secular State' in Palestine. Our objection to this slogan does not lie principally in its ambiguity (allowing several interpretations including that of a mini-state) still less in its clearly progressive aspect in prescribing no confessional basis for a future state in Palestine.

Our objection lies in the absence of any indication of which class in Palestinian society is capable of overthrowing Zionism and which class must predominate in the future state. When all the ideological trappings of religious and national mythology are stripped away, every state remains an instrument of coercion in the hands of a particular class in order to defend its particular property relations. The question of the class character of the Palestinian republic cannot be left wrapped in deceitful phrases.

It is only the proletariat, backed by the peasantry and sections of the urban petty bourgeoisie, which has the power to smash the Zionist state. In that process it must ensure that there is no return to the domination of the imperialists over the economy, its banking and agricultural sectors. The demand for a democratic secular state remains at the level of ideology utterly utopian and in practical terms would lead to a capitalist Palestine. Such a state would find itself from the first day in the vise-like grip of imperialism just as every Arab state does today.

While the PLO will be an important arena from which militants and cadres of a future revolutionary party of the Palestinian workers will be assembled, it is nevertheless a 'popular front' of varied class forces wedded to bourgeois nationalist ideology and dominated by the agents of the Palestinian and Arab bourgeoisies. It must be supplanted, politically and organisationally, if the Palestinian revolution is to move forward to final victory.

Because of the failure of the PLO to advance the cause of self-determination, Palestinian nationalism is increasingly being challenged for hegemony of the masses within the West Bank and Gaza by Islamic fundamentalism. Any moves to recognise Israel by the PLO will allow the Islamists to pose as intransigent enemies of Israel and gain credibility thereby.

This movement finds its inspiration from the Iranian revolution which brought down the Shah. In the refugee camps of Gaza, as in Lebanon, the spread of Islamic influence depends as much on the provision of funds and other supplies, as on any liberatory vision that the fundamentalists are able to conjure up. In reality, Islamic fundamentalism has a reactionary ideology, which embraces antisemitism. This has led the Israeli state to encourage the growth of the Islamic groups to lend credence to their repressive policy and to divide the Palestinian resistance.

The goal of an Islamic republic for the Palestinians would spell disaster for the Jews as it would for the mass of Palestinians. The present example of the state of Iran is testimony to this; as with Iran an Islamic republic in Palestine would involve the enslavement of women, the oppression of other religious groups, such as the Christian Arabs and the wholesale denial of the democratic rights of the masses.

While it is possible and necessary to struggle alongside these militants against Israeli repression in the Occupied Territories, a real consistent struggle for democratic rights for the Palestinians involves sharp criticism of the denial of such rights contained within the goals of fundamentalism and a fight to defend and extend such rights even against Islamic militants.

Marxism and the Jewish Question

Karl Marx (1818–1883) himself was Jewish but came from an assimilated enlightenment background. He had very little sympathy with the old ghetto culture of eastern Jewry. In addition, in the early 1840s he identified Judaism as the embodiment of the spirit of capitalism (Christianity was a more impure form of the same thing). This does not mean that Marx was an antisemite or a self-hater as Zionist apologists claim. It does mean that neither Marx nor Engels made a 'modern' (i.e. scientific materialist) analysis of the Jewish Question.

The reasons for this are simple. Both assumed a straightforward process of assimilation of the Jews as capitalism developed. Jewish culture was for them a medieval fossil, a reactionary leftover that would melt away into modern bourgeois culture. Marx died just at the moment that modern antisemitism was being born. Friedrich Engels (1820–1895) and his German Social Democratic disciples condemned it as 'the socialism of fools', that is, a fake demagogic 'anticapitalism'. In this spirit the Second International (1889–1914) in its early years condemned 'anti-Semitism and philo-Semitism alike'; it condemned incipient Zionism as well as the Tsarist pogroms and the anti-Dreyfus reactionaries. Jean Jaurès (1859–1914) and Rosa Luxemburg (1871–1919) both advocated an active labour movement involvement in the struggle against antisemitism. Yet the Marxist analysis of the Jewish question and Zionism was only to be effectively grounded with the work of Karl Kautsky (1854–1938), Vladimir Lenin (1870–1924), and later Leon Trotsky (1879–1940).

Lenin's attitude to the Jewish Question was forged in conflict with the leaders of the Jewish Bund. Founded in 1897 it began in the 1890s as a movement among the Jewish workers living in Poland under the Tsar's rule (the 'Pale'). The Bund opposed Zionism as a reactionary utopia distracting from Jewish workers' struggles against capitalism, Tsarism and antisemitism. Therefore they demanded the full political emancipation of the Jews in Russia as part of the labour movement's struggle against Autocracy. But at the historic Second Congress of the Russian Social-Democratic Labour Party (RSDLP), the Bund opposed the view of a centralised party for the whole Russian Empire.

Lenin opposed the idea of a federal party consisting of politically autonomous sections. Instead he proposed that the Bund should carry out agitation and propaganda in the Yiddish language among the communities of Jewish workers within the Pale, but as a section of the RSDLP subject to its congresses and leading bodies. In addition Lenin advocated the right of Russia's 'nationalities' to self-determination and secession if they so wished, and the free use and exercise of their language in state schools and public life as a method of fighting all national oppression. Lenin's objective was not to create a patchwork quilt of nations as a positive goal but to end national oppression as a dividing factor between the proletariats of all nations. Only if the proletariat actively fought against privilege, coercion and fraud could it achieve this.

The Bund, however, claimed exclusive rights to organise Jewish workers throughout the Russian Empire, even where they were a tiny minority. The Russian and other nationalities they would leave to other socialists. This led them to espouse the Austro-Marxist programme of 'national-cultural autonomy'—uniting the scattered Jews by demanding separate schools and cultural institutions. Lenin rejected this as a positive espousal of nationalism, calling the Bund 'nationalist socialists'. Trotsky never dissented from Lenin's view.

The Bolsheviks conducted a ceaseless struggle against the Black Hundreds and the instigators of pogroms, advocating and organising defence squads. Lenin explained the specific oppression of the Jewish workers and its consequence, the necessity for the closest unity between the workers of all nationalities. In this context he was a remorseless foe of Otto Bauer's slogan of 'national-cultural autonomy' as tending to unify each proletariat with 'its own' bourgeoisie and separate it from its class brothers and sisters of other nationalities.

Lenin insisted that Marxists must base themselves on the 'international culture of democracy and the world working class movement'. This is not an abstract non-national culture but one which takes 'from each national culture only its democratic and socialist elements; we take them only and absolutely in opposition to the bourgeois nationalism of each nation'.

Thus though the Jews are in Lenin's words 'the most oppressed and persecuted nation', the slogan of national culture even for them 'is the slogan of the rabbis and the bourgeoisie'. Worse, it tends to become the glorification of the results of oppression, for in Russia and Galicia (north east Austria-Hungary), 'backward and semi-barbarous countries' the Jews are 'forcibly kept in the status of a caste'. Lenin points to the other side of Jewish culture where the Jews have won emancipation. 'There the great world-progressive features of Jewish culture stand clearly revealed; its internationalism, its identification with the advanced movements of the epoch.'

Lenin was therefore a consistent integrationist. But he was absolutely opposed to any forced assimilation to the Russian nationality or to any cultural or linguistic privileges for a dominant or majority nation or language. With regard to minority and oppressed peoples he was in favour of full assistance and facilities for their unhindered cultural and linguistic life. The working class organisations however had to integrate the democratic and proletarian components of these cultures into a common international culture that transcended all nationalist philistinism and exclusiveness even of the oppressed peoples.

Karl Kautsky devoted a work, *Race and Judaism* (1914), to the Jewish question. Kautsky located the social roots of antisemitism in the despairing petty bourgeoisie, ground down by big capital in industry, trade and banking but unable to fight capitalism as a whole because of their own umbilical cord of private property. Kautsky before 1914 held that 'the Jews in Galicia and Russia are more of a caste than a nation and attempts to constitute Jewry as a nation are attempts at preserving a caste'.

Moreover in the countries where they have been totally politically emancipated the process of assimilation is going on apace, either through intermarriage and secularisation or through the development of Judaism into a religion and nothing else. Kautsky goes on to show that the project of settlement in Palestine is a utopia.

Here his argument is at its weakest because he underestimates and ignores two related facts; the oppression of the Jews by the Russian state, by antisemitic pogromists and the erecting of racist immigration laws by the 'advanced' democracies which were creating and would increasingly create an enormous pressure for 'exodus'. Secondly, imperialism itself had a use for emigrant populations. It had historically used them as a supplementary reserve army of labour in the independent countries themselves, and to settle and hold valuable colonies. This latter task came to predominate in the later 19th century and in this century, especially in South Africa and Rhodesia, where vital raw materials (gold, diamonds, copper etc) had to be safeguarded against the 'natives'.

Kautsky, who before 1914 had adopted a tolerant, conciliationist attitude to the Austro-Marxist position on nationalities therefore tended towards a more positive attitude to nationalisms than did Lenin. In the case of the Jews he insisted they were not a nation. Lenin was never so dogmatic and sometimes called them a nation, nationality or people. For Kautsky, a positive attitude flowed from the very fact of national existence. For Lenin and Trotsky the problem was how to overcome the obstacles to internationalism that any form of oppression—racial, national or religious—posed.

Trotsky, though Jewish himself, came from a Russian-speaking family and had no experience with the specifically Jewish labour movement. Only in the 1930s did he devote special attention to the question, having on his own admission hitherto assumed that once backward semi-feudal Tsarism had been swept away, the Jews would be painlessly assimilated into modern democratic society. By the 1930s he was obliged to recognise that imperialism—the highest stage of capitalism, the epoch of its death agony—was reviving antisemitism.

The *Transitional Programme*, adopted in 1938, pledged the Fourth International (FI) and its sections to 'an uncompromising disclosure of the roots of race prejudice and all forms and shades of national arrogance and chauvinism, particularly antisemitism' as part of the 'daily work' of the FI's sections. Thus the SWP (US) mounted a vigorous campaign against the racist immigration quotas and for the slogan 'Open the gates!' to the Jewish refugees from Hitler before, during and after the war.

However, Trotsky remained an intransigent opponent of Zionism. Palestine he called 'a tragic mirage' and pointed out that the development of military events between British and German imperialism—i.e. a Nazi victory—may well transform Palestine into a bloody trap for several hundred thousand Jews'. In the short term this fear was not realised, although Trotsky's other prediction that the war would bring with it the question of 'the physical extermination of the Jews' was amply grounded.

After the war the FI continued Trotsky's strategy of fighting for the admission of Jewish refugees into all the imperialist countries who still, despite the Holocaust, maintained their racist immigration laws and quotas. In addition the FI stood by the struggle of the Arab masses against Zionist chauvinism and the project of creating a Jewish state by robbing the Palestinian majority of the best agricultural land and the major economic resources of the country. It condemned the utopian and reactionary character of Zionism.

It was reactionary because its idea of autarchic economic development for Jewish Palestine was impossible in the context of capitalism in its death agony (here the FI was wrong at least for a whole period but this was a general problem of perspectives). It could never be able to outgrow the Arab population of the country and the region by Jewish immigration alone. It would be entirely dependent on the big imperialist powers, a pawn in their play for control of the Arab world.

Lastly it could be no answer to antisemitism which is rooted in capitalism in the imperialist epoch. Its reactionary nature was to be seen in its pro-imperialist role; because it racially divides the Jewish and Arab workers and fuels the latter's subordination to their own bourgeois and feudal exploiters by means of nationalism; because it weakens the agrarian struggle of the Arab peasants by diverting it against the Zionist land-grabbers and away from the feudal landowners (effendis). Last but not least on a world scale, it diverts Jewish proletarians away from participating in the class struggle where they live towards fantasies of immigration.

The FI defended the right to self-determination of the whole population of Palestine and called for the expulsion of the British and the convocation of a sovereign democratic constituent assembly to decide all questions, including the right of immigration and its control.

After the war, however, the FI wrongly took a position of defeatism on both sides in the 'war of independence' of 1948–49. They did so mainly because during the period of economic prosperity during the Second World War there had been growing incidences of united working class action between Jewish and Arab workers in Palestine. They believed that the 'war of independence', led by the Zionists on one side and the semi-feudal landowners of the Arab League on the other, represented a reactionary diversion from the class struggle of the Jewish and Arab workers.

In reality these special conditions of the Second World War were bound to collapse and with it the fragile basis of unity and integration. The FI underestimated the importance of the imperialist-backed offensive in the region and the revolutionary-democratic struggle against Zionism as part of the class struggle. It would have been essential to have agitated for armed self-defence committees in the Arab villages and towns; for military co-ordination with the forces of the Arab League without giving any political support for their own annexationist goals.

Programme of action

The starting point for a revolutionary party's programme in Palestine and the surrounding countries must be the struggle against imperialism and its wide variety of local agents. The world-hegemonic imperialist power—the USA—defends 'its' oil and the semi-feudal rentier regimes it props up in the Arabian peninsular with a limitless arsenal. Yet as its ignominious fiasco in Iran and its inglorious retreat from Lebanon shows, it is far from invincible when the masses are roused against it even under the most appalling leadership. This 'leadership' whether Stalinist, bourgeois nationalist or clerical reactionary can, however, only score partial and limited victories against the USA and its agents.

Militarily the Israeli state is a formidable supplement to the forces of imperialism, socially and economically rooted as it is within the region. But its massive strength derives ultimately from the huge economic support given it by the US and European imperialist bourgeoisies and the Zionist bourgeoisie worldwide. While it acts as an agent of imperialism as a whole in dividing and disciplining the Arab world, it has its own projects and interests that clash from time to time with the projects of one or other of the imperialist powers—even with those of the USA.

So essential to the USA is the existence of the Zionist state that it is repeatedly forced to adapt its overall strategy and tactics for controlling the region to the wishes of its Israeli ally. Most frequently undermined and sabotaged are its relations with its Arab clients (Mubarak, Hussein and the Saudi rulers) who it is repeatedly obliged to abandon and swindle.

The world strategic interests of the Soviet bureaucracy and its ability and willingness to give military and economic aid (armaments, advisers and loans) have enabled various bourgeois

Bonapartist regimes (Nasser, Assad, Hussein, Gaddafi) to play the anti-imperialist and even defy the USA tactically for a whole period. In turn these regimes have influenced and moulded the PLO through its various factions.

Yet these bourgeois nationalist Bonapartes, despite all their anti-imperialist and even 'socialist' demagogy, despite their claims and aspirations to unify the 'Arab nation' or Islam against the 'Yankee' and Zionist menace have repeatedly surrendered to them at the decisive moment. In reality they are competitors with Israel for imperialism's favours.

What are the real anti-imperialist objectives facing the proletariat of the Middle East? Who are its allies and who are its enemies? What demands must it take up both in its own interest and to win to its side these allies? Its open enemies and their slavish semi-colonial puppets are clear enough to millions, although illusions may exist in the Japanese and EEC imperialists who from time to time, jackal-like, try to seize some morsel from under the nose of the US lion by playing up their own 'moderate' and 'peaceable' nature.

While it is legitimate to take tactical advantage of any contradictions within the imperialist camp, to entertain any illusions in for example Britain, France, Italy or Germany—old plunderers or would-be plunderers of the Middle East and architects of its Balkanisation—could lead only to defeat and catastrophe. Nor should the workers' movement entertain any illusions in the Stalinist or social democratic lackeys of these imperialisms when they weep crocodile tears over the wrongs against the Palestinians.

Labour, Socialist and Social Democratic leaders have long supported and encouraged the Zionists and fêted their 'labour' leaders in the Socialist International—that below-stairs version of their masters' big 'thieves' kitchen', the United Nations. In neither the one nor the other will the masses of the Middle East see their violated national rights addressed let alone redressed.

Nor can the bourgeoisie and the military caste of the Arab states, which temporarily resist direct imperialist control or its dictates, provide the leadership of a successful struggle against imperialism. Firstly, neither Nasser and Sadat nor Assad were able to defeat the Israeli armies, backed as they were by US economic aid. Leaving aside their ability as strategists, Egypt and Syria alone or together were not economically or militarily able to overcome the Zionist forces. 1948, 1956, 1967 and 1973 have all proved that Israel cannot be defeated from without by conventional military means, and that the bourgeois Arab generals cannot lead the Arab masses to victory.

Still less can the battle cries of Islam and the clergy unite the Arab world in a successful jihad. Their reactionary utopian political slogans will alienate all the minority national and religious communities of the region and repulse women who have nothing to hope from them except a return to medieval conditions.

The working class alone can provide the solid social force capable of sustaining a real revolutionary party which can lead all the dispossessed and impoverished—the poor farmers, the camp dwellers, the sub-proletariat of the huge cities, the self-sacrificing intelligentsia—in an assault on imperialism and all its agents, Arab as well as Zionist.

The first step is to create the nuclei of revolutionary parties, independent of all bourgeois and petty bourgeois forces and not tied to any strategic deals with the exploiters and oppressors of the working class. Class independence is the beginning of all wisdom. From the 1930s onwards the powerful influence of Stalinism with its strategy of the popular front and the revolution by stages has led the proletariats of Palestine, Egypt, Syria and Iraq to various Bonapartist dictators or petty bourgeois parties or fronts, demanding first national liberation and a popular democratic regime, then at a later stage socialism.

The working class and its immediate and historic needs have been sacrificed on the altars of these false gods. In the 'independent' Arab states the proletariat has seen its trade unions and political parties repeatedly crushed and its best fighters martyred by 'anti-imperialist heroes', whose standing amongst the masses was sedulously promoted by the Stalinists.

Against the popular front of class collaboration and betrayal the working class must fight for class independence, for an alliance between the working class and the urban and rural poor organised in soviets, and for anti-imperialist united fronts of struggle whenever the fight reaches the stage of open conflict. The united front must be based on the principle of the right and ability of the workers' parties as well as those of the petty bourgeoisie to organise separately, openly and democratically but to fight together loyally and with iron discipline against the common enemy.

There must be no confusion of programmes and strategy and no suppression of any party's right to express them or to make criticisms of each other. As for the parties or forces tied to the bourgeoisie, we cannot expect them to ally with us or to prove a reliable ally, should exceptional attacks by imperialism momentarily force them to do so. As for the Arab bourgeois states in conflict with imperialism, their 'gifts' can be accepted only on the points of their spears, that is, with no conditions as to control of the struggle or the leadership of it.

They are the class enemy even when imperialism forces them to seek the proletariat and the peasantry as allies. In each separate country the proletariat must seek as its main support the proletariat of the surrounding states and must defend their interests as its own. No 'stage' must act as a barrier to the proletariat's advance to power. A workers' state in the Middle East would be a massive blow to imperialism, a reliable arsenal and fortress for all the oppressed. The seizure of power therefore must be the goal of our programme. But to rally the forces and create the conditions to make this possible, we must take up all the immediate and partial, the democratic and anti-imperialist demands, that are in the interests of the masses.

The Palestinian urban and rural proletariat has shown that it can fight—not only because generations of its bravest youth have taken up arms against Zionism and imperialism in guerrilla struggle and alongside the 'regular' forces in the Arab-Israeli wars but also in the mass actions of the 1987–89 uprising on the West

Bank.

Guerrilla warfare can never be a strategy for victory, despite the justification of guerrilla tactics in certain periods and the need for a defence militia to protect the mass struggle and inflict punishment on the occupiers and aggressors. While the proletariat must defend the heroes of the guerrilla forces it cannot share their strategy, which tends to oscillate between negotiations and concessions and individual acts which, though heroic, are all too often doomed to defeat from the outset.

The proletariat erects its strategy along the path of mass action; the demonstration, the strike, the uprising, the building of trade unions, workers' and peasants' councils, women's committees and a popular militia. In the present period the key factors that proletarian revolutionists have to address are:

(a) US and European imperialism's attempts to create a disarmed Palestinian mini-state on part or all of the West Bank, under the guardianship of King Hussein.

(b) The commitment of the Fatah majority within the PLO to a West Bank statelet and the recognition of the state of Israel and the abandonment of the struggle against the Zionist state that this would entail.

(c) The uprisings of the Palestinians of the West Bank and Israel proper against Zionism's military brutality and against the appalling conditions under which they live.

(d) The division of the Israeli ruling class with the Likud-led forces seeking to sabotage the US-EEC plans and with the Labour Zionists seeking to accomplish the creation of a helpless Bantustan where the 'surplus' Arab population can be used in the South African fashion to make permanent an Israeli Jewish majority in Israel and keep a pool of cheap Arab labour close at hand.

(e) The continued guerrilla actions of the Palestinian fedayeen and the interaction of the whole Israel/Palestine situation with the class struggle and inter-state rivalries of the Arab world.

Revolutionary communists must be prepared to intervene and take united actions with progressive forces on all these issues but from a strictly independent class standpoint. Thus we should oppose the imperialist project of a West Bank Bantustan.

• No PLO recognition of the Zionist state's right to oppress 650,000 Palestinians. No abandonment of these Palestinians!

• For a united struggle against national oppression. Smash the Zionist state. Support the mass uprisings against Zionist terror and occupation. Broaden it into a struggle against all aspects of national oppression and super-exploitation suffered by Arab workers and peasants!

• Strengthen the organisations of the working class, trade unions and workplace committees. Build workers', village and camp councils to forward the struggle!

• Build a mass defence militia. Down with the Zionist occupation and brutalising of all Palestinian towns, villages and camps. Israeli troops out! Jewish workers who oppose the occupation: do not avoid conscription into the reserve. Organise soldiers against the occupation inside the army. Organise within the army to get units to refuse to serve in the Occupied Territories. In the Territories fight the brutality and politicise the disaffection within the army. Organise rank and file soldiers' committees. Link up with the Palestinian resistance.

• Build fighting unity with all Jewish Israeli organisations willing to defend the democratic rights of the Palestinians and oppose repression. For solidarity wherever possible with the Jewish Israeli proletariat's economic struggles against the bourgeoisie. Defence of their democratic trade union rights. Proletarians of all nationalities unite!

• Critical support for the struggle of the guerrilla organisations against the Zionist state against imperialism and against the treacherous Arab bourgeoisie. For an active defeatist position towards the Zionist state in any conflict with an Arab bourgeois regime. Defencism with regard to both the PLO and the Arab regimes does not and must not signify abandonment of the political struggle against both, preparing the working class for their betrayals and their inability to fight Zionism and imperialism!

At no stage must the working class abandon its struggle to

unite and lead all the exploited and oppressed against the Zionist state and to create a workers' state in Palestine which would recognise and defend equality of rights for the Arab and Israeli Jewish nationalities, their language and culture. This can only be achieved by mass struggle, by the disintegration and destruction of the Zionist armed forces, that is, by an insurrection that breaks the ability and will to resist of the Zionists. To achieve this objective the working class and its revolutionary party must take up a whole series of struggles (democratic, trade union, poor peasant) that will rally forces to the workers' side and disintegrate the class alliance of Zionism.

To win the masses to action one must take up and defend their vital interests here and now whether these interests can be satisfied by the existing state or whether their realisation requires its destruction and indeed the abolition of capitalist ownership of the large scale means of production.

Thus within the whole of the borders of historic Palestine, and indeed in the surrounding states where Palestinian refugees live, we must fight for a programme of demands to abolish the awful conditions of the camps. This would require a massive programme of public works to build decent houses, hospitals, schools and centres for social life and recreation, install running water and sewers, electricity and heating to pave the roads and provide a good public transport service. Who should pay for it? The American, Zionist and European imperialists and Arab millionaire bourgeoisies and feudalists. How to force them—for certainly they will not do so out of the goodness of their hearts? Take action against their businesses in Palestine, throughout the Arab world and summon the proletariats of Europe, the USA and Asia to assist.

This must not be a call for charity but for restitution and recompense for generations of plunder of the Palestinian people. And such a massive public works programme should be under the control of the unions and local committees of the Palestinian workers and camp dwellers. They should plan and execute everything.

The Palestinian workers' unions should fight for full trade union rights and absolute independence from the state. They should be open to all workers who wish to fight for their interests on the basis of class solidarity and oppose national chauvinism and privilege. They should support Jewish workers in every progressive trade union and political struggle they undertake (i.e. for higher wages, against inflation, against rationalisation or austerity measures and in defence of their social welfare gains). In return the Palestinians should demand equal wages and equal social welfare conditions with their Jewish class brothers and sisters. Together they should fight for the full programme of transitional anti-capitalist measures (the sliding scale of wages and hours, against inflation and unemployment, workers' control of production, workers' inspection of all aspects of the economy, nationalisation of industry, commerce and banking etc.). They should fight under the slogans:

• Jewish workers break out of the company union, the Histadrut, instrument of class collaboration and Zionist chauvinism!

• For an anti-racist union movement open to all Arab and Jewish workers!

• For militant class struggle and workers' democracy!

• For a workers' party to fight for a workers' state!

A revolutionary workers' party faces a whole series of democratic demands, mainly affecting the Arab workers and peasants, but the Jewish workers should remember Marx's dictum: 'A people that oppresses another cannot itself be free'. Any serious crisis for the Zionist state will see the restriction and destruction of bourgeois democracy for Jewish workers, intellectuals and progressives too. The most important and general demand is to end the forty-year separation of millions of Palestinians from their own country:

• For the right to return of all Palestinians!

• Down with the internal borders and all restrictions on movement between Israel, the West Bank, the Gaza Strip and Jerusalem etc.

- For free elections for all municipal authorities and the legalisation of all political parties including the PLO and its constituent organisations!
- Absolute equality of the Hebrew and Arab languages in state, business, education etc.
- Repeal all repressive and emergency regulations and release all political prisoners.
- For the dissolution of the Israel Defence Force and police and the replacement of them with an integrated popular militia.
- For the summoning of a sovereign constituent assembly based on universal suffrage of all Palestinian-Israeli citizens over the age of 16.

These demands should be fought for among Jews and Arabs. No consistent or sincere democrat can oppose them. If the mass struggle around democratic slogans leads to the shipwreck of the Zionist state before the workers and peasants are convinced in their majority of the need to establish a workers' state based on soviets then revolutionaries—while giving no support to the objective of a bourgeois state (i.e. a secular democratic republic)—should fight for the convening of a sovereign constituent assembly based on an armed popular militia.

Revolutionary communists should fight in the elections to such an assembly and in it, if it were convened, for a programme that can resolve the national antagonisms; granting the fullest democratic freedoms to both nationalities now resident within Palestine and posing the only social and economic and political basis for doing this—a workers' state and a planned economy. Such a programme must be a programme of transition based upon:

- The nationalisation of all land and its working on a collective or cooperative basis with the restoration of the returning Palestinians full right to participate equally in the farming sector. To make this possible a massive development of the neglected areas of Arab land ownership would be necessary to raise its productivity. Private property on the land is an anachronism and can only be a continued instrument of national antagonism. Of course, collective ownership cannot be imposed on small peasant farmers. They must be won to it via a process of co-operative working when they see its economic superiority.

- The nationalisation under workers' management of all large scale industry and its coordination under a democratically decided upon central plan.
- The nationalisation of the banks, financial institutions and large scale commercial institutions.

A workers' state would grant absolute equality to all peoples and languages in political and cultural life, making state facilities available to fully develop and protect cultural expression in the Hebrew and Arab languages, with full rights for minority languages (Yiddish etc).

This equality and absence of all coercion would extend to the Israeli/Hebrew speaking people themselves, once the national oppression of the Palestinian Arabs had been ended and the Zionist state destroyed. Revolutionaries would of course not advocate separation. Quite the contrary. But it would be far better for the Palestinian Arabs to freely facilitate a democratic and equal separation where the Israelis wished it than to exert the slightest coercion themselves. Of course, there could be no question of yielding to an undemocratic minority of hardened Zionists in collusion with imperialism who were acting as a *Vendée* against the Palestinian workers' revolution.

The programme for permanent revolution in Palestine, for an uninterrupted strategic advance from democratic and transitional demands in today's conditions to a workers' state, should not be seen as a schema of peaceful or gradual advance. On the contrary, the Zionist bourgeoisie and the imperialist powers will not yield to persuasion—to the weapons of criticism. War, revolution and counter-revolution gave birth to the Zionist state and will undoubtedly bring about its destruction. A living, flexible but principled programme will have to be applied and re-applied in action programmes suited to every fundamental change of conditions or decisive shift in the balance of forces or the arena of struggle.

Firstly the Palestinian revolution is intimately and indeed inextricably linked with to the political fate of the immediately surrounding lands; Lebanon, Syria, Jordan and Egypt. Palestinian revolutionaries should seek the closest links with revolutionaries in these countries. The existence of huge Palestinian refugee communities in these countries makes this involvement easier, and imperialism and Zionism's repeated interventions makes Palestine almost a domestic issue in all these states. The fate of their class struggle could be of the greatest importance to the struggle within the Zionist state. The overthrow of a Mubarak or a Hussein could alter the whole balance of forces. A new Arab/Israeli war could also create conditions where the external and internal destruction of the Zionist state could coincide.

There is a political slogan which expresses the goal of a Middle East united against imperialism and led by the working class and poor peasants: the socialist united states of the Middle East. It is profoundly more progressive than other goals aimed at unifying against imperialism. We have already stated that the idea of a united Islam is a reactionary utopia. Reactionary because it would not be a democratic but a theocratic state, imposing religious law on non-believers. It would be utopian in that it could hardly unify Sunni and Shi'ite Islam let alone the many sects and minority religions. Pan-Arab nationalism, while largely a secular ideology, also has reactionary and utopian features relative to national minorities—Berbers, Israeli Jews, Kurds within Arab countries—and it cannot unite with overwhelmingly non-Arab states such as Iran. A socialist united states of the Middle East would allow for separate states or autonomous regions for every nationality, would allow for the real national consciousness that distinguishes Palestinians, Syrians, Egyptians, Iraqis to be both expressed and resolved in a state form capable of completing the struggle against imperialism. Thus and only thus could the Balkanisation of the Middle East be ended and the world proletarian revolution carried a mighty step forward.

- Down with the imperialist powers—exploiters and oppressors of the peoples of the Middle East!

- Smash the Zionist state—instrument of imperialism!
- Victory to the national liberation of the Palestinian people!
- Critical support to even bourgeois Arab states in economic or military conflict with imperialism and Israel!
- Unconditional but critical support to the PLO's military struggle by the proletariats of the imperialist countries!
- For permanent revolution in Palestine and the Middle East!
- From the national democratic struggle to the proletarian revolution!
- No to any form of confessional state! For a workers' state in Palestine!
- For a socialist united states of the Middle East!
- For revolutionary communist (Trotskyist) parties in every country as a part of a refounded international!

Movement for a Revolutionary Communist International
September 1988.

The Fourth International on Palestine

Editor's note

We reprint here an English translation of the 'Draft theses on the Jewish question today', first published in *Fourth International* in the January/February 1948 issue. They are dated January 1947 and the available evidence suggests that they were drafted by Ernest Mandel ('Walter') and first discussed by the International Secretariat in Paris at its 16 December 1946 meeting.

They first appeared in a special number of the French *Internal bulletin of the International Secretariat* in October 1947. It appears that they were not discussed at the fifth plenum of the IS in February 1948, nor the sixth plenum in October that year, nor even the seventh in April 1949. The theses were not submitted to the Second World Congress in June 1948, although there are brief passages on Palestine and the Middle East in the resolution on 'The struggle of the colonial peoples and the world revolution' which reflect the line of thought in the draft theses.

The most plausible explanation for the lack of a congress or plenum discussion on the theses is that the political situation between late 1946 and the spring of 1949 was extremely volatile. When the theses were drafted the British mandate still operated in Palestine. Ahead lay the war between the Palestinian Arab and Jewish settlers, the withdrawal of the British, the declaration and recognition of the state of Israel, the invasion by the Arab League armies, and the expulsion of over a million Palestinians. All these events took place between the last months of 1947 and the first months of 1949.

Despite this, the theses are a principled attempt to chart a path of permanent revolution. With the memory of the holocaust so fresh in the minds of Jews and progressive forces all over the world it was not easy to insist that the project of the Zionist state in Palestine was a reactionary endeavour, one which entailed a complete denial of the rights of the Palestinians to self-determination. The theses are equally harsh on those apologists for Zionism within the socialist movement. Yet this attitude is balanced by their strong call to arms against all manifestations of antisemitism, and especially that of the imperialist states, which hypocritically backed the Zionist project while restricting (or denying totally) Jewish immigration into their own countries.

Draft theses on the Jewish Question today, adopted by the International Secretariat of the Fourth International: 1 January 1947

In presenting its draft theses on the Jewish question prepared one year ago, the International Secretariat of the Fourth International has issued the following statement:

'In view of the fact that this question is being raised in our ranks for the first time and that the discussion is likely to bring forth numerous contributions, the International Secretariat presents these theses as a general line of orientation, but is ready in the course of the discussion to offer clarifications, amendments or corrections if necessary.'—Ed.

A. The Jewish Question in the Capitalist world

1. Throughout the ages the lot of the Jews, a mercantile people whose survival among other peoples has its root causes in a special social function, has been determined by the general evolution of society, an evolution which brought about changes in their relationships with the various classes. The bourgeois revolution in Western Europe opened the doors of the ghettos and merged the Jewish masses within the envi-

roning society. The assimilation of the Jews seemed to be an accomplished fact. But the countries of Central and Eastern Europe, those vast reservoirs of Jews confined for centuries to the functions of middlemen, entered upon the road of capitalist development at a time when world capitalism had already embarked on its imperialist phase. Although the age-old relations of exchange and production experienced an abrupt upheaval which robbed the Jews of the material base for their existence, there was no widespread industrialization to allow these millions of now useless middlemen to become integrated in the proletariat. Social differentiation of the Jewish masses was thus blocked. A small part of the Jews became capitalist or proletarian; a larger part emigrated, thus contravening the tendency toward complete assimilation which was going on in the Western countries. The largest part of all remained in the wretched condition of small merchants, 'crushed between feudalism and capitalism, each feeding the rottenness of the other' (A. Leon).

2. The anti-Semitic movements of the past always had a direct or indirect social base. They were movements of various social classes whose interests came into conflict at a certain time with the social function of the Jews. The anti-Semitism of the beginning of the Twentieth Century was nowise different.

In the backward countries of Eastern Europe, reactionary political forces were able to turn the discontent and despair of the masses into periodic pogroms—for the hatred of the little people toward the Jewish petty usurer and pawn-broker, the Jewish small merchant and shop-keeper, was an undeniable social reality.

In the countries of Central Europe, the anti-Semitic movements, such as that of the burgermaster Lueger in Vienna, had their social roots in the sharpening of competition within the professional and mercantile middle-classes who were being inundated by a tide of Jewish immigrants.

In France, the anti-Semitic movement which broke out at the time of the Dreyfus affair had its social origin in the hatred of the aristocracy for the Jewish bankers who had bought up their castles, and of the sons of aristocrats who saw the careers that formerly had been 'reserved' exclusively for them now occupied by these dangerous competitors. These social layers were successful for a certain time in turning against the Jews the inflamed nationalist sentiments of a large part of the petty bourgeoisie.

Rooted in specific social conflicts, these various anti-Semitic movements took on most diverse manifestations, all the way from phenomena of utter barbarism (the Russian pogroms) to the formulation of the 'subtle' nationalist theories which were characteristic of the imperialist epoch (Charles Maurras).

3. In Western Europe the social opportunities for assimilation of the Jews had created a powerful ideological movement toward complete assimilation. In Eastern Europe the impossibility of widespread assimilation of the Jews resulted in a strong current in the direction of a national renaissance and preservation of national characteristics. It was within the large concentrations of Jewish masses in Poland, Lithuania, Western Russia, Hungary, Rumania and Slovakia that there developed a new literature in Yiddish, a new folklore, an intense autonomous cultural and even political life (the 'Bund' in the workers' movement). Wherever the Jewish masses who had emigrated to the United States were again socially restricted to certain economic fields, and where they were geographically concentrated, this movement continued even in these countries. Lenin, who alone in the Second International understood how to apply Marxist strategy to the national question, rejected all pedantic formalism in his appraisal of this current. He started from the standpoint that the task of the revolutionary party was to integrate into the movement of proletarian emancipation every current of cultural and national autonomy which corresponded to a genuine aspiration of the working masses. That is why he recognized the legitimacy, from a socialist point of view, of the Jewish movement as much as of the Polish or Czech movements. The task of the Jewish workers consisted in struggling, at the side of the workers of the country where they lived, for the overthrow of capitalism, and after this they would be left completely free to carry out the organization of their national and cultural economy as they chose.

4. The epoch of decaying capitalism is also the epoch of the sharpened crisis of the Jewish problem. Inflation, the increased pressure of finance capital, and finally the profound economic crisis, ruined millions of small tradesmen and merchants and inflamed to the highest pitch their hatred of their Jewish competitors. In Central and Eastern Europe the appalling unemployment among the intellectual workers and the increasingly wretched situation of the professionals created a climate especially favorable for the appearance of vast petty-bourgeois mass movements, which found in anti-Semitism one of their ideological weapons. In the countries of Eastern Europe, these movements revealed a very deep popular current which manifested itself in many bloody outbursts. In Germany, it was the state power, fallen into the hands of the Nazi rulers, which organized from on top the persecution and later the extermination of the Jews. In this sense it is decaying capitalism, which deliberately placed power in the hands of a band of bloody criminals, that bears full responsibility for the horrible fate of the Jewish European masses during the war. The extermination of the European Jews by German imperialism is a warning to all other peoples and shows them the fate that awaits them so long as present-day society continues to decay.

5. Zionism arose among the Jewish petty bourgeoisie of Central Europe as a reaction against the rebirth of anti-Semitism at the beginning of the Twentieth Century. A typically petty-bourgeois movement, it remained for a long time without the support of the Jewish bourgeoisie and isolated from the popular masses. During the First World War, British imperialism, which wanted to use Zionism as an instrument for establishing itself in Palestine, seemed to offer Zionism the possibility of becoming a reality through the Balfour declaration. At this time there began a small flow of capital imports, and a slight movement of immigration. It was only after the coming of Hitler to power and the sudden fall of European Jewry into the abyss, that these two movements 'speeded up', though obstructed both by the nationalist outbursts of the Arabs and by the policy of British imperialism which threw

up more and more barriers against Jewish penetration into Palestine.

For the revolutionary proletariat, Zionism must be looked upon as a movement which is both utopian and reactionary.

Utopian and Reactionary Character of Zionism

Utopian:

(a) Because Zionism believes that a 'harmonious' development of the productive forces is possible within a 'closed economy' in Palestine, in the midst of a capitalist world undergoing ever greater economic convulsions. The immense development of Palestine economy that would be necessary if several million immigrants were to be absorbed, is not realizable within the framework of present-day world capitalist economy.

(b) Because Zionism considers the creation of a Jewish (or bi-national) state possible amid the open hostility of 50 million Arabs – in the face of the fact that the Arab population grows in the same proportion as the Jewish immigration and the gradual industrialization of the country.

(c) Because Zionism hopes to reach this goal by relying on the maneuverings among the great powers, all of which, in reality, want to utilize the Zionist movement simply as a pawn in their play for power in the Arab world.

(d) Because Zionism thinks it possible to neutralize anti-Semitism throughout the world by the simple grant of a nationality to the Jews – in the face of the fact that anti-Semitism has deep social, historical and ideological roots which will be all the more difficult to tear out as the death agony of capitalism is prolonged.

Reactionary:

(a) Because Zionism serves as a support for British imperialist domination, by giving to imperialism the pretext of acting as "arbiter" between the Jews and Arabs, by demanding the maintenance of the British mandate, and by developing a 'closed' miniature Jewish economy within which the working masses have a much higher standard of living and different immediate interests than those of the Arab working masses.

(b) Because it produces a nationalist reaction on the part of the Arab masses, causes a racial division of the working-class movement, strengthens the 'sacred union' both of the Jews and of the Arabs, and thus makes it possible for imperialism to perpetuate the conflict by continuing to keep its troops in Palestine.

(c) Because it retards the movement for the agrarian revolution, by buying lands from the large Arab landholders and working them, thanks to foreign subsidies, as a 'closed' Jewish agriculture within Arab Palestinian agriculture. In this way the position of the large landholders is to some extent reestablished, lands are taken from the Arab peasants, and most important of all, the Jewish masses in Palestine have no interest in fighting for partition of the lands of the effendis among the Arab masses, since this would mean the end of their land purchases.

(d) Because it acts as a brake on the participation of the Jewish working masses in the class struggle in the rest of the world, separates them from the world proletariat, gives them autonomous goals to strive for, and creates illusions as to the possibility of improving their lot within the framework of decaying world capitalism.

For all these reasons the revolutionary workers' movement has always conducted a violent struggle against Zionist ideology and practice. The arguments advanced by the "socialist" representatives of Zionism in favor of their cause are either the classic reformist arguments ('the possibility of gradually improving the situation of the Jewish masses'); or the social-patriotic arguments ('it is first necessary to resolve the national question for all the Jews before approaching the solution of the social problems of the Jewish workers'); or the classic arguments of the defenders of imperialism ('the penetration of Jews into Palestine has developed not only industry but also the workers' movement, the general culture of the masses, their standard of living, etc.')—the arguments advanced by the defenders of colonialism in every country.

B. The Present Aspect of the Jewish Question throughout the World

6. After the Second World War, the especially tragic situation of the Jews appears as a symbol of the entire tragedy of humanity slipping back toward barbarism. After the fearful tragedy of European Judaism, the Jews in every part of the world are facing a revival of the hostility of large layers of the population against them.

In Europe, two years after the 'liberation', more than 100,000 Jews are still living under the infamous regime of the concentration camps. The imperialist masters who in the course of their military operations were able to shift millions of men in the period of a few days have been unable, after searching for twenty months, to find any refuge whatsoever for these miserable survivors of the Nazi camps. Throughout the continent there are hardly a million Jews remaining.

In Palestine, 700,000 Jews face an Arab world in full eruption. The development of Egyptian and Syrian capitalism adds the factor of economic competition to the many causes for the militant anti-Zionism. British imperialism and the Arab feudal lords and bourgeoisie will for their part do all they can to turn the hatred of the oppressed Arab masses against the Jew as a scapegoat. Thus the Jews in Palestine are in danger of being wiped out in the widespread explosion which is preparing in the Middle East.

In the Soviet Union, the bureaucracy in its struggle against the opposition has made use of the anti-Semitism latent within the peasant masses and the backward working-class layers. During the period of the First and Second Five-Year Plans, millions of Jewish merchants and artisans were brought into the lower and middle ranks of the bureaucracy as engineers, technicians, directors of cooperatives, and into the upper layers on the collective farms. In Western Russia they constitute that part of the bureaucracy most directly in contact with the oppressed masses, and thus it is in large part against them that the hatred of the masses for the parasites and profiteers of the regime is concentrated. The bloody pogroms launched by the native population at the time of the German invasion furnished very clear evidence of the intensification of this hatred (70,000 Jews killed in Kiev in twenty-four hours). A sharpening of the social crisis in Russia and the purges of a civil war would certainly see the extermination of the Jewish masses if the counter-revolution were victorious.

Finally, in the United States, the confining of Jews to certain sectors of small manufacture and trade and to commercial and professional occupations will cause, in the acute economic crisis ahead, a heightening of the competition which will give a strong material base to the anti-Semitism existing now in latent form. Exploitation of reactionary prejudices against 'racial minorities' has been a long-time favorite weapon of the American fascist gangsters. Insofar as the sharpening of the social crisis, the politicization of the workers' movement and the rapid decay of American 'democracy' give birth to the development of a fascist mass party, anti-Semitism as well as anti-Negro agitation will assume gigantic proportions. The fate of the Jews in the United States is tied in the very closest way to the outcome of the tremendous struggle of the American working class against the Yankee bourgeoisie. A victory of the latter through the establishment of a dictatorship would signify within a short period a catastrophe for the Jews comparable only to the catastrophe which Hitler's coming to power meant for the Jews in Europe.

7. The endless series of ordeals undergone by the Jewish masses in Europe has without question accelerated the growth of a national consciousness, both among the survivors and among the Jewish masses in America and Palestine who feel themselves closely tied to the fate of their brothers in Europe. This national consciousness is manifested in the following ways:

The Jewish masses in general now want to affirm their own nationality as against other peoples. Violent Jewish nationalism corresponds to the violence of the persecutions and anti-Semitism.

The eyes of the Jewish masses in Europe are turned toward emigration. With all frontiers hermetically sealed, and as a result of the general conditions of the postwar world and in harmony with the engulfing wave of nationalism, the desire of the Jews to leave a continent which for them is nothing but a vast graveyard finds its expression primarily in a Zionist desire to go to Palestine.

Within the Zionist movement, the struggle for the 'Jewish state', hitherto conducted exclusively by the extreme right (the 'revisionists'), has now been taken up by all parties (the 'Biltmore program') except the centrist Hashomer Hatzair.

The rebirth of the national consciousness of the masses is the result of capitalism's decay which raises once more all the problems that had been solved in its period of expansion. The Fourth International, basing itself firmly on its program and on a scientific analysis of the situation in Palestine but at the same time taking into account the actual state of mind of the Jewish masses, must recognize that their desire to lead their own national existence is a legitimate one. The Fourth International must show concretely that the winning of their nationality cannot be realized within decaying capitalist society, and is especially unrealizable and reactionary in Palestine. The Fourth International must show that for the Jews as for all other peoples of the earth, the defense or the final winning of their own nationality cannot be achieved by building 'closed' states and economies, but that a planned world socialist economy is the only realistic framework within which the free and normal development of a people is possible today. The Fourth International must make the Jewish masses aware of the terrible catastrophes which await them if the decay of capitalism continues its course. Integration of the Jewish emancipation movement within the movement of the world working-class is the only thing that will make possible a harmonious solution of the Jewish problem. Socialist planned economy, 'completely altering the topography of the globe' (Trotsky), will assure to all who desire it their own national existence within the framework of the United States of the World.

A Program of Action

8. But the Fourth International will never win decisive influence over the Jewish masses by simply proclaiming that only the socialist revolution will bring their emancipation. Only by

taking leadership of a vast world movement of solidarity on the part of the proletariat toward the victims of imperialist and fascist persecution, only by showing the Jews in practice that the solutions proposed by the revolutionary movement offer more hope and are more realistic than the Zionist 'solution'—only in this way will the Fourth International succeed at the next turn in drawing the Jewish masses into the world struggle against imperialism. To march against the Zionist current today, and to oppose to it another immediate and concrete solution—these are the two indispensable factors in making preparations for the next stage. When the Jewish masses have gone through their disillusioning experience with Zionism and have learned the futility of their efforts and sacrifices, they will turn toward us—provided we understand how to move toward them today with our solutions as well as with an intransigent criticism of Zionism.

All sections of the Fourth International must advance the slogan: 'Open the doors of every country to the Jewish refugees! Abolish all restrictions on immigration!' This slogan must be supported especially in the United States, on the one hand, and by the English, Canadian, French and all the Latin American sections on the other. The latter, particularly the Argentine and Brazil sections, and also our Australian section, must add to this the slogan: 'Abolish all discriminatory racial and religious clauses in immigration legislation!' Every concrete occasion (complaints about the insufficiency of manpower and the population decline, partial opening of the country to certain categories of immigrants, actions in commemoration of the victims of fascism, etc.) must be utilized to arouse the working-class public opinion of the country and to demand the launching of concrete actions as the way to get immediate results. Resolutions like those of the CIO must be used as a point of departure for demanding actions from the World Federation of Trade Unions, for organizing joint movements in those sections of the economy and society which are most ready to express their solidarity in action (seamen, government employees, etc.) through slow-down strikes, organized sabotage of discriminatory measures, protest actions, joint meetings and manifestations, etc. Only insofar as our sections can prove to the Jews that they are carrying on a real and effective struggle for the opening of their own country to immigration—only thus will they succeed in getting the Jews to choose immigration into these countries rather than into Palestine, since immigration into Palestine would then be more difficult while at the same time constituting an act contrary to the interests of the anti-imperialist masses of the Middle East.

All sections of the Fourth International must devote themselves seriously to the task of combating the foul vapors of anti-Semitic ideology existing or steadily growing in large layers of the population of every country. This work of disinfection is all the more urgent because the 'official' working-class movement, whether through conservatism, cowardliness or narrow partisan calculation (the anti-Trotskyism of the French CP is expressed not infrequently in anti-Semitic arguments), does nothing to eliminate from the consciousness of the masses the anti-Jewish poison introduced by the Hitler propaganda.

On every concrete occasion our sections must demolish the fascist lies about 'Jewish capitalism' or the 'Jewish monopolists'. They must constantly warn the proletarian mass organizations against every attempt to rebuild anti-Semitic organizations. Using the tragic examples of the last years, they must impregnate the consciousness of the masses with the fundamental truth that their own fate is at stake in the struggle against anti-Semitic gangsterism. Only insofar as our sections can bring the masses to understand this truth and to translate it into action—only thus will they succeed in convincing the Jews that the integration of their emancipation movement into the world working-class movement is the only thing which will put them in a position to defend themselves effectively against new waves of anti-Semitism.

All sections of the Fourth International which are faced with an organized fascist movement making full use of anti-Semitic demagogy and proceeding to terrorist acts against the Jews, must strive to mobilize the working class in armed formations (militias, etc.) to defend the Jewish people. Wherever the Jewish population, is geographically concentrated in

Jewish quarters, they must propose and help to set up armed defense guards, while endeavoring to fuse them with the workers' militias. They must explain to the Jewish masses that only such fusion in the armed struggle can guarantee an effective defense; but at the same time they must warn the workers that only armed defense of the Jews can prevent the crushing of the entire working-class movement later on by the same fascist weapons.

C. The Present Aspect of the Palestine Problem

9. The Palestine problem has received a new and special importance since the end of the Second World War because of a number of 'new factors' profoundly changing its physiognomy:

The industrialization of the Near and Middle East has to some extent strengthened the native Arab bourgeoisie in Egypt, Palestine, Syria, Lebanon, and to a lesser degree in the other Arab countries. The social differentiation of the old feudal or patriarchal Arab society has been speeded up. An Arab proletariat much more powerful numerically and already politically conscious has appeared on the political scene in numerous countries of the Middle East (strikes in Egypt, Palestine, Syria, Iraq and Iran). Arab nationalism shows the same differentiations. Alongside feudal and reactionary pan-Islamism there now appears a progressive pan-Arab current which sees in the realization of a union of the Arab countries of the Middle East the only real framework for the development of the productive forces and for the constitution of an Arab state. The bourgeoisie can support this idea only in a hesitant way on an ideological plane, insofar as it desires expansion of the market for its industry which has been plunged in a profound crisis since the end of the war. The only force capable of accomplishing the program of the national-democratic revolution in the Arab world is the proletariat, which alone can carry out to the end, through the mechanism of the permanent revolution, the struggle against feudalism, for the agrarian revolution, for the emancipation of the Arab world from imperialist intervention, and for the constitution of the unity of the Arab world.

Growth of anti-imperialist movements within the framework of the colonial revolutions, the most significant upheavals of the immediate postwar period. The weakening of the old imperialist powers (Great Britain, France, Italy) had the result that the bourgeoisie and even certain feudal layers seized the opportunity of obtaining by pressure—and without having to unloose genuine mass struggles, from which they always recoil—important concessions from the occupying powers, such as withdrawal of French troops from Syria and Lebanon and preparatory steps for withdrawal of British troops from Egypt. These various retreats on the part of imperialism are an incentive for the anti-imperialist struggle in the other colonial or semi-colonial countries of the Middle East. They strike a powerful blow at the prestige of imperialism and they increase the confidence of the native masses in their own strength.

Transformation of Palestine into the key position in the system of imperialist defense in the Eastern Mediterranean. After the withdrawal of British troops from Egypt, Palestine will be the main base for the British fleet, air force, land army and secret services in the Eastern Mediterranean, and the key position for defense of the Suez Canal and the imperialist route to India. The terrorist actions are used simply as a pretext for the large concentrations of British troops in Palestine. In reality, what is involved for British imperialism is constructing a strong base with a view to the coming conflicts and for defense of the Empire.

Transformation of the Middle East into one of the main stakes in the rivalry between the 'Big Three'. Before the war the Middle East was the part of the world where the predominant influence of British imperialism was least menaced. Since then, the drive of Rommel all the way to El Alamein, the installing of American 'observers' in the kingdom of Ibn Saud, the outbreak of the Anglo-American dispute over Arabian oil and the Russo-Anglo-American dispute over Iranian oil, the Russian penetration into Iranian Azerbaijan, the Russian attempts to threaten the integrity of Turkish territory, the organizing of the Orthodox Church throughout the Middle East as a powerful agency of the Kremlin diplomacy—all these have brought into question the exclusive domination of Great Britain in this part of the world and have transformed it into an arena of constant conflicts between the great powers. And since the Middle East is, moreover, the least tapped and most important source of oil in the entire world, it is now becoming the principal contested area in the world struggle for this strategic raw material, the reserves of which in the United States and the Soviet Union are greatly reduced. The various "tactical" movements of American and Soviet diplomacy toward the Zionist movement must be seen as elements in their intrigues to supplant British domination in the Arab world.

The demand for immigration into Palestine—advanced by the mass of Jewish refugees in Europe and supported by a powerful protest movement on the part of American Zionism, and culminating in the 'peaceful' actions of the Hagana in Palestine as well as the terrorism of the Irgun Zvai Leumi and the Stern group.

Our Point of Departure

10. The starting point for the position of the Fourth International on the Palestine problem must be an understanding of the necessity for the anti-imperialist struggle waged by the Arabs, setting as the goal of this struggle the establishment of a union of the Arab countries of the Middle East. The Arab masses, the workers and poor peasants, constitute the revolutionary force of the Middle East and also of Palestine, because of their numbers, their social conditions and the material conditions of their existence which set them in direct conflict with imperialism. The revolutionary party must base itself first of all on the dynamics of the class struggle waged in defense of their interests. The Middle East section of the Fourth International, growing as the Arab proletariat develops and grows in strength, and built on the base of the existing nuclei in Palestine and Egypt, must lead the actions of the masses in defense of their daily interests, must raise the workers' consciousness to an understanding of the necessity of political action, and must strive to weld a bloc of all the exploited around the revolutionary proletariat through a struggle for the four

following essential demands:

• Immediate withdrawal of British troops. Complete independence for Palestine.

• Immediate calling of a single and sovereign Constituent Assembly.

• Expropriation of the lands of the effendis, with management of the expropriated land by committees of poor peasants.

• Expropriation of all enterprises which are the property of foreign capital, with workers' management of the nationalized enterprises.

Through the struggle for these four central objectives the revolutionary party will educate the masses on the need for setting themselves increasingly in opposition to the Arab bourgeoisie which is so closely tied to the effendis. When the struggle of the masses reaches its peak, when committees of workers and peasants cover all the Middle East and the question of seizure of power by the Arab proletariat is placed on the order of the day, the revolutionary party will have sufficiently educated the masses to be able to lead them on to expropriation of the 'national' bourgeoisie.

11. Can these four objectives be realized at the present stage in a common struggle of the Arab masses and the Jewish working-class masses? To answer this question we must start not from abstract formulas but from the social and ideological realities of Jewish life in Palestine. With the exception of several thousand Jewish workers employed on the railroads, in the IPC, the refineries and the port facilities, the entire Jewish industrial and agricultural proletariat of Palestine is employed in 'closed' Jewish industry, which operates on the basis of the steady imports of foreign capital and guarantees the Jewish workers a standard of living far above that of the Arab workers. Moreover, the Jewish community in Palestine lives in constant fear of an Arab uprising, and in the face of this danger places all its hopes in continuous immigration and maintenance of the British occupation. We can therefore assert the following:

(a) Far from desiring the immediate withdrawal of the British occupation forces, the Jewish masses on the contrary wish to have them maintained in the country. The only thing demanded by the Zionist leaders, bourgeois as well as workers, is concessions on immigration and on the setting up of a Jewish state. But the overwhelming majority of Jews in Palestine (primarily the Hagana) are not ready to 'act' against imperialism except insofar as such 'action' does not endanger the fundamental 'security' of the Jewish community as against the Arab world. That is why armed struggle or even large-scale sabotage undertaken by the Jewish masses is at the present stage virtually excluded. The aim of Zionist action today is simply to exert pressure on British imperialism in order to win concessions, and not to strive to expel British imperialism from Palestine.

The terrorist movement and the so-called 'Hebrew Committee of National Liberation' do set forth the objective of expelling British imperialism from Palestine. But they cannot conceive of such expulsion except in the form of a general arming of the Jews in Palestine who would hold the Arab world in check until such time as large-scale immigration of Jews would give them the military strength to oppose the 'Arab menace'. These ideas, an abstraction formed out of complete utopianism, are ultra-reactionary and can only deepen still further the gulf separating the Jewish and the Arab workers in Palestine.

(b) All the Jews in Palestine are opposed to the immediate calling of a Constituent Assembly, which would place power in the hands of the Arab majority of the population.

The terrorists claim that they are struggling for a free, independent and democratic Palestine. But since they are the most ardent partisans of a 'Jewish state', they also have to find an excuse for depriving the majority of the population of sovereignty. They say they are not ready to organize general elections until the Jews in exile have been given 'the opportunity within a certain period of time' to return to their country. In other words, they do not support general elections until such moment as the Jews constitute an absolute majority of the population.

(c) The Jews have no interest in expropriation of the effendis, for this would actually deprive them of any possibility of buying new lands and enlarging their 'closed Jewish economy' in Palestine.

(d) They are even more violently opposed to expropriation of the enterprises built with foreign capital and to the closing of the country to capital imports, since this would be a deathblow to their Jewish economy.

Thus the conclusion is inevitable that at the present stage the Jewish masses in Palestine do not as a whole constitute an anti-imperialist force, and that the establishing of a Jewish-Arab anti-imperialist bloc cannot become a slogan for immediate agitation.

12. The question of Jewish immigration into Palestine must be viewed in the light of the foregoing considerations. As long as the Jewish and Arab economies exist as two separate economies in Palestine, the Arab working population will consider every new influx of Jewish immigrants as an act of open hostility. With the entire population of Palestine living under the perspective of the outbreak of a bloody conflict in the Middle East, the Arab masses must necessarily look upon the arrival of new immigrants as the arrival of enemy soldiers; and this point of view is confirmed, moreover, by the way in which the Jewish masses look upon this, immigration. That is why we must recognize the fact that continuance of Jewish immigration into Palestine widens the breach between the Jewish and the Arab workers, strengthens the positions of and prolongs the presence of British imperialism, and cannot but prepare the ground for the complete extermination of the Jewish minority when the Arab uprising comes in the next stage.

The Fourth International must therefore do its utmost to dissuade the Jewish refugees from immigration to Palestine; it must endeavor, within the framework of a movement of world solidarity, to get the doors of other countries opened to them, and must warn that Palestine is for them a terrible trap; and in its concrete propaganda on the question of Jewish immigration, it must start from the sovereignty of the Arab population. Only the Arab population has the right to determine whether or not immigration into Palestine should be open or closed to the Jews. The immigration question must be decided by the Constituent Assembly elected by all the population from the age of 18. That is the only democratic position on this question—and at the same time it is a position which fits into the framework of general revolutionary strategy in the Middle East.

Furthermore, the Fourth International must condemn and combat the British repression of Jewish immigration, denounce all their police measures and constantly oppose to these the concrete demand for withdrawal of the British troops. It will not be hard to explain to the Arab masses that this imperialist repression, now limited to the Jews, is only the preparation for much more savage repression of future Arab movements. It is in the interest of the Arab masses that every protest movement against British police terror should be utilized to bring forward concretely the question of withdrawal of British troops. Moreover, it would then become clear that the very 'victims' of the repression would not at all accept a consistent struggle against their 'oppressors'.

Similarly, the Fourth International must oppose all the 'solutions' proposed and perhaps carried out by imperialism, with or without the help of its agents in the Jewish Agency. All these solutions, such as division of Palestine, limited immigration of 100,000 Jews, surrender of the British mandate to the UN, have the aim of prolonging the presence of British troops in the country, and they all deprive the majority of the population of its right to self-determination.

13. At the present stage, large-scale unity between the Jews and the Arabs in Palestine is unrealizable; only on a very limited scale and to the extent that a section of the Jewish workers is employed outside the 'closed' Jewish economy, has it been possible for Jewish-Arab strikes such as those of the past year to occur. But this does not mean that such unity is excluded for all time. Up to now the Jewish population in Palestine has bent all its efforts toward strengthening its autonomous economic and political positions. But already the radical section of the Jewish nationalist youth has recognized the futility of the Jewish Agency's efforts at 'conciliation' and 'maneuvering' in order to win from imperialism or from the great powers unlimited immigration and establishment of a Jewish state.

The present waves of terrorism on the part of the Irgun Zvai Leumi and the Stern group are acts of despair on the part of this minority which is first utilized and then abandoned by the bourgeois leaders of the Zionist movement and which arose because of the blind alley into which the entire movement has wandered. Obviously this terrorism of despair is not in itself the road to a solution of the Palestine problem. Quite the contrary. Against this terrorism, the Arab feudal lords and bourgeoisie are able to create an atmosphere of artificial 'solidarity' between the masses and imperialism, and to aggravate the hostility between the Arab and the Jewish workers. From a military standpoint, the terrorist acts can only hasten the establishment of a British police force in Palestine, the goal of the entire postwar imperialist policy. But as the ultimate phase of Zionism, terrorism, achieving no concrete results, may make the most conscious and most active elements among the Jewish masses more disposed to reconsider the whole question of Zionism and the solution of the Jewish problem. This reconsideration of the entire question is what the Fourth International must work for today.

Any possible unity between the Jews and the Arabs must first of all move along the road of the abolishing of all racial ideology and practice on the part of the Jews.

• Down with exclusively Jewish enterprises! For the employment of Arab workers in every industry in the country!

• Down with separate Jewish and Arab trade unions! For the establishment of Jewish and Arab trade unions!

• Down with the hidden boycott of Arab or Jewish products! Down with the 'closed Jewish economy'! For the mutual integration of the Jewish and Arab economies!

• Down with the idea of a 'Jewish state' imposed on the majority of the population! For the elimination of Zionist concepts from the workers' movement! For the integration of the Jewish workers into the national-democratic revolutionary movement of the Arab masses!

• For the breaking-away of the Jewish trade unions and working-class organizations from the Jewish Agency, and the publication in full of all the secret proceedings of the Agency.

- For the breaking-away of the Arab trade unions and working-class organizations from the Arab League and the Arab High Committee for Palestine, and the publication in full of all the secret proceedings of these organizations.

All these slogans, which today can be advanced only as general propaganda slogans, will necessarily meet with furious opposition from the Zionists, not only for ideological reasons but also and especially because the privileged material situation of the Jews in relation to the Arab masses is thus threatened. But as the bankruptcy of Zionism becomes more and more strikingly revealed to the masses; as immigration slows down and the terrible danger of the Arab explosion comes nearer; as our propaganda helps in getting the masses to realize that it is a life-or-death question for them to find a common ground with the Arab masses, even at the price of temporarily giving up certain privileges—under these conditions our slogans will be able to pass from the propaganda stage to the stage of agitation, and will help in bringing about a split between the workers' movement and Zionism. This is the condition sine qua non for the realization of Jewish-Arab unity of action against imperialism. This alone can prevent the Arab revolution in the Middle East from passing over the corpse of Palestinian Judaism. In Palestine as well as among the Jewish masses in the rest of the world, a firm position today against the current is the only thing which will make it possible to work toward a reversal of the current in the next stage.

This means also that it is necessary for the sections of the Fourth International to carry on preliminary propaganda work within the Zionist organizations of the extreme left. While showing that the slogan of a 'bi-national state' is a nationalist and anti-democratic slogan, running counter to both the right of self-determination and the immediate needs of the anti-imperialist struggle in Palestine, our members must at the same time constantly put on the order of the day the question of concrete realization of the slogan of Jewish-Arab unity. They must confront the centrist leaders with their responsibilities, they must put on the order of the day the adoption of the anti-racial program outlined above, and thus speed the development of the consciousness of the Jewish working-class vanguard beyond the stage of Zionism.

INDEX OF NAMES

A

Abbas, Mahmoud – 37, 78, 86, 96, 124
Abdel Aziz al-Rantisi – 116
Abdul Hamid II – 23
Abdullah I (Abdullah bin Al-Hussein) – 36, 42, 51, 59, 225
Abu Ali Mustafa – 123
Abu Iyad. *See* Khalaf, Salah
Abu Jihad. *See* al-Wazir, Khalil
Adani, Mahmoud – 123
Aflaq, Michel – 88
Agranat, Shimon – 77
Ahimeir, Abba – 36, 48
bin Ali, Hussein – 31
Al Saud, Mohammed bin Salman – 173
Arafat, Yasser – 92–93, 96, 99, 101, 103, 111, 112–113, 113, 118, 121, 124, 141, 231
Arlosoroff, Haim – 48
Ashrawi, Hanan – 111–112
al-Assad, Bashar – 88, 112, 142, 145
al-Assad, Hafez – 88, 103, 104, 106, 243
Attlee, Clement – 61, 150, 157
Atzmon, Gilad – 153
Avigdor Lieberman – 138

B

Baker, James – 112
Balfour, Arthur – 25, 28, 32, 194
al-Banna, Hassan – 224
Bannon, Steve – 153
Barak, Ehud – 81, 121–122, 138
al-Barudi, Fakhri – 49
Begin, Menachem – 62, 64, 104, 106, 139, 140, 220
Ben-Gurion, David – 36, 47–48, 52, 53, 58, 59, 60, 62, 64, 65, 196
Benn, Tony – 150, 151
Ben-Yair, Michael – 81
Bevin, Ernest – 150
Bialik, Hayim Nahman – 37
Birnbaum, Nathan – 19
Bisharat, Odeh – 74
von Bismarck, Otto – 191
Black, Edwin – 163
Blair, Tony – 151
Bolivar, Simon – 90
Bonaparte, Napoleon – 90, 224
Borochov, Ber – 26, 192, 193
Brenner, Lenni – 163
Brezhnev, Leonid Ilyich – 92, 104
Brown, Gordon – 151
Bush, George H. W. – 112
Bush, George W. – 124, 136

C

Cabet, Étienne – 22
Cabral, Amilcar – 92
Carter, Jimmy – 81, 104
Chamberlain, Joseph – 25
Chávez, Hugo – 90
Churchill, Winston – 28, 32
Corbyn, Jeremy – 83, 151–152, 160, 169
Curzon, George Nathaniel – 28, 40

D

Dayan, Moshe – 65
Debray, Régis – 92
Dreyfus, Alfred – 19
Drumont, Édouard – 19
Duke, David – 152
Duterte, Rodrigo – 145, 159

E

Eisenhower, Dwight – 90
Eisen, Paul – 153
Erdogan, Recep Tayyip – 145, 159

F

Faisal I (Faisal bin Al-Hussein bin Ali al-Hashemi) – 42, 229
Falk, Richard A. – 80
Foot, Michael – 150
Fourier, Charles – 22
Frangieh, Suleiman – 106
Freedland, Jonathan – 149
Freilich, Chuck – 82–83

G

de Gaulle, Charles – 137
Gemayel, Bachir – 106
Gemayel, Pierre – 105–106
Ghazi of Iraq (Ghazi ibn Faisal) – 51
Gichon, Mordechai – 63
Gilmour, Ian – 150
Glubb, John Bagot – 59
de Gobineau, Arthur – 16
Goldmann, Nahum – 65
Gorbachev, Mikhail Sergeyevich – 112
Gordon, Aaron David – 25
Griffin, Nick – 152
Grunis, Asher – 77
Guevara, Ernesto 'Che' – 92

H

Habash, George – 87, 89, 92, 99, 100, 130, 170
al-Hafiz, Amin – 94
Haidar Abdel-Shafi – 111
Hananu, Ibrahim – 50

Herzl, Theodor – 19, 19–23, 27, 32, 38, 44, 155–156, 162, 191, 202
Hess, Moses – 18
Hitler, Adolf – 44, 47, 54, 56, 113–114, 200
al-Husayni, Musa – 41
al-Husri, Sati' – 226
Hussein, bin Ali (King of Hejaz) – 225
al-Husseini, Mohammed Amin (Grand Mufti) – 41, 51, 59, 113–114, 198, 204
Husseini, Faisal – 111–112, 225
Hussein of Jordan (Hussein bin Talal) – 102–103, 234
Hussein, Saddam – 88, 104, 112, 243

I

Ibn Saud, Abdulaziz – 51
Itzchaki, Arieh – 62

J

Jabotinsky, Ze'ev – 36, 48, 192
Jadid, Salah – 94
Jaurès, Jean – 20, 237
Joseph II (Josef Benedikt Anton Michael Adam) – 12

K

Kanafani, Ghassan – 92
Kant, Immanuel – 12
Kautsky, Karl – 11, 237, 239
Kelman, Moshe – 62
Kerry, John – 81
Khalaf, Salah – 93
Khaled, Leila – 92
Kinnock, Neil – 151
Kushner, Jared – 66

L

Lenin, Vladimir Ilyich – 79, 237, 238
Leon, Abram – 11, 188
Lieberman, Avigdor – 138–141, 145
Livingstone, Ken – 47
Livni, Tzipi – 137, 138

Lloyd George, David – 28, 32
Locke, John – 12
Lueger, Karl – 17
Luxemburg, Rosa – 237

M

MacDonald, Malcolm – 54
Mahmoud Darwish – 111
al-Din al-Mamun, Sayf – 49
Mao, Zedong – 138
Marr, Wilhelm – 16
Marx, Karl – 18, 85, 236
Mashal, Khaled – 116
May, Theresa – 29
McMahon, Henry – 31
Melcer, Hanan – 77
Mendelssohn, Moses – 13
Mikardo, Ian – 150
Miliband, Ed – 149
Mitzna, Amram – 136
Modi, Narendra – 145, 159
Montague, Edwin – 28
Morris, Benny – 145
Morsi, Mohamed – 114
Lord Moyne – 56
Mussolini, Benito – 36, 48, 50, 193

N

al-Nashashibi, Raghib – 41
Nasser, Gamal Abdel – 89, 89–91, 93, 99, 101, 103, 104, 115, 226–230, 231, 243
Netanyahu, Benjamin – viii, 62, 69, 78, 113, 119, 122, 137, 140, 145, 159, 173
Nicholas II (Nikolai Alexandrovich Romanov) – 17, 32
Nicosia, Francis R. – 163
Nixon, Richard – 104, 137

O

Obama, Barack – 158
Olmert, Ehud – 69, 137, 138, 140
Ornan, Uzzi – 78
Owen, Robert – 22

P

Pappé, Ilan – 62
Peel, William – 53
Peres, Shimon – 119, 137
Peretz, Amir – 137
Georges-Picot, François – 31
Pinsker, Leon – 18
von Plehve, Vyacheslav – 24, 44
Proudhon, Pierre-Joseph – 22
Putin, Vladimir Vladimirovich – 145, 159

Q

al-Qassam, Izz ad-Din – 50
Qutb, Sayyid – 115

R

Rabbath, Edmond – 226
Rabin, Yitzhak – 106, 110, 113, 138, 170
al-Rantisi, Abdel Aziz – 123
Regev, Mark – 159
al Rihani, Amin – 226
Rodinson, Maxime – 11
Rothschild – 16
Rothschild, Lionel Walter (Baron Rothschild) – 29, 32, 194

S

Sadat, Anwar – 104, 114
Samuel, Herbert – 28, 32, 40
Schocken, Gershom – 158
Shah (Mohammed Reza Pahlavi) – 104, 157, 158
Shamir, Israel – 153
Shamir, Yitzhak – 62, 112, 140, 220
Sharon, Ariel – 69, 75, 106, 121–123, 124, 135, 137–138, 140
Shawkat, Sami – 226
Shehade, Salah – 116, 123
Shoshani, Neta – 63
Shukeiri, Ahmad – 95
el-Sisi, Abdel el-Fatteh – 145, 159, 173
Spencer, Richard – 152, 162
Stern, Avraham – 56
Storrs, Ronald – 40, 156

Sykes, Mark – 31

T

Tonge, Jenny – 149
Traverso, Enzo – 11
Treitschke, Heinrich – 15
Trotsky, Leon – 43, 85, 237, 240
Trump, Donald – 66, 69, 85, 145, 152, 158, 173

W

al-Wazir, Khalil – 93
Weisglass, Dov – 136, 137
Weizmann, Chaim – 28, 32, 36, 42, 53, 156, 195
Wilhelm II (Friedrich Wilhelm Viktor Albert) – 23
Wingate, Orde – 52
Woodhead, John – 54

Y

Yassin, Ahmed – 116, 123

Z

Zettler, Yehoshua – 63
Zinoviev, Grigory – 43
Zola, Émile – 20

Books published by Prinkipo Press

Richard Brenner	LEON TROTSKY: AN INTRODUCTION 2020, 188 pages, £5.00 Selected bibliography
Workers Power	MARXISM AND TRADE UNIONS First edition 1978, second edition 2023, 216 pages, £8.00 Glossary of names, bibliography ISBN 978-1-7395059-0-5
Workers Power	PALESTINE: A MARXIST ANALYSIS First edition 2018, second edition 2024, 284 pages, £10.00 Index of names ISBN 978-1-7395059-1-2
Workers Power / Irish Workers Group	THE DEGENERATED REVOLUTION First edition 1984, second edition 2012, 600 pages, £14.00 Full index ISBN 978-0-0553664-5-1